THE
UNQUENCHABLE
LIFE

THE
UNQUENCHABLE
LIFE

What the Apostles Teach Us About
Victorious Christian Living

A Study of Acts Chapters 8 to 28[1]

RUSSELL M. STENDAL

---

1   My commentary on the first eight chapters of the book of Acts is contained
    in other writings; for instance, see *Until the Day Breaks and the Shadows Flee
    Away* (formerly *The Mystery of the Will of God*), Russell Stendal, ANEKO Press,
    Abbotsford, WI.

We love hearing from our readers. Please contact us at www.anekopress.com/questions-comments with any questions, comments, or suggestions.

Visit Russell's website: www.cpcsociety.ca

The Unquenchable Life – Russell M. Stendal

Copyright © 2017

First edition published 2017

Cover Design: Natalia Hawthorne, BookCoverLabs.com

Cover Painting: Matt Philleo

eBook Icon: Icon design/Shutterstock

Editors: Bronwen Jorel and Paul Miller

Printed in the United States of America

Aneko Press – *Our Readers Matter*™

www.anekopress.com

Aneko Press, Life Sentence Publishing, and our logos are trademarks of Life Sentence Publishing, Inc.

203 E. Birch Street

P.O. Box 652

Abbotsford, WI 54405

RELIGION / Biblical Commentary / New Testament

Paperback ISBN: 978-1-62245-496-9

eBook ISBN: 978-1-62245-497-6

10 9 8 7 6 5 4 3 2 1

Available where books are sold

Contents

To all the true disciples of our Lord Jesus Christ.

Preface

Twice a week, in the midst of a bitter fifty-two-year civil war, I addressed a live audience at the Salon Los Heroes auditorium in Bogotá (right next to the memorial of the Colombian Revolutionary War, twenty meters from the statue of Simon Bolivar mounted on his horse and holding his sword aloft). My purpose was to preach extemporaneously through all sixty-six books of the Bible before a live audience, speaking in Spanish and limiting myself to one chapter (or so) per message. These messages were also broadcast on dozens of radio stations all across the war zone and on short wave and Internet all over the world. After eighteen years, this task is almost completed (only the book of Job is pending).

Fifteen years ago, I preached twenty-three messages on the book of Acts. (My wife, Marina, surprised me with an extraordinary statement: "I think the devil hates the book of Acts more than almost anything else.")

I had spent the previous ten years (from 1990 to 2000) editing the Spanish and English versions of the Bible in accordance with the scholarship of the anointed men of God from the early Reformation – men like Francisco de Encinas, Juan Pérez de Pineda, William Tyndale, Casiodoro de Reina, and Cipriano de Valera.

In short, no one could accuse me of not doing my scriptural homework. And yet, despite all my diligence, those messages lacked something very important, something that could have given extra depth to the characters I described. I'm talking about their names.

In biblical times, people's names had a meaning and a significance. Today we might name a child after a grandparent, a public figure we admire, or even a movie star, but names were once weightier matters. "Isaiah," for example, means "salvation of the Lord," "Salome" means "perfect peace" (which might explain why her dance affected Herod so strongly), and God changed Jacob's name to Israel (meaning "God prevails" or "he who prevails with God") as a token of Jacob's conversion after he had wrestled all night with the angel of the Lord. Over the years, Bible scholars have attempted to determine the meaning of the proper names in Scripture, yet up to one-third of the names in the New Testament, including many of the names mentioned in the book of Acts, have defied explanation. For the most part, they are not of Greek or Roman derivation. Rather, they come from pre-Greek or pre-Roman civilizations whose languages, by and large, have been lost. Modern Europeans, despite living in towns and cities that are often built upon layers and layers of ancient ruins, have no idea what the names of these places really mean.

Two years ago I began my own search, beginning with the extensive Bible translator's library left to me by my late father, Chadwick M. Stendal, who from 1966 to 1974 was in charge of forty-two Bible translations in Colombia and Panama for Wycliffe Bible Translators. His collection included a number of ancient leather-bound volumes, most of them in tatters. My research among these venerable books resulted in the publication last year of an extensive English Bible dictionary that defined almost 90 percent of the approximately three thousand proper names in Scripture, including difficult ones, which are of Chaldean, Persian, or Egyptian background, many of which only occur once.

This year, during our massive Bible distribution into former guerrilla strongholds in rural Colombia and into Venezuela, I felt an urgency to compile a Spanish Bible dictionary. Using Spanish reference materials that for the most part have not been available to English scholars, I was able to pin down the meanings of some of the most elusive terms, including almost all of the formerly uninterpreted proper names in the book of Acts. I consider these names to be among the crown jewels of the New Testament. Each name put me, like a detective, on the trail of an ancient mystery. It is clear that in the eyes of God each person is unique and valuable, and the conditions regarding the name of each person recorded in Scripture (along with its meaning) help form living parables that are of spiritual and prophetic value to every serious student of the Bible.

You, the reader, are the jury. Consider this treatise and tell me if, under the inspiration of the Holy Spirit, I have truly discovered the missing values of these names.

Russell M. Stendal
September 23, 2017
Bogotá, Colombia

Introduction

I've been called a wide range of derogatory names over the years, and in some sectors I've even been denounced as the antichrist (Matthew 5:10-12), but I'm not alone in being vilified this way. Mockers referred to Jesus himself as Beelzebub (Satan). So we know we're in good company when we're denigrated. One of the more interesting titles conferred on me (and not always intended as a compliment) is that of the Lone Ranger. As this name continued to crop up in one form or another, I decided to do a little research. According to Wikipedia[2]:

> The Lone Ranger was named so because the character is the only survivor of a group of six Texas Rangers, rather than because he works alone (as he is usually accompanied by Tonto). While details differ, the basic story of the origin of the Lone Ranger is the same in most versions. . . . A posse of six members of the Texas Ranger Division pursuing a band of outlaws led by Bartholomew "Butch" Cavendish is betrayed by a civilian guide . . . and is ambushed in a canyon named Bryant's Gap. Later, an Indian named Tonto stumbles onto the scene and discovers one Ranger is barely alive, and he nurses the man back to health. In some

2   https://creativecommons.org/licenses/by-sa/3.0/

versions, Tonto recognizes the lone survivor as the man who saved his life when they both were children. According to the television series, when Tonto left the Reid place with a horse given him by the boy Reid, he gave Reid a ring and the name Kemo Sabe, which he said means "trusty scout." Among the Rangers killed was the survivor's older brother, Daniel Reid, who was a captain in the Texas Rangers and the leader of the ambushed group. To conceal his identity and honor his fallen brother, Reid fashions a black domino mask from the material of his brother's vest. To aid in the deception, Tonto digs a sixth grave and places at its head a cross bearing Reid's name so that Cavendish and his gang would believe that all of the Rangers had been killed.

Hmm. So the Lone Ranger was a survivor? My thoughts immediately went back to August 6, 1969.[3] Our family was home on furlough from the mission field of Colombia, and I went on a ministry trip to the West Coast with my father, while some of the other young people of our church community (Bethany Fellowship of Bloomington, MN) went on a retreat at a camp in northern Minnesota. Tragically, a tornado hit the camp and the two other young people in my class were killed, leaving me a survivor. These were kids with whom I had gone to confirmation class. They would've grown up to be my friends, associates, and contemporaries in ministry. However, some of their parents, friends, and relatives have had a special place in their hearts for me ever since and have prayed for me and supported me in ministry over the past fifty years.

My thoughts also went back to the 80s and 90s when so many missionaries and pastors – many of them my personal friends and associates – were killed in Colombia. Again, I was

3   I was thirteen.

the survivor, having been captured by the FARC guerrillas (Revolutionary Armed Forces of Colombia) in 1983 and tied to a tree for 142 days before being unexpectedly released after one of the guerrilla commanders realized that I was the person who had saved his mother. After my release, my brother Chad and I remained at the missionary base at Lomalinda where we had grown up. These were difficult and dangerous times, however, and by the year 2000, close to 850 foreign missionaries had been withdrawn from eastern Colombia. My brother and I watched as the last missionary airplane departed, leaving the two of us alone at the base. After the missionaries left, intervals of heavy fighting mixed with looting soon destroyed two-thirds of the missionary base and a third of the nearby town of Puerto Lleras. An untold number of church buildings were destroyed, hundreds of pastors were gunned down, and according to recent UN figures, over six million people were displaced (second only to Syria).[4] On a personal level, my brother and I lost more than five hundred friends, every one of them killed in the dirty war. Yet in spite of all this death and destruction, God used us to raise up powerful radio stations at Lomalinda that to this day cover even the most remote border regions of Colombia.

So, like the Lone Ranger, even though many of my friends had died, I had lived. Wondering whether we had anything else in common, I continued my research on the Lone Ranger. It turned out that he was generally depicted as living by a creed that the show's writer, Francis "Fran" Striker, drew up at the very beginning. This creed read:

I believe . . .

That to have a friend, a man must be one.

That all men are created equal and that everyone has within himself the power to make this a better world.

4   See *Rescue the Captors 2*, chapter 12, "The Last Bible Translator," ANEKO Press.

*That God put the firewood there, but that every man
must gather and light it himself.*

*In being prepared physically, mentally, and morally to
fight when necessary for what is right.*

*That a man should make the most of what equipment
he has.*

*That "this government of the people, by the people, and
for the people" shall live always.*

*That men should live by the rule of what is best for the
greatest number.*

*That sooner or later . . . somewhere . . . somehow . . . we
must settle with the world and make payment for what
we have taken.*

*That all things change but truth, and that truth alone,
lives on forever.*

In my Creator, my country, my fellow man.

I like the moral code of the Lone Ranger, but if I were writing
that creed, I'd clarify a couple of points.

In order to have within us "the power to make this a better
world," we must be dead to our own plans and ambitions so that
Jesus Christ can be alive in us by the power of the Holy Spirit.
The apostle Paul wrote, *For to me to live is Christ and to die is
gain* (Philippians 1:21). Or in the words of the psalmist, *Cause
me to live according to thy mercy, so I shall keep the testimony of
thy mouth* (Psalm 119:88). In the highest sense, the truth that
never changes but lives on forever (to paraphrase Mr. Striker)
is the Lord Jesus Christ. He said, *I AM the way, the truth, and
the life* (John 14:6). While we may all wish "to make this a better world," I disagree with Mr. Striker's belief that the power

to do so lies within ourselves. Without God's help, we have no
such power. God's way for us to fight evil is to overcome it with
good (Romans 12:21).

Our country needs an abundance of people who understand
this truth and the significance of what that sixth grave meant
to the Lone Ranger; otherwise "this government of the people,
by the people, and for the people" will surely fail. For the health
of any society and any nation, there must always be those who
will stand – alone, if need be – for truth and justice, and who
are willing to go against the groupthink of the secular or religious crowd and against corrupt special interests and private
kingdoms in order to set an example for others to follow.

Over the course of the fifty-two-year war in Colombia,
my brother and I had many conversations with well-meaning
officials from the US embassy, as well as other friends who, in
the interests of our personal safety and that of our families,
wanted us to leave the war zone. They were, for the most part,
unable to understand that – then as now – we considered ourselves already "dead in Christ," and therefore no enemy has
been able to overpower us with fear, even if at times we must
stand alone. Of course, I've never really been alone; the Lord
has always been with me, and so have my wife, my brother,
my children, and countless others (friends and guides) whom
God has always provided to fulfill the role of "Tonto" or even
to restore the original "posse."

Does the Lone Ranger have any other characteristics that
I might share or wish to emulate? Well, it turns out that Fran
Striker (the show's writer) and George W. Trendle (a radio station owner who was the legal owner of the Lone Ranger and
associated characters and who may have conceived the radio
show in which the Lone Ranger first appeared) drew up guide-
lines that embody who and what the Lone Ranger is, including
the following:

The Lone Ranger was never seen without his mask or some sort of disguise.

He was never captured or held for any length of time by lawmen, avoiding his being unmasked.

He always used perfect grammar and precise speech devoid of slang and colloquialisms.

Whenever he was forced to use guns, he never shot to kill, but instead tried to disarm his opponent as painlessly as possible.

He was never put in a hopeless situation; e.g., he was never seen escaping from a barrage of gunfire merely by fleeing toward the horizon.

He rarely referred to himself as the Lone Ranger. If someone's suspicion were aroused, the Lone Ranger would present one of his silver bullets to confirm his identity; but many times someone else would attest on his behalf. The origin of this name was, following the Bryant's Gap ambush, Tonto observed him to be the only ranger left – the "lone ranger." Tonto's choice of words inspired him to call himself "The Lone Ranger."

Even though the Lone Ranger offered his aid to individuals or small groups facing powerful adversaries, the ultimate objective of his story always implied that their benefit was only a by-product of the development of the West or the country. . . .

The Lone Ranger never drank or smoked, and saloon scenes were usually shown as cafes, with waiters and food instead of bartenders and liquor.

Criminals were never shown in enviable positions of wealth or power, and they were never successful or glamorous.

The Lone Ranger is a symbol of the brave circuit-riding preachers, judges, and marshals (riding alone or with one or two sidekicks, unless circumstances warranted a posse) who feared only God and tamed the Wild West. Their work ushered in well over a century of peace and safety for women, children, and minorities, and their heroic actions ensured liberty for everyone to pursue happiness and worship God according to each individual conscience. This is unique in world history.

I certainly can't claim to have tamed the Wild West, but from 1974 – when I returned from the University of Minnesota at age nineteen to begin our Chaparral Ranch project in untamed eastern Colombia and to start my work as a missionary jungle pilot – until the guerrillas kidnapped me in 1983, I almost always carried a weapon (either a Smith & Wesson Highway Patrolman .357 Magnum or a .38 Chief's Special, with a concealed carry permit). My first sidekick (taking the role of Tonto) was Guillermo Romero, whose one uncle was the Colombian minister of defense, while his other uncle was director of the National Police. In addition, my brother Chad sometimes rode with us, carrying his Colt .44, and on several notable occasions he stopped merciless bands of rustlers from taking our cattle or from raping or otherwise harming innocent people.

In the lawless environment of the eastern Colombian cattle country, we had many encounters with desperate criminals, but we always came out on top without ever having to shoot to kill. In one such encounter, I successfully faced down a notorious bad guy who had come to our place to wreak havoc. What he didn't know was that I only had one "silver bullet" left in my gun at the time! These were special, precise bullets that I molded and reloaded on my own. After morning chores, I used to sit in the bushes beside a salt lick (reading C. S. Lewis books while I waited for my prey) and shoot pigeons that were attracted to the salt. These pigeons always made a good lunch, and I remember that on one occasion, using a box of fifty of my special bullets, I shot fifty-one pigeons through the neck or head (two of them helpfully lined up for one shot). I also dropped a wild bull with one shot to the head, won shooting contests against nefarious characters, and shot an untold number of snakes through the head, including a bushmaster over ten feet long that had killed one of my horses (the horse died fifteen minutes after being struck). My brother was also a good shot. I recall one time when a twenty-two-foot anaconda had a stranglehold on his dog, and he killed that snake with a single shot, in the middle of a swamp, in the dark, without a flashlight.

Not everyone cared for that sort of lifestyle, of course. For the Chaparral project, my father had carefully selected the best pastors and evangelists that he could find in the big cities, but when they found themselves facing intense community life in a rustic, wild, and hostile rural environment, most of them failed miserably and soon returned home. The only one who didn't get into serious moral trouble, a man named Paco, whom I greatly respected, accidentally drowned in the river. So, in late 1974, at the age of nineteen, I was the only remaining spiritual "elder" who wasn't morally deviant. I stuck it out until August 14, 1983, when I was kidnapped by the FARC.[5]

On January 3, 1984, I was miraculously released by my kidnappers. My liberation had been brokered by my brother Chad, and at this point I turned the ranch over to him and entered full-time ministry, traveling all over North America and Colombia.[6] Since that time (thirty-three years ago) I've never carried another firearm, except on special occasions. Now my "silver bullets" are facets of the truth of God that I've been able to share, witnessing to the men and women and leaders on all

---

5   See *Rescue the Captors*, Life Sentence Publishing.
6   See *Rescue the Captors 2* and *God's Plan for Spiritual Battle*, ANEKO Press.

the sides in the conflict. In fact, so many of these people have come to Christ that the FARC conflict has ended.

Some of the most dangerous trips I have ever made were over the *paramo*, or high alpine Andes, above the tree line, into territory that had been held by rebels since 1917. No churches or religious meetings of any kind were allowed in the region, but from 2007 to 2012 we went in with ten thousand children's backpacks filled with books, solar-powered radios, toys, clothing, school supplies – and Bibles. We gave these backpacks as gifts to every child that we could find, and in this way we recruited the children to evangelize their parents, the guerrillas, and the army soldiers. I had planned to place a radio station somewhere remote, where the rebels would be unlikely to find it and destroy it, and the Lord provided me with two brothers who, in their capacity as my guides, not only found me the ideal location on top of a 13,500 ft. high peak, but also offered to run the station that I set up there. In addition to that, after I had been through several experiences with horses that failed me and almost killed me, my guides bought me a wonderful high-mountain stallion that I named Silver.

On February 17, 2015, I was arrested in Bogota as a result of false charges apparently trumped up by enemies who didn't understand the importance of the guerrillas being converted to Christ. Twenty-four hours later a judge released me, and ultimately the government was forced to apologize and withdraw the charges. Twenty random *campesinos* (tenant farmers or farmworkers) from Sumapaz who had helped me distribute the children's backpacks were also arrested, as were my guides, and all of them were held for an entire year without formal charges being filed. They were offered their freedom if they would give testimony against me (the prosecutor wanted them to testify that I was a guerrilla), but all of them stuck to the truth about me, even when threatened with long prison terms. Our lawyers were finally able to obtain their release by filing a writ of habeas corpus. Although it ended well (the case against all of us was finally precluded September 4, 2017), this incident was a horrible miscarriage of justice and cost us quite a bit in legal fees and other expenses.

My enemies thought that they would use the law to "unmask" me and discredit our work, but what happened at the trial showed what God had been doing all along. One million Bibles, almost three million good books, and a hundred and twenty thousand Galcom radios fix-tuned to our frequencies had been distributed throughout the war zones, in addition to the thousands of backpacks we gave to children who had never been to church or Sunday school.

My horse, Silver, never let me down. He could power through the treacherous peat bogs and was surefooted on the slippery shale rock precipices, even in the dark. Silver could jump chasms and traverse seemingly impossible slopes, and unlike his predecessors, he never caused me to fall. Eventually we put him out to pasture in the beautiful mountain valley pictured in our movie, *La Montaña*.[7] The valley is filled with sweet grass and clover and is as close to horse heaven as anywhere I have seen on earth (there are no ticks or horse flies). Therefore, when people who would belittle us or warn others not to follow our example call me a Lone Ranger, I really don't mind. In fact, I take it as quite a compliment.

Of course, we know that God's end game is for the body of Christ to come to maturity and to function corporately in

---

7 To date, this movie (in Spanish with English subtitles) has more than four million views on www.youtube.com, making it the most watched Colombian film of all time, even though it was banned from theaters in that country by misguided government officials who seemed to want the guerrillas dead instead of evangelized and converted. In addition to soldiers, paramilitaries, *campesinos*, and policemen, many guerrillas of the FARC discreetly became Christians, and secret peace talks began in Havana, Cuba, in late 2011. This led to open peace negotiations by the end of 2012, with Cuba, Norway, Venezuela, and Chile as sponsoring countries.

perfection, and he has placed ministry to aid this purpose (Ephesians 4). The day will soon come when Jesus returns with the armies of heaven and all of his saints (Jude 14-15). When that happens, we'll be caught up to meet him in the air and deputized as part of the real posse that will hunt down all the bad guys.

In the meantime, however, it may be necessary on repeated occasions to stand – alone if necessary – for the truth in the midst of this godless world and even among so-called people of God who have become compromised due to their selfish ambition and private kingdoms. The heroes of faith in Hebrews 11 stood seemingly alone in their day. Let's join them.

Hebrews 11

11:1 *Faith, therefore, is the substance of things waited for, the evidence of things not seen.*

11:2 *For by it the elders obtained a good report.*

The heroes of faith who are described in the succeeding verses started out alone, yet they're called "elders" here in Scripture. They're in God's hall of fame because they submitted to him instead of blindly following human counsel. They look forward to the perfection of the body of Christ as *the substance of things waited for, the evidence of things not seen.*

11:3 *Through faith we understand that the ages were framed by the word of God, that which is seen being made of that which was not seen.*

God has used each age to fulfill his purpose and has used men and women of faith to demonstrate his will and character.

11:4 *By faith Abel offered unto God a more excellent sacrifice than Cain, by which he obtained witness that*

he was righteous, God testifying of his gifts, and by it he
being dead yet speaks.

Abel stood alone in his generation. Does this make him a Lone
Ranger?

11:5 By faith Enoch was translated that he should not
see death, and was not found because God had trans-
lated him, for before his translation he had this testi-
mony, that he pleased God.

Enoch walked alone with God. Does this make him a Lone
Ranger?

11:6 But without faith it is impossible to please God; for
he that comes to God must believe that he is and that
he is a rewarder of those that diligently seek him.

If we believe that God is and that he rewards those who diligently seek him, why would we want to trust in man?[8]

11:7 By faith Noah, having received revelation of things
not seen as yet, with great care prepared an ark to the
saving of his house, by which he condemned the world
and was made heir of the righteousness which is by
faith.

Was Noah a Lone Ranger? (Every other human authority in
the ancient world was condemned by Noah's faith.)

11:8 By faith Abraham, being called, hearkened to go
out into the place which he should afterwards receive
for an inheritance; and he went out, not knowing where
he went.

What if Abraham had listened to the elders of Ur of the Chaldees

---

8   And yes, we understand that children are to obey their parents in the Lord
     (Ephesians 6:1) and that young people are to respect and submit to their elders
     (1 Peter 5:5), but ultimately each of us will be held personally accountable to
     God according to the responsibility he has bestowed upon us (Matthew 12:36;
     Luke 12:48b).

instead of hearkening to the call of God? Shem was still alive, and there must have been other patriarchs who were also wise and from whom Abraham could have sought counsel; yet there is no mention in Scripture that Abraham sought advice or counsel from anyone other than God.

> 11:9 *By faith he sojourned in the promised land, as in a strange country, dwelling in booths with Isaac and Jacob, the heirs with him of the same promise;*

> 11:10 *for he looked for a city which has foundations, whose builder and maker is God.*

Even after it was established that he walked with God and was his friend, Abraham refused to build his own city. He refused to attempt to control others. *He looked for a city which has foundations, whose builder and maker is God.* The only everlasting foundation is the Lord Jesus Christ.

Does this make Abraham a Lone Ranger?

> 11:11 *By faith also Sara herself being sterile received strength to conceive seed and was delivered of a child when she was past age, because she believed him to be faithful who had promised.*

It should be very clear by now that faith begins as a very personal, individual thing. Each of us must believe God for ourselves and personally respond to his voice and promises. Only after our hearts and minds have been cleansed can we be properly joined to others in the body of Christ.[9]

> 11:12 *Therefore there sprang even of one, and him as good as dead, so many as the stars of the sky in*

---

9   And even then we must be very cautious not to make commitments to others unless those commitments have been approved by God. Otherwise our commitment to a given group or individual(s) may supersede our commitment to the Lord Jesus Christ and begin to quench the liberty of the Spirit.

multitude and as the sand which is by the sea shore innumerable.

Abraham started off alone in response to God's call.[10] He was promised spiritual descendants (as a father of faith), *so many as the stars of the sky in multitude*, and natural descendants, *as the sand which is by the sea shore innumerable.*[11]

11:13 *These all died in faith, not having received the promises, but seeing them afar off and believing them and embracing them and confessing that they were strangers and pilgrims on the earth.*

What people *died in faith, not having received the promises?*

Were they "strangers and pilgrims"? People in those categories mostly travel in ones or twos, like the Lone Ranger and Tonto (Jeremiah 3:14).

Does the term "these all died in faith" refer only to Abel, Enoch, Noah, Abraham, Isaac, Jacob, and Sara?[12] Does it also apply to their spiritual and natural offspring, including us? (Are we like unto the stars of the sky and the sands of the sea?)

Some seem to think that instead of God cleansing individuals by his Spirit and joining them together after they're clean, he brings forth his people in "clusters" (or in community in perfect "order" under the authority of "elders"). Bear in mind, however, that in order for elders like Abel, Enoch, Noah, Abraham, or many others to participate in such wonderful wholesome clusters, a very important prophetic event called the first resurrection must come to pass (Revelation 20:4-6). We're still in the time in which wheat and tares grow together in the same field,

---

10 Approximately 2,000 years of human history had elapsed before the time of Abraham, and in that whole period, Scripture only mentions three individuals (Abel, Enoch, and Noah) prior to Abraham as outstanding and pleasing to God.

11 The spiritual and natural descendants of Abraham have been increasing for the past four thousand years, and the promises have still not been completely fulfilled.

12 And according to verse 2, it certainly seems that all of them (including Sarah) are considered "elders" in Scripture.

seemingly indistinguishable as they both come to maturity. At the time of the harvest, however, the "wheat" bears good fruit and the "tares" produce deadly poison.[13]

Moses spent forty years virtually alone in the desert, tending sheep. God used this time as training for him, to prepare him to spend another forty years leading the children of Israel through the wilderness.

Was Moses a Lone Ranger?

What about David? He singlehandedly protected his sheep from lions and bears and then at a very young age stood up to Goliath when every other man in Israel cowered in fear.

Throughout Scripture, God is seen to anoint "lone" individuals.

If the enemy can entice us to submit our ministry to a committee, the wind will begin to be taken out of our sails with regard to being led by the Holy Spirit, because the committee will come to usurp the authority of God. This is especially true if one or more members of the committee are spiritually immature or unclean. Scripture is clear that the apostle Paul always took personal responsibility before the Lord for his ministry, even while contemplating advice and counsel from others.

The book of Acts gives excellent examples of how the authority of God flows and of how a ministry team of two or three people (similar in some ways to the Lone Ranger and Tonto) can blossom into wonderful, vibrant congregations in which each member of the body of Christ is encouraged to come to maturity with a direct unbroken relationship with Jesus Christ as their only head (as their government).

In the Old Testament, the elders were determined by the

---

13 I recently did a study of the 192 Scriptures that mention "elders" (see Appendix A) and found that even though God's goal and plan is for each of us to come to maturity in Christ, many of the examples in Scripture are of ungodly elders (who have come to maturity in the nature of Adam). The word "elder" has to do with maturity, but we must keep in mind that maturity as "wheat" is one thing and maturity as "tares" is quite another. Acts 11:30 marks an important turning point, with the first mention of reliable elders in the NT.

people according to such factors as age, number of progeny, character, genealogy, etc.[14] Even in the New Testament, God doesn't directly name elders. Rather, he decides whether or not to put his seal of the Holy Spirit upon them, and the ministry that God has placed discerns this.

Apostles, prophets, evangelists, pastors, and teachers are given directly by God (Ephesians 4:7-16). They are a gift from God to the body of Christ, and their role is not to lord it over everyone else, but to serve. They represent the authority of God, but unlike the Levites and priests of the Old Testament, they're not an intermediate clergy class between the people and God, for there is only one mediator of the New Covenant (1 Timothy 2:5; Hebrews 8:6).

There are examples in Scripture where those involved in ministry, such as Paul, Barnabas, Timothy, Titus, or others could discern, recognize, and therefore ordain elders or set them in the congregations, based at least in part on human initiative. There are, however, no examples where the people or the ministry could decide for themselves who was an apostle or a prophet or an evangelist or a pastor or a teacher. This takes a sovereign act of God, accompanied by signs that can only be witnessed to and accepted (or rejected).

In the broadest sense, all those among the people of God (men or women) who come to maturity in Christ are elders; those who come to maturity in Christ aren't interested in church politics. The twenty-four elders in Revelation cast their crowns at the feet of the Lord (Revelation 4:10-11). They know that he deserves all glory and honor and virtue[15] and that they are only an extension of his government. Even though it's easy to imagine twenty-four literal elders (the twelve sons of Israel

---

14 See Appendix A.
15 Virtue, in this sense, has to do with godly character that by the work of God has been developed in us and that the elders attribute to him.

plus the twelve apostles of Jesus), they also symbolize all those who have come to maturity in Christ.

Unless we come to maturity in Christ, it's difficult for us to do anything worthwhile, because without him we can do nothing. Attaining this maturity isn't difficult, because Jesus Christ is already mature (perfect), and if we are hid in him, this solves the problem of our inadequacy. It doesn't necessarily take decades for us to learn this. It may happen quickly, or we may struggle unnecessarily for a very long time against the government of God (Acts 9:5). The children of Israel could have travelled from Egypt to the Promised Land (symbolic of our inheritance in Christ) in as little as eleven days, but they finally got there more than forty years later, after an entire generation died off along the way (Deuteronomy 1:2-3).

Let's consider the words of a man who also had his struggles with coming to maturity.

Psalm 144

A Psalm of David

144:1 *Blessed be the LORD my strength, who trains my hands for the battle and my fingers for the war:*

David's fingers (trained by the Lord) were used for his bow, his sling, his sword – and his harp.

144:2 *My mercy and my fortress; my high tower and my deliverer; my shield and he in whom I trust, who subdues my people under me.*

Even though he was king, David didn't want to subdue the people of God under him; he let God take care of that. David was an example of prophet, priest, and king, all in the same person and anointed by God for ministry. If the Lord has anointed any of us for ministry, which is our inheritance in Christ, then we don't have to be concerned with subduing the people under us. If God has indeed given us authority, he'll take care of this at the proper time.

144:3 *LORD, what is man that thou knowest him? or the son of man, that thou esteemeth him?*

Jesus came as Son of God, but also as Son of Man. He is both the promised seed of Abraham and the son of David. Although Jesus overcame as a man, the fullness of the presence of God dwelt inside him. Anyone who loves the truth will love Jesus.

144:4 *Man is like unto vanity; his days are as a shadow that passes away.*

144:5a *Bow thy heavens, O LORD, and come down;*

One definition of the heavens is "the place where God dwells."

When Jesus came in flesh and blood, he was the temple of God. He received the Spirit without measure, and the fullness of the Father dwelt within him (John 3:34, 14:9-11).

How could this happen?

It happened because the heavens "bowed" and touched the earth as the Father descended and dwelt within his only begotten Son.

Jesus's guidance was internal. His heart was indivisibly linked to the heart of his Father. There is no evidence in Scripture to suggest that Jesus ever depended on external guidance from man once he came to maturity (at about thirty years of age) and began his ministry. Jesus didn't consult with or depend on elders or prophets (or even his own disciples) with regard to his plans, his journeys, or any other facet of his ministry.

Jesus depended upon his Father, and this total dependency made everyone who loved the truth rally around him in solidarity. Those who hated the truth, on the other hand, became his mortal enemies.

Most of the priests, scribes, elders, and Pharisees undoubtedly saw Jesus as a Lone Ranger. They thought that if they could kill him, the war would be over.

144:5 *Bow thy heavens, O LORD, and come down; touch the mountains, and they shall smoke.*

What do the mountains represent?

Mountains can represent the kingdoms of men or the kingdoms of this world.

When Jesus touched the kingdoms of the religious leaders, everything began to smoke. The elders of the priests, scribes, Pharisees, and Sadducees began to lose control, and their world started coming apart. The kingdoms of men couldn't survive in Jesus's presence.

144:6 *Cast forth lightning and scatter them; shoot out thine arrows and destroy them.*

The presence of God is as lightning, and his arrows project truth that is deadly to the systems of man. (And remember that what was not fully accomplished at the first coming will certainly be fulfilled at the second coming.)

Who does *them* refer to?

The mountains of any kingdom that is not the kingdom of God.

144:7 *Send thine hand from above; redeem me and deliver me out of many waters, from the hand of the strange sons,*

Who are the *strange sons*?

If the world is the field and the wheat is the sons of God who have been planted by him (or by those he has sent), then the *strange sons* are the tares, the sons of the wicked (Matthew 13:38).

144:8 *whose mouth speaks vanity, and their right hand is a right hand of falsehood.*

Jesus's enemies claimed to be sons of Abraham, but Jesus told them the truth: *Ye are of your father the devil, and the desires of your father ye desire to do. He was a murderer from the beginning and abode not in the truth because there is no truth in him* (John 8:44).

> 144:9 *I will sing a new song unto thee, O God; upon a psaltery and an instrument of ten strings I will sing praises unto thee.*

Scripture contains nine references to a *new song*. The ninth and final reference is *and they sang as it were a new song before the throne and before the four animals and the elders; and no one could learn that song but the hundred and forty-four thousand, who were redeemed from the earth* (Revelation 14:3).

Only the redeemed may sing the *new song*, and Jesus came to redeem us.[16]

The new song is sung upon *a psaltery and an instrument of ten strings*. The law of sin and death is based on the Ten Commandments, but the "psaltery" of the grace of God brings forth the startling notes of deliverance and freedom by *the law of the Spirit of life in Christ, Jesus* (Romans 8:2).

> 144:10 *Thou, he who gives salvation unto kings, who redeems David his slave[17] from the evil sword.*

King David is an example of the Messiah (Christ), yet even so, he needed redemption like everyone else.

What is the *evil sword*?

---

16 Twelve is a number that symbolizes divine order (as opposed to man's order, represented by humanistic elders). Twelve squared, which is one hundred and forty-four (and remember, we're in Psalm 144 here), represents the results of divine order (i.e., redemption). One thousand represents perfection. Therefore, one hundred and forty-four thousand represents the perfect number of all of the redeemed. They are the only ones who can sing the new song.

17 Servants are paid a salary and can quit, but a slave belongs to an owner. When Jesus redeems us (from being slaves to sin), he becomes our owner. The sign or seal of his ownership is the Holy Spirit, and where the Spirit of the Lord is, there is liberty (freedom to do the will of God).

There is the good double-edged sword of the truth of God, but there is also an evil sword with which our enemies try to destroy us. They attempt to trap us with their version of the truth and cause us to fall.

Look at this little exchange between Jesus and the elders:

Then the Pharisees and scribes asked him, Why do thy disciples not walk according to the tradition of the elders but eat bread with unwashed hands? He answered and said unto them, Well has Esaias prophesied of you hypocrites, as it is written, This people honours me with their lips, but their heart is far from me. Howbeit in vain do they honor me, teaching for doctrines the commandments of men (Mark 7:5-7).

144:11 Redeem me, and save me from the hand of strange sons, whose mouth speaks vanity, and their right hand is a right hand of falsehood:

The native tongue of our adversary, the devil, and his (strange) sons is the language of vanity (excessive pride that is worthless and futile). They derive their authority (the right hand is symbolic of authority) from falsehood, and they attempt to trap us by holding us to their lying version of the truth. They are essentially lawless, but they want to trap us if we don't comply with their interpretation of the letter of the law.

They know nothing of the way of the cross or of the promises of God. Those who are led by the Spirit are the sons of God (Romans 8:14); those who are led by the Spirit are not under the law (Galatians 5:18).

Jesus didn't come to comply with the traditions of the elders. He fulfilled the law by the fullness of the Spirit because his Father dwelt within him and God cannot lie (Titus 1:2).

The elders, on the other hand, used the law – specifically, the law of blasphemy, which stated that pronouncing the sacred name of God (literally, I AM) was a capital offense – to condemn him to death. When Jesus was put on trial before the Sanhedrin (the council of seventy elders) on trumped-up charges, no one defended him. The elders' false witnesses contradicted each other, however, and so the elders finally asked Jesus, *Art thou then the Son of God?*

Jesus decided to tip the balance of the trial so that he could legally die for us; accordingly, he responded, *Ye say that I AM.*[18] When Jesus pronounced the sacred name, the trial ended (Luke 22:70-71). Jesus was the only human being who could truthfully pronounce that name, declaring his eternal existence; but regardless of the fact that he spoke the truth, his words enabled the vain elders to sentence him to death.

Why did he decide to redeem us and save us from the vanity and falsehood of the "strange sons"?

Here are some reasons prophesied by King David a thousand years before:

> 144:12 *That our sons may be as plants grown up in their youth; that our daughters may be as corner stones, polished after the similitude of a palace;*

The sons were to mature quickly and the daughters were to become part of the polished foundation of the glorious new thing that God would accomplish with his people (Isaiah 42:9, 43:19).

> 144:13 *that our garners may be full, affording all manner of store; that our sheep may bring forth thousands and ten thousands in our streets;*

God desires to store up his word in the hearts of his people. We are the sheep of his pasture, and he will cause us to be fruitful and multiply instead of being sterile. When God apprehends us from our own crooked ways, as he did with Saul of Tarsus,

---

18 I AM is the sacred name of God (Exodus 3:13-14). This name written in the ancient manuscripts with four consonants YHWH is translated as LORD (in caps) in many English Bibles.

he immediately conducts us to the *street which is called Straight* if we genuinely desire to follow him (Acts 9:11). Then he may multiply us into thousands and tens of thousands. (God refuses to multiply anyone or anything that is unclean or incomplete.)

> 144:14 *that our oxen may be strong to labour; that there be no breaking in nor going out; that there be no shout of alarm in our streets.*

The cherubim (special angels or living creatures) that minister unto the Lord and are associated with the realm of the Holy of Holies and with the throne of God have four faces, one of which is that of an ox (Ezekiel 1:10), an animal that can be symbolic of ministry (both in heaven and on earth). The book of Acts portrays members of the ministry selected by God who are *strong to labour,* like an ox. They are humble, hard-working servants and help make sure *that there be no breaking in nor going out* (that the people of God are secure from attack and that no one would have reason to flee God's sheepfold) and *that there be no shout of alarm in our streets* (no complaint of injustice). Jesus said, *And I have other sheep which are not of this fold; it is expedient that I bring them also, and they shall hear my voice, and there shall be one fold and one shepherd* (John 10:16). This is what God began to accomplish in the book of Acts with ministry like that with Peter and Paul, as the gospel was extended to the Gentiles. The fullness of this promise, however, is reserved for our day.

> 144:15 *Blessed is that people, that is in such a case; yea, blessed is that people, whose God is the LORD.*

Throughout more than six thousand years of human history, there has never been a unified people of God with the fullness of the blessing. There have been many excellent individuals and even some excellent groups here and there, but God's people have had a penchant for choosing human leadership while gradually turning their backs on the Lord. The book of Acts narrates an important inflexion point in which, by the Holy Spirit, God offers to place his government within any and every person who persuades him.[19] It is by the power of the Spirit (not by our submission to man) that we are to put to death the deeds of the flesh so that we may live.

The battle between the leadership and government of the Spirit on the one side and the leadership and government of man on the other has raged in Christendom for almost two thousand years, but this is about to change.[20] The tares (or "strange sons" who spew poison at harvest time) are about to be removed from among the wheat, giving way to a beautiful bride without *spot or wrinkle or any such thing* (Ephesians 5:27) at our Lord's return, coupled with the first resurrection. This bride will produce consistent good fruit of the Spirit that is readily discernable to anyone with eyes to see.

Let Us Pray

Lord, May we not only understand your message, but may we live it in the power of the Holy Spirit so that men may see our good works and praise our Father in heaven. Amen.

---

19 *And we are his witnesses of these things, and so is also the Holy Spirit, whom God has given to those that persuade him* (Acts 5:32).

20 The last two chapters of Acts, in addition to being historically accurate and spiritually inspiring, are also a prophetic picture of the end of our present age. I recently compiled an accurate "Dictionary of Proper Names in Scripture" (published as an Appendix to the latest edition of the Jubilee Bible in Spanish and in English), having been able to discover the meanings of almost all of the proper names used in the book of Acts. My source for this research was old Spanish reference material that has not, for the most part, been available to English, Greek, Hebrew, or Latin scholars. The names in question were pre-Greek and pre-Roman, and discerning their meanings was very helpful in unlocking this prophetic picture. Every church structure built by man, even if it was deemed necessary and served a useful purpose at the time, is a ship that will ultimately founder and fail in the end-time storm as we enter the imminent day of the Lord. The heart of God, however, is to save all of his people.

Chapter 1

Sent Ones: God's Definition of a Missionary or Apostle

The scene is a dramatic one: *and the witnesses laid down their clothes at a young man's*[21] *feet, whose name was Saul. And they stoned* [the disciple] *Stephen calling upon God and saying, Lord Jesus, receive my spirit. And he kneeled down and cried with a loud voice, Lord, impute not this sin to their charge. And having said this, he fell asleep in the Lord* (Acts 7:58-60).

This callous young man named Saul, who seems unmoved by Stephen's fate and makes no attempt to save his life, is none other than the man who was later converted and became that passionate Christian, the apostle Paul.

Stephen, too, had been a passionate Christian, *full of faith and power,* who *did great wonders and miracles in the people* (Acts 6:8). His preaching had left even the best-prepared Jews without an adequate answer, so they did the same thing to him that they had done to the Lord Jesus: they put up false witnesses and had him killed.

After Stephen's death, there were two interesting developments:

---

21 Most historians and commentators date this as happening within a year of Jesus's death and resurrection (AD 33 or possibly 34). Saul is referred to as a "young man," meaning that he was most likely less than thirty years of age at this time.

1) Philip began doing what Stephen had been doing, and 2) God touched Saul, who was leading the campaign against the Christians by persecuting them, putting them in jail, and killing them. Stephen's death opened the door for these changes to take place.

Many people were converted under Philip's ministry, and even more chose to follow Jesus under Paul's ministry after his dramatic conversion. We see a progression, and we also see that in order to fulfill God's purpose, unity is required. The Enemy sees this too, of course, and since that time, he has developed one of his most efficient strategies against Christians; if he can't overcome them with a frontal onslaught, he'll seek to join and infiltrate their groups so that he's in a good position to produce divisions and separate sects that don't get along with one another.

Acts 8

8:1 *And Saul was consenting unto his [Stephen's] death. And at that time there was a great persecution against the congregation²² which was at Jerusalem, and they were all scattered abroad throughout the regions of Judaea and Samaria, except the apostles.*

Having killed Stephen, that same day his persecutors attacked the Christians in Jerusalem, and all of them except the apostles fled the city. Apostles, or "sent ones," only go where Jesus sends them.

8:2 *And devout men carried Stephen to his burial and made great lamentation over him.*

8:3 *As for Saul, he made havoc of the congregation; entering into the houses and dragging out men and women, he committed them to prison.*

22 Greek *ekklesia*; i.e., called-out ones.

8:4 *But those that were scattered abroad went everywhere preaching the word of the gospel.*

8:5 *Then Philip went down to the city of Samaria and preached the Christ unto them.*

8:6 *And the people with one accord gave heed unto those things which Philip spoke, hearing and seeing the signs which he did.*

8:7 *For many unclean spirits, crying with a loud voice, came out of those who were possessed with them, and many paralytics and that were lame were healed.*

8:8 *And there was great joy in that city.*

Samaria, like Jerusalem, was a religious city. When the Lord entered Jerusalem, one of the distinctive features of his ministry, not only there but in all of Judaea, was that many demons came out of the people – and often out of the people who were the most religious. Evidently the religion of Samaria was even more contaminated than that of Jerusalem, such that when Philip arrived, many unclean spirits had to flee.

The sequence of events is interesting. The Jews who didn't receive the Lord attacked the Christians in Jerusalem, and all except the apostles fled. The Christians (including Philip) who escaped to different places began to give testimony of Christ, and wherever they went, the demons fled. Thus, the Jews scattered the Christians, and the Christians scattered the demons.

What's even more interesting is that when Paul's ministry reached the Gentiles, there were fewer demons in that region than there were in Judaea, Jerusalem, or Samaria – places that supposedly had the truth. This has parallels with today's situation, where many apparently supernatural events are taking place among many groups that claim to be Christian, and yet an observer with the gift of discernment may well conclude that much of this activity is not of God. This is reminiscent of Simon the magician:

> 8:9 *But there was a certain man called Simon, who before this in the same city used magic arts and amazed the people of Samaria, giving out that he himself was some great one,*

> 8:10 *to whom they all gave heed, from the least to the greatest, saying, This is the great virtue of God.*

When the real presence of God was absent, Simon the magician seemed like *the great virtue of God.* From the least to the greatest, the people gave heed to him, until Philip arrived.

In how many places do deceivers pass themselves off as great leaders when they sway multitudes by claiming their actions are the virtue of God?

If it really is the virtue of God, the fruit of the Holy Spirit will be found. When it's not the Holy Spirit, however, there may be many "wonder works," but there will be no good fruit. Instead, the "fruit" will be unscrupulous hypocrites seeking power and control, like the religious leaders of the Jews who added to the Scriptures, held endless meetings that God had not ordered, established synagogues that God had not authorized, and filled them with religious rituals that God had not ordained.

There are many examples of meetings in the Scriptures, but a specific statement that we *must* attend a meeting every Sunday or every Saturday is nowhere to be found. So why do we do it? Because it's been done for so many centuries that we've become conditioned. It's true, of course, that the Holy Spirit can congregate the people, and likewise it's true that in the book of Acts, many people attended meetings where someone preached. However, these meetings are recorded because that was what God decided to do in a given moment in time.

On the day of Pentecost when Peter preached, three thousand people were converted, but it wasn't because someone passed out flyers, announced the meeting in the local media, and told everyone of the time and place where the miracles would happen. Likewise, when Peter and John raised up the paralytic, they preached to a multitude in the temple, and many believed. Admittedly their message was interrupted when they had to answer to the so-called religious authorities and were thrown into jail; but God had them miraculously released, and they continued preaching the next day.

The message that led to Stephen's death was one he delivered to a group of people who had been brought together, not for a religious event, but as the result of a trial. Known for being *full of faith and power* and performing *great wonders and miracles in the people*, Stephen had alienated Jews from other synagogues by besting them in debate; in revenge, they brought false witnesses to accuse him of blasphemy, and they began a biased trial. This aroused such interest that it turned into a big meeting, with a message that is recorded in a long chapter in Scripture, ending with Stephen's death (Acts 6:8-7:60).

The messages that Philip delivered in Samaria weren't the result of the apostles and Christian leaders in Jerusalem having a get-together to plan where and how to extend the work. Rather, due to an unexpected attack, all the believers except the apostles fled the city in disarray, and Philip, having ended up in Samaria, continued flowing in what the Holy Spirit had ordained for his life. His preaching had a great effect on all those who had been oppressed by the devil, and the demons began to flee. Very few of the evangelistic campaigns that take place today can stand comparison with Philip's ministry.

Philip's actions in Samaria were in accordance with the advice Jesus gave the apostles prior to his ascension; namely, to wait until they received power from on high. There has been confusion, however, regarding the power that they were to receive. The word used (*dunamis*) indicates not raw power, but power *under control*. The Lord has no desire to combine gifts from the Holy Spirit with rash, out-of-control human arrogance. That which comes from heaven by the Spirit should also remain under the control of the Spirit.

The apostles in Jerusalem were in the ministry, the ministry was multiplied into many people, and many were cared for in both the natural and the spiritual realms: widows, orphans, people in need. Those who had excess sold their possessions and gave the funds to the apostles so that no one remained in want. The apostles were dedicated to spiritual work, and with many demands on their time, they decided to establish seven deacons ("deacon" means "servant") to wait on tables and minister to the widows and others who were being cared for by the new believers. This decision had been taken because there were complaints that the Greek widows weren't getting the same attention as the Jewish widows, but it's actually quite remarkable that Greek widows were being cared for in the first place, as previously this would probably not have occurred to the average Jew. This is further evidence that the Spirit of God had genuinely touched the people.

Although these seven men were chosen to be servants, Jesus had taught that in the kingdom of God, the one who is the least – that is, the one who is everyone's servant – is really the greatest, and the caliber of these seven servants certainly bore out that teaching. Given that the first person on the list of servants was Stephen and the second was Philip, it's hardly surprising to learn that soon the men who had been selected to wait on tables were performing signs, wonders, and miracles. What's more, they were preaching with such zeal that the Pharisees and Sadducees who were attempting to derail the gospel were at a loss. That kind of preparation for ministry is quite a contrast to our own day, where after studying in a fine and comfortable place for four or eight years, the students graduate as doctors of divinity and are given the title of *reverend* (compare this to Psalm 111:9).

Those who were moving in the center of what the Holy Spirit was doing here were the disciples whom Jesus had chosen during his life on earth. They had become apostles when he sent them forth. The next group named in the Scriptures after the twelve apostles is the waiters; first one, then the other came into renown, and we can be sure that many more followed in powerful ministry because they *turned the world upside down* (Acts 17:6). What an exciting time to be alive!

In contrast to these servant preachers in Jerusalem, Philip found that Simon the magician had duped the entire city of Samaria, convincing the residents that he was grand and important and that his magic tricks were really the virtue of God. How many Simons do we have in Christendom today?

Simon let the cat out of the bag eventually, because his heart was concerned with money above all else, just like the hearts of the modern-day Simons. They're very interested indeed in money, but not interested at all in risking their lives for the gospel and for the Lord. So in the difficult places where it can cost people their lives if they mention the Lord Jesus, we tend not to find a "Simon the magician." Such types are only attracted to places where money is plentiful and where they can easily influence naïve people with the supernatural (or the seemingly supernatural).

Speaking of Simon the magician:

8:11 *And to him they had regard because for a long time he had amazed them with magic arts.*

Even today we have great buildings full of those who have long been amazed and continue to be amazed at the spectacle of the modern Simons who appear to be exercising the virtue of God.

8:12 *But when they believed Philip preaching the gospel of the kingdom of God and the name of Jesus Christ, they were baptized, both men and women.*

They were baptized after the unclean spirits fled and the demons left. When the people saw the real power of God working through Philip, the magic tricks of Simon the magician were revealed for what they were.

8:13 *Then Simon himself believed also; and when he was baptized, he continued with Philip and wondered, beholding the miracles and signs which were being done.*

The magic of Simon couldn't hold a candle to what Philip was doing under the power of the Holy Spirit. Today some so-called spiritual leaders fill large stadiums and perform what appear to be great miracles, but if we compare this show-business approach with the real presence of God, we'll find that it leaves much to be desired.

8:14 *Now when the apostles who were at Jerusalem heard that Samaria had received the word of God, they sent Peter and John unto them,*

Samaria was not really Gentile. Its residents were the residue of the northern ten tribes of Israel who had been removed from the land. Some had trickled back and mixed their beliefs with those of others, producing an even greater spiritual contamination than was found in the descendants of Judah, Benjamin, and part of Levi who continued to worship in Jerusalem. The Samaritans worshipped in Bethel (which means "house of God") where Jacob (who later became Israel) had sacrificed. The difference between the Samaritans and the Jews in those days is roughly parallel to our modern differences between Catholics and Protestants, or Catholics and Orthodox Christians. The two groups had a common root, but over time they had separated, and each group contained its own leaven. The only way to really cut through this is with the Holy Spirit and fire, and this formed part of Peter and John's mission in Samaria.

8:15 *who, when they were come down, prayed for them that they might receive the Holy Spirit.*

8:16 *(For as yet he was fallen on none of them; they were baptized only in the name of the Lord Jesus.)*

In the Jewish world and in every issue related to Israel, as laid out in the books of Moses, if anyone recognized that they were unclean and contaminated, their remedy was to be washed in water. There were many ways in which a person could become unclean, some of them avoidable and some of them not. For example, you could sin, become sick, touch someone who was unclean, or touch a dead body. The ingrained reaction of any Jew finding himself in an unclean state was to seek the remedy described in the law of Moses. There were many ways to become contaminated, but only one way to be decontaminated – wash in water.

This is where water baptism comes from. The Israelites knew that when the Messiah came, he would find them all unclean, so tradition said that when he came, they would all need to be washed. (This is why they asked John the Baptist why he was baptizing people if he wasn't the Messiah.[23]) So when Philip spread the gospel in Samaria, the reaction was automatic. The Samaritans' way of manifesting repentance with Philip mirrored that of the Jews with John the Baptist; that is, they were baptized in water (but not in the Holy Spirit). Even though there were no dealings between the Jews and the Samaritans,

---

23 John 1:25.

both groups clearly understood the meaning of water baptism: it was a public declaration that they were not clean.

It's very sad that in the Christian era, even though almost all the different groups and sects have followed some form of water baptism, the significance of this rite has for the most part become unclear. For many, it's simply a formality denoting membership into the group, and they don't know and aren't informed of the significance that it had for the Jews in the time of the New Testament. These people know even less about the symbolism relating to the true gospel – that the old (carnal) man must be buried so that the resurrected Christ can live in us. Today many Christians are in the same straits as the Samaritans. They were baptized in water and they came out wet, but the Spirit of God, the life of God, has not yet entered into them.

Verse 17 speaks of what happened when Peter and John arrived in Samaria:

8:17 *Then they laid their hands on them, and they received the Holy Spirit.*

In this case, it's obvious that the Holy Spirit didn't come by the water baptism. The Spirit came when the apostles laid their hands on those who had believed, repented, and had been baptized with water.

8:18 *And when Simon saw that through the laying on of the apostles' hands the Holy Spirit was given, he offered them money,*

8:19 *saying, Give me also this power, that on whomsoever I lay hands, he may receive the Holy Spirit.*

This is where Simon the magician showed his true colors, but today we have something worse than Simon's shenanigans. We have people who want to utilize a human method to confer gifts and ministry on believers (provided they are willing to pay) instead of depending directly upon God. If you go where these people are, they'll sell you an expensive book or charge an entrance fee at the door so that you can enter a room along with several hundred other people, the vast majority of whom don't know each other, and you'll be told that everyone is going to learn to prophesy. The leaders are going to pray for you, and each one of you is going to become a "prophet." And just how do you prophesy? According to them, you just put your hand on the stranger standing next to you and say good things, and that's prophecy. Then they tell you that if you want to be sure that your prophecies will come true, you will have to come back, take a second course, buy another expensive book, and learn about apostles. The degree to which you submit to your "apostle" will determine the degree to which your "prophecies" will come true, you're told, and this cycle goes on and on and on. Not even Simon the magician would have tried to get away with this.

8:19 *Give me also this power, that on whomsoever I lay hands, he may receive the Holy Spirit.*

8:20a *But Peter said unto him, Thy money perish with thee.*

Peter didn't say, "Look, Brother Simon, I don't feel that you're in perfect spiritual shape, but give us a nice offering and I'm sure God will bless you. Come with us, Simon, you clever magician, and we'll give you the opportunity to share all that money you spent years collecting in this town. Just finance the Great Crusade of the Peter and John Ministries, and God is bound to bless you. We're the 'real' apostles. Come along with us, Simon, and after a while, you'll learn how we do things."

Peter's response was much more blunt and honest than that. What he said was:

8:20b *Thy money perish with thee because thou hast thought that the gift of God may be purchased with money.*

8:21 *Thou hast neither part nor lot in this matter, for thy heart is not right in the sight of God.*

8:22 *Repent therefore of this thy wickedness and pray God, if perhaps this thought of thine heart may be forgiven thee.*

8:23 *For I perceive that thou art in the gall of bitterness and in the prison of iniquity.*

Had Peter been a different sort of man, he might have said coaxingly, "Look, Simon, you don't understand. When a bad desire like this one surfaces, you have to kneel down and ask for forgiveness. In fact, it's a good idea for you to do this every night, because we all sin in word, thought, and deed, as well as by omission. And if you confess your sins to the Lord Jesus, he'll always be faithful and just to forgive your sins."

Did Peter say this? No! He told Simon in so many words to repent and pray if *perhaps* this wicked thought could be forgiven. He told him in plain but vivid terms that he was in the gall of bitterness and the prison of iniquity. (Iniquity is what happens when the person knows he's in sin, yet is trying to cover it up and pretend that he's fine.) Peter made Simon understand that God didn't *have* to forgive him; God could decide to forgive or not to forgive, according to his sovereign will. In other words, Peter scared the living daylights out of Simon the magician.

8:24 *Then Simon answered and said, Pray ye to the Lord for me that none of these things which ye have spoken come upon me.*

What Simon didn't want to come upon him was God choosing

not to forgive his wicked thought. Peter had told him, in effect, that this was a distinct possibility. How many preachers would dare to say this to someone today? Very few, I suspect.

> 8:25 And they [Peter and John], *when they had tes-tified and preached the word of God, returned to Jerusalem and preached the gospel in many villages of the Samaritans.*

Peter and John didn't speak again to Simon the magician. He had been badly frightened, but we don't know if he really repented and if God forgave him. But later in the book of Acts a similar scene took place, this time involving the apostle Paul and an individual identified as Elymas the wise man. This false prophet tried to prevent a local proconsul from hearing Paul's words, but what Elymas didn't realize was that when Paul was talking about his beloved Jesus, he was virtually unstoppable. Paul left this so-called wise man blind, and everyone knew what had happened (Acts 13:8-12).

One unusual thing about the Samaria situation is the Holy Spirit aspect. As we know, Philip was full of the Holy Spirit, which meant that because of his preaching, the demons were fleeing and so many signs, wonders, and miracles were happen-ing that even Simon the magician could see a huge difference between what Philip was doing and what he had been doing. And yet, under Philip's ministry, the Holy Spirit didn't enter into the Samaritans. It was only when Peter and John came that the Spirit entered into the people there. Why was this?

I wish I could offer a simple answer, but as John 3:8 suggests, the Holy Spirit is sovereign and, like the wind, may be unpre-dictable in human terms. For instance, although Philip was performing great works in Samaria, God sent him to another site, where the Holy Spirit was about to touch the treasurer of Queen Candace. In the coming pages, you'll find several examples of how different people were baptized in (Greek "into") the Holy Spirit, and each case is different. For example, when Peter visited the centurion Cornelius and his family, they received the Holy Spirit before he even laid hands on them or baptized them in water.

Or consider the case of Saul (Paul), who became filled with the Holy Spirit in a very curious way, as we will examine in detail later. After Saul – who had been the worst persecutor of the Christians – was blinded on the road to Damascus, God sent him a disciple named Ananias, who told him, *Brother Saul, the Lord Jesus . . . has sent me, that thou might receive thy sight and be filled with the Holy Spirit* (Acts 9:17). Apparently, Ananias didn't consider himself an apostle ("sent one") at the time, but even so, he feared the Lord more than he feared man. So when God sent him, Ananias went and accomplished the work of an apostle as an agent of the Holy Spirit.

God may deal directly with us, as he did with Saul, but he may also incorporate those he desires to use as part of a larger whole. When Philip fled to Samaria out of fear, God used him there. After Philip had established a beachhead against the powers of darkness, God brought Peter and John to Samaria and used Philip in the role of an apostle to the Ethiopian eunuch.

> 8:26 *And the angel of the Lord spoke unto Philip, saying, Arise and go toward the south unto the way that goes down from Jerusalem unto Gaza, which is desert.*

What happens when the Lord sends someone forth with a specific purpose? Well, Jesus sent his disciples on a journey to spread the gospel, and when they returned, the Scriptures called them apostles (Mark 6:30). When the persecution arose that caused Philip to flee to Samaria, the apostles didn't flee, because apostles only go when and where God sends them. Nevertheless, the Lord used many people like Philip, the gospel was spread throughout the region, and the Holy Spirit came in power. The apostles then arrived in Samaria, and at this point, according to verse 26, *the angel of the Lord spoke unto Philip.*

The angel of the Lord spoke to the prophets throughout the Old Testament, and he continued to speak in the New Testament. For example, when Paul was on a ship in the midst of a severe storm (Acts 27), it appeared that all would be lost, but he was able to calm everyone down by revealing to them, "The angel of God stood by me tonight and told me that this is what will happen."

Where is the angel of the Lord today?

> 8:26 *And the angel of the Lord spoke unto Philip, saying, Arise and go toward the south unto the way that goes down from Jerusalem unto Gaza, which is desert.*

What happened? The angel of the Lord sent him. And who is the angel of the Lord? One who represents the LORD and is like the Lord (to confirm this, read Revelation chapters 1 and 10). When the Lord sends, what happens? The sent one is an apostle (Greek "sent one"). The Lord sent Philip – previously a waiter – to represent him. Scripture says that he who is faithful in little will receive more (Luke 16:10). Philip was faithful waiting on tables, and look what God did with him!

> 8:27 *Then he arose and went, and, behold, a man of Ethiopia, a eunuch of great authority under Candace queen of the Ethiopians, who had the charge of all her treasure and had come to Jerusalem to worship,*

> 8:28 *was returning and sitting in his chariot reading Isaiah the prophet.*

This was a man of high rank who was returning to his home from a nearby country. He was obviously wealthy, since a copy of the book of Isaiah would have cost a small fortune. He must also have been well educated, since he was able to read it in Hebrew, which was quite an accomplishment for a foreigner.

8:29 *Then the Spirit said unto Philip, Go near and join thyself to this chariot.*

The angel of the Lord had sent him, and the Spirit now told him to zero in on a specific chariot. Many people say that the Lord has spoken to them, when in fact it is only the vain imaginings of their heart. Philip, however, had a direct encounter with the angel of the Lord, and the Spirit was fine-tuning the guidance along the way. Many today claim to be apostles of the Lord, even though he didn't send them (most likely they were sent by a group). Perhaps they have done some studies, or maybe they have gifts that allow them to convince multitudes, and based on these factors, they have launched out. A true apostle, however, has had a direct encounter with the Lord. A true apostle has been sent by the Lord. An apostle cannot be set into place by men.

8:30 *And Philip ran there to him and heard him read the prophet Isaiah and said, Dost thou understand what thou readest?*

8:31 *And he said, How can I, except someone should guide me? And he besought Philip to come up and sit with him.*

How many of us read our Bibles every day? People have been taught that it's necessary to read a chapter every day or to follow a plan that will get them through the Bible in a year. They are told which chapters to read each day. The most splendid plans have a chapter out of the books of Moses, a chapter of history, a chapter out of the Psalms, one out of the Prophets, a chapter out of the Gospels, and one out of the writings of Paul. Those who follow such plans may be able to read the whole Bible in a certain amount of time, but most of them wind up like this poor eunuch, reading without understanding. They don't realize that they're in the same situation as the Jews whom Paul describes, who have a veil over their hearts and thus can't understand that the law of Moses is really about the Lord Jesus Christ (2 Corinthians 3:13-18).

Many Christians today read the New Testament with the same veil over their hearts. They read it because they've promised to do so, and if they don't follow through, they feel great pangs of guilt. Yet a great many don't really comprehend what they're reading.

> 8:31 *And he said, How can I, except someone should guide me? And he besought Philip to come up and sit with him.*
>
> 8:32 *The place of the scripture which he read was this, He was led as a sheep to the slaughter, and like a lamb dumb before his shearer, so opened he not his mouth;*
>
> 8:33 *in his humiliation his judgment was taken away, and who shall declare his generation? for his life is taken from the earth.*
>
> 8:34 *And the eunuch answered Philip and said, I pray thee, of whom does the prophet speak this? of himself or of some other?*
>
> 8:35 *Then Philip opened his mouth and began at the same scripture and preached unto him the gospel of Jesus.*
>
> 8:36 *And as they went on their way, they came unto a certain water; and the eunuch said, See, here is water; what hinders me to be baptized?*

The eunuch had studied the Old Testament. He knew that if you were unclean, you had to be washed. When he saw the water, he wanted to take the step with the Lord that he knew about.

> 8:37 *And Philip said, If thou dost believe with all thine heart, thou may. And he answered and said, I believe that Jesus Christ is the Son of God.*

Philip might have responded, "Wait a minute, that's above my pay grade. I'm only the waiter, the guy who waits on the tables over at the church of Jerusalem. We've got to get Peter and John to come from Jerusalem. Sorry, but if you want to be baptized in water or in the Holy Spirit, we need to call for an apostle." But of course, he didn't say any such thing. He was in direct contact with God.

> 8:38 *And he commanded the chariot to stand still, and they went both down into the water, both Philip and the eunuch, and he baptized him.*

> 8:39 *And when they were come up out of the water the Spirit of the Lord caught away Philip, so that the eunuch saw him no more, and he went on his way rejoicing.*

The eunuch went on his way filled with joy, which is a fruit of the Holy Spirit. Logically, since it would have been important to seize this opportunity to open a work in the land of Ethiopia where the queen's trusted right-hand man was now saved, at this point Philip should have arranged to go to the court of the queen or to send someone there in his place. But that would have been human logic. Instead, once the eunuch was in direct contact with God, the Spirit of the Lord caught Philip away. He had fulfilled his apostolic mission, and the eunuch saw him no more because the Holy Spirit would continue to guide and comfort the eunuch. Curiously, history bears out that one of the places on earth where there has always been a faithful band of believers is Ethiopia.

In all that we do, it's much better to leave the plans and details under the care of the Holy Spirit and not think that we must coordinate everything down to the last detail. It's important to explain, teach, and preach under the anointing of the Holy Spirit, but we should not and must not maintain a people who need to hear from God through us. The person who is truly immersed in the Spirit of God has the possibility of direct communion with God and direct teaching from the Lord. The Holy Spirit can guide us into all truth.

It's also true, of course, that the Lord uses his people as a team. He can send Philip first, and then Peter and John or whatever other person seems best to him. The choice is his.

What happened to Philip after his encounter with the eunuch?

8:40 But Philip was found at Azotus, and passing through, he preached the gospel in all the cities until he came to Caesarea.

Philip was relocated to another place, but Scripture doesn't give details about how this was accomplished except to say that the Spirit of the Lord caught him away. The rapture that happened to Philip wasn't intended to take him out of a place of danger and put him in a spot where he would be secure from the problems of this world. He was deposited into another region that had problems and dangers of its own, but where people were open and ready to hear the message. Later in the book of Acts, there is mention of a Philip (undoubtedly this same person) who had daughters who prophesied, so it seems that his children were also spiritually gifted.

At the beginning of the events described in the book of Acts, the ministry was conducted through men who had come of age, but later on, women were also directly involved. At first the gospel was just for the Jews, and then it was extended to the Samaritans and the Gentiles (who were considered to be pagans). God opened horizons and borders.

After this episode with Philip, the Lord revealed himself to the very person who was implementing most of the persecution of the Christians, and Saul was converted to Christianity. Although it's often assumed that he changed his name to Paul (meaning "small" or "little") at this point as a token of his new life and humbled spirit, in fact he continued to be called Saul for more than ten years after his conversion. He was still called Saul even as he preached and worked for the Lord. But one day, some of the Lord's men were praying in a situation where the only ministries that had been mentioned were those of prophets and teachers, and the Holy Spirit said, *Separate me Barnabas and Saul for the work unto which I have called them* (Acts 13:2). Several verses later, Saul became Paul (Acts 13:9). It was God who made the change.

The congregation at Antioch (where the word "Christian" was coined) knew that the Lord had said the gospel must be preached to all nations, but they didn't hold a meeting to figure out how to extend the gospel and evangelize the rest of the world. They didn't decide to search for potential missionary candidates to implement the Great Commission. The ministry leaders at Antioch didn't conclude that they were indispensable to the congregation at Antioch (or that they were the cradle of Christianity) and that therefore they needed to make an appeal to the young people and send out missionaries.

No, nothing like that. They were simply praying, and the Holy Spirit said, *Separate me Barnabas and Saul for the work unto which I have called them.* God had a plan for how to evangelize, and his plan included sending Paul as an ambassador to the house of Caesar (where Scripture tells us that some were converted). To our way of thinking, though, God carried out that plan backwards, since Paul arrived at the palace as a prisoner in chains. According to tradition, Paul ultimately paid with his life, but he left a clean, untainted gospel planted everywhere he went.

Someone said that Paul's greatest mistake was not listening to the prophets who told him what was going to happen to him if he went back to Jerusalem. A big mistake in Paul's ministry! Well, it depends. God had Ananias tell Paul, right at the beginning, that he would show him how much it would behoove him to suffer for the cause of Christ, and Paul was willing. He knew what was going to happen to him, and he went and did it anyway, just as Jesus knew what would happen to him but did not shrink from accomplishing the will of his Father. This is how we got the New Testament! If Paul hadn't gone to Jerusalem over the objection of the prophets, we would be missing his prison epistles, which have encouraged countless generations of persecuted Christians right up to our present time and will continue to encourage them in the future.

Our natural, physical life isn't everything, and those who would judge God fail to understand this. Those who would accuse God of injustice or even of genocide (as when he ordered entire nations wiped out in the Old Testament) don't understand that there will also be a general resurrection. There will be a fair trial for everyone with an eternal possibility and potential for God to right every unjustice and a promise to wipe away every tear.

Why did God do away with Ananias and Sapphira (Acts 5:1-10)? Why did he speak to Simon the magician so abruptly, not even giving him an assurance that he would be forgiven? Simon was told that he was *in the gall of bitterness and in the prison of iniquity* (Acts 8:23). He was called to repentance and told that *perhaps* he might be forgiven and restored.

We can't judge God, because we haven't been behind the veil; we have not yet seen the reality that he is. We haven't seen him face-to-face, much less listened to all that he has to say. We must take by faith the fact that God may do with us as he pleases, and yet at the same time we are required to be responsible for our actions, for the Lord has all eternity to straighten out the effects of the free will that he has bestowed upon us. We're told that all people will have to give account not just for their actions, but for every idle word that comes out of their mouths (Matthew 12:36-37). God will leave nothing unresolved, and whoever has suffered injustice will have his day before God's throne.

There came a time when God had to change Peter's theology. Peter had been brought up and trained to have nothing to do with Gentiles, but because God wanted to send the gospel to the Gentiles, he showed Peter in many ways that he had to accept them as clean, and therefore he had to deal with them. As far as Peter was concerned, if God said that these people were clean, they were unarguably clean, no matter how wrong this appeared to his natural judgment. As we'll see later, when he sent Peter to the house of the Roman centurion (at the same time as he was preparing Saul), God wiped out a huge number of symbols that Peter had considered indispensable rites and traditions, and Peter had to accept this change.

The Lord already knows everything, and he's much more interested than we are in changing the situation of this world. The real question has always been, "Who is willing to do what God wants, the way God wants it done, and according to the timing of God, without trying to protect their own lives and their own interests?" This is what has held us back, because so many of us desire to do the work of the Lord in our own way and not his way. The book of the Acts of the Apostles demonstrates God's work being done God's way. This is diametrically opposed to the plans for evangelization drawn up by man. *Woe unto you, scribes and Pharisees, hypocrites! for ye compass sea and land to make one proselyte, and when he is made, ye make him twofold more a son of hell than yourselves* (Matthew 23:15).

When men try to indoctrinate adept candidates with their religion, their attempts don't flow by the Spirit or improve people in any way. Instead, according to the Lord, those whom they are trying to indoctrinate (along with the indoctrinators) go from bad to worse.

Where will we be found?

Those who were used by the Lord were found faithful with whatever they had at hand. Stephen and Philip were tending tables and waiting on widows. They became good "waiters" before the Lord. This cost Stephen his life, but it launched Philip as an evangelist. The Lord is the one who decides how these things turn out. One thing, however, is certain: If we're led by the Spirit of God to decide that our own life isn't important and that what *is* important is the life of the Lord, then we can come to a place where we will no longer make decisions based on fear of what others may do to us. Instead, we will be guided by the fear of the Lord, which according to Scripture is the beginning of wisdom (Proverbs 9:10).

Let Us Pray

Heavenly Father, We want to understand, and we desire that what we learn may be fulfilled in actual practice in our lives so that we may be found doing your work and not our own. We ask this in the name of our Lord Jesus Christ. Amen.

Chapter 2

The Path to Maturity

The persecution of the Christians at Jerusalem by the religious authorities had many consequences. Although the apostles stayed in Jerusalem, everyone else fled to Judaea, Samaria, and elsewhere, and Scripture says that the congregations were multiplied. It's important to understand that the word *ekklesia*, which is translated as "congregation" (or "church" in many English Bibles) is used in the plural in many verses. The book of Acts doesn't speak of a single congregation or church; it speaks of many congregations and of the congregations or churches being multiplied.

The congregations or churches referred to in Acts are not institutions. This word *ekklesia* means "those who are called out" (of the institution), those who have come out of organized religion. They met in homes for the first two centuries after Jesus's death. *Ekklesia* always identifies people or a congregation, never a building or institution. It's not perfectly in line with Scripture to refer to an "early church" or to a "first-century church," for there were many churches or congregations. In fact, our English word "church" is most unfortunate in that it's of dubious pagan origin.[24] This is why the Jubilee Bible translation uses the word "congregation" in italics, with an explanatory footnote.

Scripture is clear that there is but one body of Christ, of which the Lord Jesus is the head. He is the only mediator of the new covenant. He is the government of the many members of the body of Christ. However, although there is only one body of Christ, there are many congregations (churches) in the book of Acts (Acts 9:31, 16:5).

Over the centuries, man has twisted things by saying that there is only one universal church, with many local bodies. This is not true. If there are local bodies of Christ, then someone may claim to be the local head of the local body. No, the fact is that the Lord Jesus is the head, and there is only one body (Ephesians 4:4). There are not many *bodies* of Christ; there are many *congregations*. There are many groups of people called by God to leave the system of this world, the system of men, and the system of religion organized by man. Such groups may be as small as two or three people (Matthew 18:20).

This is not to say that all congregations, or even all members of any given congregation, are properly aligned with the Lord. We can find a metaphor for this situation in Matthew 13:24-40, which describes the Enemy sowing tares (the sons of the wicked) in the same field as wheat (the sons of the kingdom), and the master of the house allowing the tares to remain in the field (which represents the world). At the time of the harvest, however, the tares are bundled and burned before the wheat is harvested.

In Acts chapter 9, we will see that there are important details that can be overlooked only too easily by the casual reader.

---

24 The English word *church* is definitely not of Hebrew origin. *Webster's Unabridged Dictionary* suggests that it is of some form of Greek origin very distinct from the Greek word *ekklesia* used in the NT.

Acts 9

9:1 And Saul, yet breathing out threatenings and slaughter against the disciples of the Lord, came unto the prince of the priests

9:2 and asked him for letters to Damascus to the synagogues, that if he found any of this way, whether they were men or women, he might bring them bound unto Jerusalem.

9:3 And as he proceeded, he came near Damascus; and suddenly there shone round about him a light from heaven;

9:4 and falling to the earth, he heard a voice saying unto him, Saul, Saul, why dost thou persecute me?

9:5 And he said, Who art thou, Lord? And the Lord said, I AM Jesus whom thou dost persecute; it is hard for thee to kick against the pricks.

9:6 And he trembling and astonished said, Lord, what wilt thou have me to do? And the Lord said unto him, Arise and go into the city, and it shall be told thee what it behooves thee to do.

The Lord Jesus revealed himself to Saul, who was persecuting the true congregation (church). He was dragging men and women off to prison. He had participated in the death of Stephen. But when Saul arrived in Damascus, he was in no fit state to persecute anyone. Blinded by his direct encounter with the Lord Jesus, he had to have someone lead him by the hand.

9:7 And the men who journeyed with him stood speechless, hearing indeed the voice, but seeing no one.

9:8 Then Saul arose from the earth; and opening his

eyes, he saw no one; so they led him by the hand and brought him into Damascus

9:9 *where he was three days without sight, and neither ate nor drank.*

Jesus had told him to *Arise and go into the city, and it shall be told thee what it behooves thee to do.* Saul was so shaken by his encounter with God and his subsequent blindness that he did nothing but wait for instructions. For three days, he neither ate nor drank while he waited.

9:10 *And there was a certain disciple at Damascus, named Ananias; to whom the Lord said in a vision, Ananias. And he said, Behold, I am here, Lord.*

9:11 *And the Lord said unto him, Arise and go into the street which is called Straight and enquire in the house of Judas for one called Saul, of Tarsus; for, behold, he prays*

9:12 *and has seen in a vision a man named Ananias coming in and putting his hand on him, that he might receive his sight.*

Saul and Ananias had each received a vision with instructions from the Lord. ("Ananias" means "the LORD is gracious.")

9:13 *Then Ananias answered, Lord, I have heard by many of this man, of how much evil he has done to thy saints in Jerusalem,*

9:14 *and even here he has authority from the princes of the priests to bind all that call on thy name.*

9:15 *But the Lord said unto him, Go; for he is a chosen vessel unto me, to bear my name before the Gentiles and kings and the sons of Israel;*

9:16 for I will show him how much it behooves him to suffer for my name.

Ananias had his doubts about whether Saul deserved to be helped; he told the Lord about all the evil that Saul had been doing and how great a threat Saul was (as if God didn't already know!). But when the Lord told him to go anyway, Ananias didn't feel any need to go and consult with some elders or clergy in order to get permission to follow God's instructions and minister to Saul. No, he simply went, risking his life, but he was secure in the word that he had received directly from the Lord. Had he been mistaken in what he heard from God, Ananias could have been in real trouble, since Saul had come to Damascus for the express purpose of harming believers.

Saul, too, was risking his life, because after the Lord Jesus spoke to him, he refrained from doing anything on his own until he had a word from the Lord. He didn't even drink any water. How long can people last in the desert without water? Three days is probably close to the limit. This was a test of faith for Ananias, but it was also a test of faith for Saul.

You'll recall that after Philip went to Samaria, many signs, wonders, and miracles took place and many people believed, but the Holy Spirit was only imparted when the apostles came from Jerusalem and laid their hands on the believers. In the case of Saul, three days after his direct encounter with Jesus, the Lord sent a disciple (Ananias), not an apostle, to minister to him. Based upon what happened in Samaria, there should have been no question of imparting the Holy Spirit. And yet:

9:17 Then Ananias went and entered into the house; and putting his hands on him said, Brother Saul, the Lord Jesus who appeared unto thee in the way as thou didst come, has sent me, that thou might receive thy sight and be filled with the Holy Spirit.

9:18 *And immediately there fell from his eyes as it had been scales; and he received sight immediately and arose and was baptized.*

9:19a *And when he had received food, he was comforted.*

"Comforted" is a word that's linked with the action of the Holy Spirit, because he is the Comforter.

In the book of the Acts of the Apostles, the word "disciple" is used frequently. What's the difference between a disciple and an apostle? A disciple is one who leaves everything to follow the Lord. He doesn't count on having anything of his own; everything is in the hands of the Lord. And when the disciples became apostles, the process was even simpler. The Lord sent them out to represent himself, and after they came back, having done what the Lord sent them to do, Scripture simply says, *Now the names of the twelve apostles are these . . .* (Matthew 10:2). Nowhere in the Gospels is there a ceremony where apostles are appointed. Interesting!

Here was the disciple Ananias, and the Lord sent him to do what only an apostle could do, yet everything went perfectly. It's a great example of how the Lord can send whomever he wants to do whatever he ordains whenever he chooses. *For he whom God has sent speaks the words of God; for God does not give the Spirit by measure unto him* (John 3:34).

What does this mean? It means that the person who is sent by God to do God's will is going to receive an unlimited anointing to fulfill whatever is in God's heart for him or her to accomplish. This isn't an anointing by measure, such as the formula for the carefully prepared oil described in Exodus chapter 30 – oil that was to be poured over every prophet, priest, and king in Israel. (I'm told that the exact formula yields two gallons of anointing oil.) Nor is it the anointing of Pentecost that provided gifts of the Spirit, or even a double portion such as Elisha received. No, it's the anointing described in Psalm 133. It's the anointing that Jesus had from his Father. He only came to speak the Father's words and to do the Father's deeds. We're able to catch glimpses of this in the book of the Acts of the Apostles, but the fullness is reserved for the time of the end (Revelation 10 and 11).

The problem we have today is that many who claim to be Christians aren't even disciples. In the book of Acts, in God's terminology, there's no word to describe those who don't walk the talk. Those who follow the Lord Jesus are called disciples, and if they follow the Lord, they can't be following their own whims and desires. (Simon the magician found out about that!)

However, following Jesus doesn't always mean that people must change their occupations. Late in the book of Acts, for example, after it was confirmed that God had designated Paul as the apostle to the Gentiles, with wonderful results in many places, Paul kept doing what he had always done: he made tents and sold them to meet his expenses (Acts 18:2-3). In this way, he could present the gospel without cost to the Corinthians or others. He chose to work with his hands and not ask for money, so he continued with his occupation as a tentmaker.

A call to follow the Lord, even if it involves him sending you out as an apostle, isn't necessarily a call to stop working with your hands and operate only within the spiritual realm. There is no example in the book of Acts of any follower of Jesus seeking higher education with rabbis or wanting to be a rabbi. To be a disciple means that Jesus is directly in charge and the disciple is willing to be like Ananias. If the Lord tells a disciple to risk his life, that's his prerogative. The disciple's life isn't his own; it belongs to the Lord. And if the Lord sends us on an apostolic mission such as the one he assigned to Ananias, we will flow in the apostolic realm.

Returning to Acts 9:

9:19(b) Then Saul was certain days with the disciples who were at Damascus.

9:20 And straightway he preached Christ in the synagogues, that he is the Son of God.

9:21 But all that heard him were amazed and said, Is not this he that destroyed those who called on this name in Jerusalem and came here for that intent that he might bring them bound unto the princes of the priests?

9:22 But Saul increased the more in strength and confounded the Jews who dwelt at Damascus, proving that this is the Christ.

9:23 And as many days passed, the Jews took counsel among themselves to kill him;

9:24 but their ambushes were understood by Saul. And they watched the gates day and night to kill him.

It didn't take very long for the Jews to decide to kill Saul, and this wouldn't be the last time they attempted to ambush him.

9:25 Then the disciples took him by night and let him down by the wall in a basket.

9:26 And when Saul was come to Jerusalem, he tried to join himself to the disciples; but they were all afraid of him and did not believe that he was a disciple.

9:27 But Barnabas took him and brought him to the apostles and declared unto them how he had seen the Lord in the way and that he had spoken to him and how he had preached boldly at Damascus in the name of Jesus.

9:28 *And he was with them coming in and going out at Jerusalem;*

9:29 *and he spoke boldly in the name of the Lord Jesus and disputed against the Greeks; but they went about to slay him,*

9:30 *which when the brethren knew, they brought him down to Caesarea and sent him forth to Tarsus.*

9:31 *Then the congregations had rest throughout all Judaea and Galilee and Samaria and were edified, walking in the fear of the Lord, and with the comfort of the Holy Spirit they were multiplied.*

After Saul (the main persecutor of the Christians) was converted, the Enemy turned his wrath against him, and the congregations had rest, at least for a while. During this time, they were edified *walking in the fear of the Lord*. There's no mention of Bible schools, seminaries, headquarters, or even a church building, and yet *with the comfort of the Holy Spirit they were multiplied*.

9:32 *And it came to pass, as Peter passed throughout all quarters, he came down also to the saints who dwelt at Lydda.*

9:33 *And there he found a certain man named Aeneas, who had been in bed eight years, for he was a paralytic.*

9:34 *And Peter said unto him, Aeneas, the Lord Jesus, the Christ, makes thee whole; arise and make thy bed. And he arose immediately.*

9:35 *And all that dwelt at Lydda and Saron saw him and turned to the Lord.*

Here we have an example of how the meaning of names can offer an extra dimension to our understanding of Scripture.

"Lydda" means "contention." In this place of "contention," Peter found a man named Aeneas, "worthy of praise." Despite his excellent name, Aeneas had been paralyzed and in bed for eight years. Eight is a number that could symbolize new beginnings in Christ, but instead, this man had been bedridden in "Lydda," just as the capability of God's people can become paralyzed in the midst of strife and contention, even if they are individually "worthy of praise." However, the Lord used Peter to create a breakthrough by commanding Aeneas to arise (just as paralyzed Christians must break away from contention, rise to their feet, and make a stand for the Lord). Then *all that dwelt at Lydda and Saron ["plains" or "flat land"] saw him and turned to the Lord.*

9:36 *Now there was at Joppa a certain disciple named Tabitha, which by interpretation is called Dorcas; this woman was full of good works and alms-deeds[25] which she did.*

"Joppa" means "height" and "beauty" or "victory." "Tabitha" means "grace" or "a gazelle."

9:37 *And it came to pass in those days that she was sick and died, whom when they had washed, they laid her in an upper chamber.*

9:38 *And since as Lydda was close to Joppa and the disciples had heard that Peter was there, they sent unto him two men, asking him that he not delay to come to them.*

9:39 *Then Peter arose and went with them. When he was come, they brought him into the upper chamber: and all the widows stood by him weeping and showing*

---

25   Lit. "acts of mercy."

*the coats and garments which Dorcas had made them
while she was with them.*

Lydda (representing strife and contention) was close to Joppa
(representing victory). Even though Tabitha (representing
grace) had been very active in good works, she died. *Coats and
garments* are coverings, and we are all to be covered by grace
through the Holy Spirit. If, however, we get too close to what
"Lydda" represents, disaster can befall us. Strife and contention can cause us to lose our covering of grace and can bring
about spiritual death.

9:40 *Then Peter put them all out and knelt down and
prayed and turned to the body [and] said, Tabitha,
arise. And she opened her eyes; and when she saw Peter,
she sat up.*

God used Peter to minister resurrection life into this tragic
situation. Throughout the book of Acts, God used real events to
teach important object lessons, just as Jesus did in the Gospels.
Tabitha, or "grace," is also known as Dorcas, or "gazelle," and
by God's grace we can bound over any obstacle like a gazelle.

9:41 *And he gave her his hand and lifted her up; and
calling the saints and widows, he presented her alive.*

9:42 *And it was known throughout all Joppa; and many
believed in the Lord.*

9:43 *And it came to pass that he tarried many days in
Joppa with one Simon a tanner.*

Peter was now well positioned in God's will for what would
happen next. "Simon" means "to hearken" (that is, to hear and
obey). The apostle Simon Peter was in Joppa ("victory") in the
house of Simon the tanner (the gist of this is that they were all

hearing and obeying God and walking in victory in the resurrection life of Jesus Christ).

Acts 10

10:1 There was a certain man in Caesarea called Cornelius, a centurion of the company called the Italian,

Cornelius was a Roman centurion commanding Roman troops. This is noteworthy because soldiers from other nations wouldn't have had the power or prestige of the Romans, and thus the events recounted in this chapter would have had less impact. "Cornelius" means "of one horn" (or "of one purpose"). Cornelius commanded the Italian company. "Italy" means "like a calf" (symbol of humanism), and Caesarea ("of Caesar") is a symbol of the world system.

10:2 a devout man and one that feared God with all his house, who gave many alms to the people and prayed to God always.

In the midst of a very intense humanistic, worldly environment, Cornelius was focused on pleasing God. "Alms to the people" in this context means "acts of mercy" (both "alms" and "mercy" are derived from the Greek word *eleemosyne*, meaning "pity, mercy"), just as when the Lord Jesus saw people who were in need as he walked along the way, and the Scriptures say that he had mercy or compassion on them and he healed them. Sometimes he also told them they were saved and their sins were forgiven. Jesus told people that he did nothing on his own but only spoke what the Father was saying and did what the Father was doing. In other words, it was the Lord Jesus who felt compassion and performed the miracle, yet because he was completely in tune with his Father's heart, he wasn't doing anything that his Father wasn't doing.

Cornelius, too, was performing acts of compassion; he was a person who feared God, and Scripture says he was a devout man ("devout" means "like God").

> 10:3 *He saw in a vision evidently about the ninth hour of the day an angel of God coming in to him and saying unto him, Cornelius.*

The part about the ninth hour is interesting because of what else was happening at that time. According to the first chapter of the gospel of Luke, it was the turn of a priest named Zacharias to tend the altar of incense, which was located in the Holy of Holies but was tended from the Holy Place. While he was doing this, people were outside praying. Later in the New Testament, we're told that the prayer time in the temple was the ninth hour, and since it appears that the Jews counted the hours from dawn, the ninth hour would be about 3:00 p.m. Many events in the Gospels and in the book of Acts occur at this hour (just as many things in Jesus's ministry take place on the seventh day, the Sabbath, which caused much controversy). For instance, it was at the ninth hour that Peter and John raised up the paralytic and gave a message to the multitude congregated there for prayer. (Or rather, they gave part of their message at that time, before being arrested; they gave the rest of their message later to the Sanhedrin after being put on trial.)

So at the ninth hour, Cornelius was in his house, praying, just as the Jews were doing at the temple. One thing that most people forget, however, is that prayer is not just us making petitions to God; prayer is also God's response to us. The plan of God is that his temple will be not a building, but the people who surrender to him. Cornelius hadn't yet received the Holy Spirit, but God sent him an angel, just as he sent an angel to Zacharias and to Mary.

Now, given that Cornelius was a Roman centurion, you

might expect that the angel had been sent to deliver him a stern warning. Even though he was reported to be a good and devout man, he was still part of an imperialist army with a bad record, an army that was oppressing the entire world and treading the people of God underfoot. It wouldn't have been surprising if the angel had ordered him to resign from the army immediately.

Instead, having addressed him by name, the angel spoke to him kindly.

10:4 *And when he looked on him, he was afraid and said, What is it, Lord? And he said unto him, Thy prayers and thine alms*[26] *are come up for a memorial before God.*

The angel's answer was similar to the response given to Daniel when God heard his prayer (Daniel 10:12).

10:5 *And now send men to Joppa and call for one Simon, whose surname is Peter;*

10:6 *he lodges with one Simon a tanner, whose house is by the sea side; he shall tell thee what it behooves thee to do.*

To our human minds, this seems a rather convoluted way to go about things. An angel came from the presence of God directly to Cornelius, and instead of passing on a straightforward message, the angel commanded him to send for Peter in order to learn what God wanted of him. However, we know that God often chooses to work through people to accomplish his goals, as he did when he sent Ananias to Paul to restore his sight. What God has placed into the hands of human beings who have repented, are converted, have been born again, and are full of the presence of the Holy Spirit is greater than what is taking place with the angels in these circumstances. After all,

---

26 Lit. "thine acts of mercy."

Scripture says that God has never called any of the angels his Son (Hebrews 1:4-8). The Lord Jesus Christ is the Son of God, and God's plan is for Jesus to have many brethren.

Incidentally, Scripture declares that the angels are watching us with great interest to see what God does with us (1 Peter 1:12). Scripture also indicates that those who are born again and have the Spirit of God will become greater than the angels. That's quite a prospect!

> 10:7 *And when the angel who spoke unto Cornelius was departed, he called two of his household servants and a devout soldier of those that waited on him continually;*

> 10:8 *and when he had declared all these things unto them, he sent them to Joppa.*

> 10:9 *On the morrow, as they went on their journey and drew near unto the city, Peter went up upon the house-top to pray about the sixth hour;*

This was about noon, which means that Peter was going to begin his prayers about three hours before the prayer time of the Jews.

> 10:10 *and he became very hungry and would have eaten; but while they made ready, he fell into a rapture of understanding*

> 10:11 *and saw the heaven opened and a certain vessel descending unto him, as it had been a great sheet knit at the four corners and let down to the earth,*

> 10:12 *in which were all manner of fourfooted beasts of the earth and wild beasts and reptiles and fowls of the air.*

> 10:13 *And there came a voice to him, Rise, Peter, kill and eat.*

10:14 *But Peter said, Not so, Lord; for I have never eaten anything that is common or unclean.*

10:15 *And the voice spoke unto him again the second time, That which God has cleansed, do not call common.*

10:16 *This was done three times, and the vessel was received up again into heaven.*

10:17 *Now while Peter doubted in himself what this vision which he had seen should mean, behold, the men who were sent from Cornelius had made enquiry for Simon's house and stood before the gate*

10:18 *and called and asked whether Simon, who was surnamed Peter, were lodged there.*

10:19 *While Peter thought on the vision, the Spirit said unto him, Behold, three men seek thee.*

10:20 *Arise therefore and get thee down and go with them, doubting nothing; for I have sent them.*

The Holy Spirit had clear communication with both Peter and Ananias, and the revelation of the Lord Jesus to Saul had been done in such a way that there could be no misunderstanding. Today, many claim to be led by God and insist that God has spoken to them, yet they continue to have a great deal of confusion. God may indeed have spoken to them, but desiring things that are not the will of God (as many of us tend to do) tends to drown out the still, small voice of the Lord. I recall that I once complained about not hearing the voice of the Lord with clarity. However, a few weeks later I was kidnapped, and after several days of being tied to a tree out in the jungle, I was able to hear him much better!

Those who are hearing the voice of God in the book of Acts are the disciples who had made the decision to follow the Lord without looking back. They had counted the cost, and they knew that the price could be their own lives. When things are defined as starkly as this, it's much easier to hear the voice of God. Even Saul, breathing out threats and slaughtering the disciples of the Lord, thought that he was leaving all his personal ambitions behind in order to rid Israel of the heretics of this new "way" (as Christianity was then often called). The Lord changed Saul's mind by giving him an unmistakable message, not just with his voice (which Saul's companions also heard) but also with the light of his presence, which left Saul blind.

10:19a *While Peter thought on the vision,*

He had seen something, he had heard something, and as he turned things over in his mind, the Holy Spirit continued to speak to him; this was continual communion.

10:21 *Then Peter went down to the men who were sent unto him from Cornelius and said, Behold, I am he whom ye seek; what is the cause for which ye are come?*

10:22 *And they said, Cornelius the centurion, a just man and one that fears God and of good report among all the nation of the Jews, was warned from God by a holy angel to send for thee into his house and to hear words of thee.*

10:23 *Then he called them in and lodged them. And on the morrow Peter went away with them, and certain brethren from Joppa accompanied him.*

10:24 *And the next day they entered into Caesarea. And Cornelius waited for them and had called together his kinsmen and near friends.*

10:25 And as Peter was coming in, Cornelius met him and fell down at his feet and worshipped him.

10:26 But Peter took him up, saying, Stand up; I myself also am a man.

10:27 And as he talked with him, he went in and found many that were come together.

10:28 And he said unto them, Ye know how that it is an abominable thing for a man that is a Jew to keep company or come unto one of another nation; but God has showed me that I should not call any man common or unclean.

10:29 Therefore I came unto you without doubting, as soon as I was sent for; I ask therefore for what intent ye have sent for me?

10:30 And Cornelius said, Four days ago I was fasting until this hour; and at the ninth hour I prayed in my house, and, behold, a man stood before me in bright clothing

10:31 and said, Cornelius, thy prayer is heard and thine alms are had in remembrance in the sight of God.

We know that our own good works can't save us, but a person who is moved by the heart of God to do the will of God is in a very different situation. The work that God does in our heart and the work that he does through us after changing our heart is "good work" that is acceptable to him.

10:32 Send therefore to Joppa, and call here Simon, whose surname is Peter; he is lodged in the house of one Simon a tanner by the sea side, who, when he comes, shall speak unto thee.

10:33 *Immediately therefore I sent to thee, and thou
hast done well to come. Now therefore we are all here
present before God to hear all things that are commanded thee of God.*

According to the Jews, the presence of God was in Jerusalem,
in the Holy of Holies. Cornelius, however, had the great revelation that God was present in Caesarea, in his house, with his
family. Nothing like this is previously recorded in Scripture.

How did Cornelius know he was in the presence of God? He
knew it by revelation, because God had already done a work in
his heart. He understood that God no longer lived in temples
made of stone, built by the hand of man; thanks to the birth,
life, and sacrificial death of Jesus, the temple of God was now
his people. Jesus had said that wherever there were two or three
gathered together in his name, he would be there in the midst
of them. Now Peter was there with two or three brethren from
Joppa, and they all – including Cornelius – felt the presence
of the Holy Spirit. And Cornelius knew that they all felt it. Yet
there are still many people who lead meetings in man-made
temples and tell their congregations that they are coming to
what they call the house of God.

10:33(b) *Now therefore we are all here present before
God to hear all things that are commanded thee of God.*

10:34 *Then Peter opened his mouth and said, Of a truth
I perceive that God is no respecter of persons;*

10:35 *but in every nation he that fears him and works
righteousness is acceptable to him.*

The Jews had taught that in order to be accepted by God, people
had to go to Jerusalem, be ceremonially washed (this is where
baptism comes from), undergo circumcision, and comply
with many other rituals. Peter, however, is saying here that it's

enough to fear God and work righteousness ("righteousness" and "justice" are the same word in the original).

When soldiers challenged John the Baptist to tell them what they should do, he didn't tell him to leave the army, but only to *Oppress no one, neither accuse anyone falsely; and be content with your wages* (Luke 3:14). For you to surrender to God, it's not usually necessary to leave your country or resign from your social group or your profession. It *is* necessary, however, to change the way you've been doing things and learn the ways of the Lord. *In every nation he that fears him and works righteousness is acceptable to him* [God].

> 10:36 *The word which God sent unto the sons of Israel, preaching the gospel: peace by Jesus Christ (he is Lord of all),*
>
> 10:37 *that word, I say, ye know, which was published throughout all Judaea and began from Galilee, after the baptism which John preached,*
>
> 10:38 *how God anointed Jesus of Nazareth with the Holy Spirit and with power, who went about doing good and healing all that were oppressed of the devil, for God was with him.*
>
> 10:39 *And we are witnesses of all things which he did both in the land of Judea and in Jerusalem, whom they slew hanging him on a tree.*
>
> 10:40 *This same one God raised up the third day and showed him openly,*
>
> 10:41 *not to all the people, but unto witnesses chosen before of God, even to us, who ate and drank with him after he rose from the dead.*

10:42 *And he commanded us to preach unto the people and to testify that it is he who is ordained of God to be the Judge of living and dead.*

10:43 *Unto him all the prophets give witness, that whosoever believes in him shall receive remission of sins through his name.*

This is a simple gospel of telling who the Lord Jesus really is.

10:44 *While Peter yet spoke these words, the Holy Spirit fell on all those who heard the word.*

10:45 *And those of the circumcision who believed were astonished, as many as came with Peter, that also on the Gentiles the gift of the Holy Spirit was poured out.*

10:46 *For they heard them speak with tongues and magnify God. Then Peter answered,*

10:47 *Can anyone forbid water that these should not be baptized, who have received the Holy Spirit as well as we?*

10:48 *And he commanded them to be baptized in the name of the Lord Jesus. Then they begged him to tarry certain days.*

It's possible to hear people speaking in tongues in religious meetings even today, but the vast majority of the time no one hears God being magnified because no one understands what's being said. The tongues that were being spoken under the anointing of the Holy Spirit in the book of Acts were known languages (Acts 2:1-12). The speakers didn't previously know the language, but there were people around them who knew it and could interpret and verify that what was being said magnified God.

The apostle Paul wrote to the Corinthian congregation, *If anyone speaks in an unknown tongue, let it be by two, or at the most by three, and that by course; and let one interpret. But if there is no interpreter, let him keep silence in the congregation, and let him speak to himself and to God* (1 Corinthians 14:27-28). Why? Because if many are speaking in tongues and there is no interpretation, it will sound like the events at the Tower of Babel instead of the day of Pentecost. Also, with no interpretation and no confirmation that this is a known language (albeit a language unknown to the speaker), it would be much harder to discern and weed out false spirits.

If someone were to come in and hear a message expressed in his native language that magnified God but was delivered by a person who didn't know that language, he would be edified.

There are many spirits loose today among those who call themselves Christians who organize what appear to be supernatural events. In many cases, these spirits are not related to the Holy Spirit. When this sort of activity goes unchecked, the Holy Spirit begins to withdraw from a given individual or group. Where the Spirit of the Lord is, on the other hand, there is liberty – liberty to serve God and liberty to do the will of God. The fruit of the Spirit will be evident.

Peter and the other Jews were amazed when the true Holy Spirit fell over Cornelius and those in his house who were listening. They spoke with other tongues, but these were tongues that were understood. It was evident that the speakers were magnifying God with their words, which confirmed that the real Holy Spirit had fallen on Cornelius and on his household and close friends.

The news of this supernatural event caused quite a stir when Peter got back to Jerusalem. For a start, he had a lot of explaining to do about why he had fellowshipped and eaten with uncircumcised Gentiles. This controversy continued for some time, and eventually Peter had to be corrected by Paul for acting like a hypocrite; that is, when alone with the Gentiles, he behaved like a Gentile, including eating the foods that the Lord had shown him were acceptable; but if strict Jews were present, he followed Jewish rules of behavior and even withdrew from his friends among the Gentiles.

This serious controversy over implementation of the Jewish law continued, and God used the turmoil to further extend the gospel to the Gentiles. All of those walking in the center of the will of the Lord in this matter came under death threats from the Jews. This in turn helped produce and maintain a clean nucleus of believers whom God multiplied all over the known world. Attacks and adversity came from all sides – sometimes from without, sometimes from within.

The Jews as a nation continued to reject the gospel, and the Lord continued to offer the gospel to the Gentiles. Jesus had declared that the gospel must be preached in all the world and that they were to be witnesses of him in Jerusalem, Judaea, Samaria, and unto the uttermost part of the earth (Acts 1:8). The apostles were determined to fulfil that Great Commission, but they didn't hold a meeting so that they could strategize about whom to send and how to go about it. Nothing like that is mentioned. God was moving them, and they followed where he led. It was the great persecution that caused the message to go out to Judaea and Samaria, where congregations formed and were multiplied by the power of the Holy Spirit.

Then God dramatically converted an enemy of the gospel who was coordinating the persecution. He put Saul into real-life training by the Holy Spirit for almost fifteen years, until the Holy Spirit commissioned him not as Saul, but as Paul, the apostle to the Gentiles. Soon after Saul was converted, Barnabas wanted to introduce him to the apostles in Jerusalem, but at first they distrusted him, and in light of his reputation, they wanted nothing to do with him. God put it in the heart of Barnabas to befriend Paul, however, and they worked at Antioch until God decided to send both of them out as missionaries to the Gentiles. Incidentally, nowhere in the first ten chapters of the book of the Acts of the Apostles are elders appointed or even named. The first mention of elders is when the Gentile congregations took up an offering and sent it to the elders after a famine in Jerusalem had been prophesied. The book of Acts doesn't give a detailed explanation of how the position of elder came to be recognized, but the word "elder" has to do with the word translated as "maturity" or "perfection." At the beginning of the new program that God was implementing, no one had this maturity. After fifteen or twenty years under the discipline of the Holy Spirit, however, elders in the congregation began to be mentioned, starting in Acts 11:30, although it's only after Acts 14:23 that they're recognized or "ordained."

In a letter to Timothy, the apostle Paul describes elders and deacons. Many who have read Paul's instructions to Timothy and Titus have taken them as a license to appoint elders and deacons in congregations that they have started or for which they somehow feel responsible. This almost invariably leads to a number of complications with highly gifted or trained individuals who are not yet mature and are not chosen directly by God, but who then leaven the lump. True shepherds, on the other hand, will lay their lives down for their sheep.

We must remember that the New Testament does not operate as law; it operates by grace and by faith. If we think that we can study the New Testament as if it were a book of law and then implement it with our own ability and understanding, we'll soon find that we have fallen into a trap, because this approach will never work. Unless God is directly involved, unless the Holy Spirit is presiding over every move, unless Jesus is pleased with the way we're operating, all our endeavors will be doomed as the Enemy infiltrates our lives with what appear to be "angels of light."

People with good hearts, like Cornelius, can be found in many places, and God is no respecter of persons; that is, he shows no partiality. God understands that the people who love truth and light really love Jesus, who is the way, the truth, and the light – even if they may be confused about scriptural history and terminology at first. When the Lord decides to clear things up for these people, he isn't limited in how he approaches the matter. As we've seen, he may send the person an angel, he may strike the person with temporary blindness, or he may do something else entirely.

If God sent an angel to Cornelius, can't he just send his angels anywhere and to anyone? Of course he can, but the Lord doesn't do everything through angels. In fact, 1 Timothy 4:1 specifically warns us about *spirits of error and doctrines of demons* (fallen angels). And while we're on the subject, let me point out that we're never instructed to pray to angels. We pray to the Lord, and he instructs his angels. God has his reasons for not ordering angels to share doctrine with us; he has ordered this to be done in a different manner, through people like us who have been converted, who are selected by him, and who demonstrate the fruit of the Holy Spirit.

Many who think they've been converted – or who think that they have the Holy Spirit – are still planting confusion and not speaking of God with clarity. The result is that people who follow God today must make their way through a religious labyrinth where they hear many different voices in many places, and where humans attempt to put themselves in the place of God, control others, and take what belongs to God for themselves or for their congregation.

God has permitted this for a time and for a season so that the consequences might be demonstrated, but we see already that this is all going nowhere. The only way out of our present predicament is to stop everything and submit again to the Lord the way Saul did. After Jesus stopped him in his tracks, Saul did nothing; in his state of shock, he didn't even take a drink of water until the Lord sent someone to open his eyes and impart the Holy Spirit.

The Lord Jesus told the disciples whom he had converted into apostles that he was leaving them a mission, but they had to wait for a while and do nothing until they received power from on high. We can't cause God to reflexively do what we wish. He does *what* he wants *when* he wants. If it seems that the things that we want to happen aren't taking place, we must stop acting without his orders and direction.

Cornelius, with his soft, sensitive heart, had spent years fearing God, praying, and doing what he could for others. After a time – we don't know how many months or years – God chose to communicate with him using an angel and a human being (Peter). The result was that those of Cornelius's household were all filled with the Holy Spirit and placed into direct communion with God so that he could speak to them at any moment, guide them, work in and through them, and spread his work among the Jews and Gentiles.

The Lord didn't pick someone at random. He chose a Roman centurion with a track record of commanding troops in a very dangerous place. Cornelius worked for superiors who must have given him horrible orders from time to time in their desire to oppress the Jewish people. But he had spent years behaving in a manner that caught the attention of God, not only with his prayers, but also with his acts of mercy (alms), until the time was right and the Lord sent an angel to him.

The things of God have inherent risks for everyone; this meeting at the centurion's home was a risk for Peter as well as for the centurion. If we begin to walk with the Lord, the risk is great. Indeed, we must risk everything, but the Lord doesn't command us to withdraw from the world. When Peter arrived in Cornelius's home, he didn't tell Cornelius to withdraw from the army; in fact, he didn't mention the army at all. It appears that there were other members of the Roman army present on that occasion (one of them had even gone on the mission to bring Peter to the house), and they, too, received the Holy Spirit. As we said above, God is no respecter of persons.

As far as we know, the Holy Spirit didn't tell any of these people that they needed to go to theological school or read the Bible more. No, it was sufficient for them to be filled with the Spirit. It's interesting to note that as time went by, there were known to be Christian elders in Jerusalem. Elders? How? By following the Holy Spirit, the time came when individuals could be identified as having come to maturity in Christ, and their lives could be held up as an example for others to follow. When a large offering was sent, it was delivered into their hands because there was no danger that they would use it for personal gain or fight over it. They could be trusted to use the money according to God's leading. How many of us have reached this level of maturity in the Lord?

Let Us Pray

Heavenly Father, May we see things from your perspective, may we share your priorities from the heart, may we not be respecters of persons, and may we have discernment to identify the real Holy Spirit. We ask this in the name of our Lord Jesus. Amen.

Chapter 3

Jewish Theology Upended

Acts 11

11:1 And the apostles and brethren that were in Judaea heard that the Gentiles had also received the word of God.

11:2 When Peter was come up to Jerusalem, those that were of the circumcision contended with him,

11:3 saying, Why didst thou go in to men uncircumcised and eat with them?

It seems that up until this point, everyone who was converted under the gospel of Jesus Christ had been Jewish, and so obviously every male would have been circumcised; here, however, the Scripture mentions *those that were of the circumcision*. While this is one way of describing them, it's very dangerous to be of something other than Christ. Even today, embedded among the believers, we find people who are of this or that doctrine or persuasion, and such people continue to spread dissension.

Upon his return to Jerusalem, Peter had to explain what had really happened in the house of Cornelius.

11:4 *But Peter rehearsed the matter from the beginning and expounded it by order unto them, saying,*

11:5 *I was in the city of Joppa praying, and in a rapture of understanding I saw a vision: A certain vessel descended like a great sheet let down from heaven by the four corners, and it came unto me,*

11:6 *upon which when I had fastened my eyes, I considered and saw fourfooted beasts of the earth and wild beasts and reptiles and fowls of the air.*

11:7 *And I heard a voice saying unto me, Arise, Peter, slay and eat.*

11:8 *But I said, Not so, Lord, for nothing common or unclean has at any time entered into my mouth.*

11:9 *But the voice answered me again from heaven, What God has cleansed, do not call common.*

11:10 *And this was done three times, and it was all drawn up again into heaven.*

As the Jews were well aware, when God confirms something three times, he's telling us that the matter in question is of the utmost importance.

The law of Moses lists a number of unclean animals that were not to be eaten. God was using natural things to teach the people of Israel that what we eat is very important, hoping that they (and we) would apply these lessons in the spiritual realm. Nevertheless, after fifteen hundred years, they had become such legalists regarding the details of the natural symbols God had given them that they overlooked the most important thing about the law: *He has declared unto thee, O man, what is good and what the LORD requires of thee: only to do right judgment, and to love mercy, and to humble thyself to walk with thy God* (Micah 6:8).

Similarly, among Christians today there are those who are more interested in the details of legalism than in the true essence of the Word. It was God himself who began to show Peter that he, the Lord, was and is the owner of everyone and everything. When he wants to make a change, he may do so. If he wishes to order his people not to eat reptiles or pigs, if he wants to impose rules regarding what food is clean or unclean, and if he desires these instructions to endure for fifteen hundred years in order to set an example, that is his prerogative; and when he decides to reveal the true meaning and significance of these things, that's his prerogative as well.

Jesus said, *Think not that I am come to undo the law or the prophets; I am not come to undo, but to fulfil* (Matthew 5:17). *Not that which goes into the mouth defiles the man; but that which comes out of the mouth, this defiles the man* (Matthew 15:11).

God desires for us to be clean and for us to feed on that which is clean. Prior to his death, Jesus told his disciples, *Now ye are clean through the word which I have spoken unto you* (John 15:3). The way for us to become clean and remain clean is to hear and obey the Spirit of God, not to blindly adhere to religious rites and rituals.

Returning to Acts 11:

11:11 *And, behold, immediately there were three men already come unto the house where I was, sent from Caesarea unto me.*

11:12 *And the Spirit bade me go with them, doubting nothing. Moreover these six brethren accompanied me, and we entered into the man's house:*

Now that Peter had explained his actions, the vision God gave him in Joppa (about not being afraid to kill and eat creatures considered unclean under the law) would be applied under the witness and leading of the Spirit. This meant that Peter and other Jews would be brought into fellowship with Gentiles who were being cleansed by the same Holy Spirit.

> 11:13 *And he showed us how he had seen an angel in his house, who stood and said unto him, Send to Joppa and call for Simon, whose surname is Peter,*

> 11:14 *who shall tell thee words, by which thou and all thy house shall be saved.*

> 11:15 *And as I began to speak,*[27] *the Holy Spirit fell on them, as on us at the beginning.*

> 11:16 *Then I remembered the word of the Lord, when he said, John indeed baptized in water, but ye shall be baptized in the Holy Spirit.*

> 11:17 *So then, if God gave them the same gift as he did unto us, who have believed on the Lord Jesus Christ, who was I, that I should withstand God?*

> 11:18 *When they heard these things, they were silent and glorified God, saying, Then God has also granted repentance unto life to the Gentiles.*

This happened to Cornelius the centurion, some of his men, and many of his family members and servants, as Peter began to speak. The Roman army was the enemy of the Jews. How astounded Peter's listeners must have been to learn that the Holy Spirit had fallen on members of the enemy camp!

This upended the theology of many of the Christian Jews, so the controversy was bound to continue. Even so, when he saw

---

27 The Holy Spirit fell on them at the beginning of Peter's message, not at the end. Remember that Jesus put the emphasis on receiving those whom he sends. When it was clear that Cornelius (a Gentile) and his household had received and welcomed Peter, God poured out the Holy Spirit upon them.

that the Holy Spirit had been poured out upon the Gentiles, Peter quickly commanded them to be baptized in water. He did not, however, order them to be circumcised.

Peter may have thought that the water baptism would make it easier to explain all this to *those of the circumcision* back in Jerusalem. As we walk with the Lord under the leading of the Holy Spirit, God doesn't take away our autonomy. We follow the Lord of our free will and can either do his will or reject him. We are also free to propose or even to implement our own "good" ideas, which may have negative consequences beyond those that we are initially able to discern.

The fact that God continued to pour out the Holy Spirit upon the Gentiles (or Greeks) made this a transitional moment in history. It's interesting that this occurred approximately three and a half years after Jesus's death and resurrection. If the seventieth week (of years) prophesied by Daniel began to be counted at the start of Jesus's ministry (about the time he was baptized by John in the Jordan River), then this is about when the seven years literally ended. *Seventy weeks are determined* [Hebrew "cut"] *upon thy people and upon thy holy city to finish the prevarication and to conclude the sin and to make reconciliation for iniquity and to bring in everlasting righteousness and seal the vision and the prophecy, and to anoint the Holy of Holies* (Daniel 9:24).

The seventy weeks (of years) are cut upon Daniel's people (the Jews), and it's certainly possible to interpret that they end here[28] when the Holy Spirit is poured out on the Gentiles as

---

28 Some think that it's the last half of the last week of Daniel's prophecy that was cut off and that it will continue sometime in the future. There is, of course, the possibility for all prophecy to be fulfilled on multiple levels. However, it's clear to me that Jesus's work and ministry were not cut off when he was killed (even though his physical life was ended). His ministry was actually greatly multiplied by the coming of the Holy Spirit. Therefore, I believe that the seventieth week of Daniel continued straight through until God cut off the Jewish nation and poured out the Holy Spirit upon the Gentiles, beginning with the household of Cornelius.

God starts to cut his ties with the Jewish nation (Daniel 9:27) and send his faithful Jewish remnant throughout the entire world with the gospel.

The full implications of what had happened at Joppa and at the house of Cornelius took quite a while to sink in (and they never did sink in among the sect later referred to as the Judaizers, or with many modern prophecy teachers).

11:19 *Now those who were scattered abroad by the tribulation that arose about Stephen travelled as far as Phenice and Cyprus and Antioch, preaching the word to no one except only the Jews.*

11:20 *And some of them were men of Cyprus and Cyrene, who, when they came into Antioch, spoke unto the Greeks, preaching the gospel of the Lord Jesus.*

11:21 *And the hand of the Lord was with them, and a great number believed and turned unto the Lord.*

11:22 *Then tidings of these things came unto the ears of the congregation which was in Jerusalem, and they sent forth Barnabas that he should go unto Antioch.*

11:23 *Who, when he came and had seen the grace of God, was glad and exhorted them to all remain in their purpose of heart in the Lord.*

Barnabas (meaning "son of consolation" or "son of exhortation") witnessed the grace of God that was being poured out upon the Gentiles and didn't complicate things with legalism.

11:25 *Then Barnabas departed to Tarsus to seek Saul, and when he had found him, he brought him unto Antioch.*

11:26 *And it came to pass that for a whole year they*

*gathered themselves together with the congregation
and taught many people. And the disciples were called
Christians first in Antioch.*

Barnabas and Saul (who would soon become Paul) witnessed
and encouraged what the Holy Spirit was doing among the
Gentile believers at Antioch. They helped join the people to the
Lord and nurture them in Christ. They were literally able to
see the power of the grace of God. The fruit of the Spirit was of
such magnitude that this is where the disciples were first called
Christians (a term linked to the name or nature of Christ).

11:27 *And in those days prophets came down from
Jerusalem unto Antioch,*

11:28 *And one of them named Agabus stood up and
signified by the Spirit that there should be great famine throughout all the world, which came to pass in the
days of Claudius Caesar.*

11:29 *Then the disciples, each one according to what he
had, determined to send relief unto the brethren who
dwelt in Judea,*

11:30 *which they likewise did and sent it to the elders*[29]
by the hands of Barnabas and Saul.

As discussed earlier, this is the first mention of "elders" in the
book of Acts. However, there is no mention of asking for tithe
money (or even of taking up offerings, for that matter). We're
simply told that when a need arose, each of the disciples *according
to what he had, determined* what he would give. The donation
of money was due to the Lord moving their hearts by the Holy
Spirit, not the result of some human leader twisting their arms.

The famine prophesied by Agabus came *throughout all the
world* and affected everyone. The Christians in Jerusalem received

29   See Appendix A, number 160 (Use of the word *elders* in Scripture).

help from the Christians in Antioch; but what about the Jews who were persecuting the Christians? Who would help them? They were in the process of seeing the fulfillment of the very law they were blindly attempting to defend. The consequences of abomination and the shedding of innocent blood would soon cause the land to vomit out its inhabitants (Leviticus 18:24-30; Deuteronomy 19:10), and only the Christians would be prepared. The end of the age of the law was at hand. Today we're rapidly approaching the end of the age of grace, and there are some similarities (Matthew 24; Mark 13; Luke 21).

Let Us Pray

Heavenly Father, We ask that we may move through the realm of mere theory and into the realm of actual practice. May we leave behind the discussions regarding symbolic rites and rituals – even though they were necessary for a time. May we walk with you in obedience until we actually see the power of your grace. We ask this in the name of our Lord Jesus Christ. Amen.

Chapter 4

Persecution from Herod

Acts 12

12:1 *Now at that time Herod the king stretched forth his hands to mistreat certain of the congregation.*

12:2 *And he killed James the brother of John with the sword.*

12:3 *And because he saw it pleased the Jews, he proceeded further to take Peter also. (Then were the days of unleavened bread.)*

12:4 *And when he had apprehended him, he put him in prison and delivered him to four quaternions of soldiers to keep him, intending after the Passover to bring him forth to the people.*

U p to this point, the persecution of Christians had come from religious Jews with ties to the Sanhedrin and the high priest. Now, however, King Herod, the secular authority, realized that persecuting Christians pleased the Jews and was therefore politically expedient for him.

12:5 *Peter therefore was kept in the prison, and the congregation made prayer without unto God for him.*

12:6 *And when Herod would have brought him forth, the same night Peter was sleeping between two soldiers, bound with two chains, and the guards before the door that kept the prison.*

God allowed Herod to kill James the brother of John, and it now appeared that Peter would soon suffer a similar fate. There are many in history who have been killed for the cause of Christ, and many are being killed today for the same cause.

Why does God allow this?

And when he had opened the fifth seal, I saw under the altar the souls of those that had been slain because of the word of God and for the testimony which they held: And they cried with a loud voice, saying, How long O Lord, holy and true, dost thou not judge and avenge our blood on those that dwell in the earth? (Revelation 6:9-10).

The martyrs themselves ask God to intervene.

And white robes were given unto each one of them; and it was said unto them, that they should rest yet for a little while until their fellow servants and their brethren, that should be killed as they were, should be fulfilled (Revelation 6:11).

Genuine martyrs will reign and rule with Christ (Revelation 20:4). These martyrs will include all who are willing to lay down their own lives for the Lord, such as the apostle John (even though, according to tradition, he died a natural death). When we belong to the Lord Jesus, it's up to God whether we live or die, for we have given up our own ambition. Throughout history, there have been some, like James, who have literally given their lives for the Lord. Others, like his brother John, have been faithful witnesses[30] for Jesus until their natural death.

With regard to Peter in prison, let's not forget that the congregation (of saints) was praying without ceasing for him, and *the effectual prayer of the righteous is very powerful* (James 5:16). Returning to Acts 12:

> 12:7 *And, behold, the angel of the Lord*[31] *came upon him, and a light shone in the prison,*[32] *and he smote Peter on the side and woke him up, saying, Arise quickly. And his chains fell off from his hands.*

Throughout Scripture, *the angel of the Lord* is linked to the direct presence of God. When the presence of God lit up the prison, Peter was sleeping peacefully – so peacefully that it took a strong touch from the angel to awaken him. Immediately afterwards, in the face of the light of God and the word of God, the chains that bound him fell off his hands.

> 12:8 *And the angel said unto him, Gird thyself and bind on thy sandals. And so he did. And he said unto him, Cast thy garment about thee and follow me.*

The order to *Gird thyself* and then to *Cast thy garment about thee* symbolizes that Peter was aware that he was under covenant with God (in this case, the New Covenant in Jesus's blood).[33]

In Scripture, sandals or shoes are symbolic of the preparation required to journey through the desert or wilderness. By

---

30 The Greek word for "witness" is the same as the word for "martyr."

31 This is the next-to-last reference in Scripture to the angel of the Lord (out of 69 total) and the second time that the angel of the Lord released Peter from a prison.

32 To unregenerate man, however, the Shecaniah glory of God may appear as gross darkness (1 Kings 8:12; 2 Chronicles 6:1; Psalm 97:2).

33 In a covenant, each party has responsibilities. Peter (like all of us) was responsible to walk according to the way Jesus had trained him and to stay under the covering of the Holy Spirit. From early on, the prophets of God were linked to having a leather girdle indicative of a blood covenant, priests had a linen girdle indicating purity, and there is also reference in Scripture to a golden girdle representing the righteousness of Christ. In Christ we are called to be prophets, priests, and kings, and our intimate parts are to be covered appropriately.

telling him to gird himself and bind on his sandals, the angel is signaling to Peter that the preparation (discipleship) he gained by walking with Jesus is adequate for the ministry he is being called to accomplish.[34]

Peter's outer garment, or covering, represents the Holy Spirit.

12:9 *And he went out and followed him and knew not that it was true which was done by the angel, but thought he saw a vision.*

The angel of the Lord comes from and projects the direct presence of God. This is a realm from which fallen humanity has been banished. The ancients feared that they would die if they ever came face-to-face with the angel of the Lord. What took place in that prison was real, but it was also a vision symbolizing that Peter (and all those represented by him) was being called to follow the direct presence of God.

12:10 *When they were past the first and the second guard, they came unto the iron gate that leads unto the city, which opened to them of its own accord, and they went out and passed on through one street, and then the angel departed from him.*

Peter was being delivered from almost certain death at the hands of wicked King Herod, and at the same time God was showing him key aspects of the future of his particular ministry and of ministry in general. The angel of the Lord represents the realm of the Holy of Holies of the direct presence of God. If we were to journey forth from the Holy of Holies, we would come to two "guards" or veils. The first is between the Holy of Holies

---

34 Moses and (later) Joshua were both told to take off their sandals when standing in the presence of God (in the form of the angel of the Lord). Their sandals represent their preparation for their journey, Moses's preparation in the house of Pharaoh had to be dispensed with in order for him to lead the children of Israel through the wilderness, and Joshua's preparation in the wilderness under Moses had to be discarded in order for the Israelites to take possession of the fullness of their inheritance in the Promised Land.

and the Holy Place (of the ministry of the priests), and the second is between the Holy Place and the outer court. Then, if we were to continue our journey, we would come to an iron gate leading to the Court of the Gentiles, outside the Jewish temple.

Iron is a symbol of the law. The "iron gate" opened of its own accord, showing Peter that his ministry would definitely now be in the realm of grace and no longer under law. After going through the iron gate, Peter and the angel of the Lord *passed on through one street*. One street (this phrase could have been translated "one way") refers to salvation by grace through faith in Jesus Christ and not by self-righteous works under the law. This entire experience was further confirmation to Peter that God was pulling the plug on the entire Jewish system of law and that Peter and the remnant of Jews who were saved would now be used by God to reach the Gentiles instead.

> 12:11 *And when Peter was come to himself, he said, Now I know of a surety that the Lord has sent his angel and has delivered me out of the hand of Herod and from all the people of the Jews who waited for me.*

> 12:12 *And considering this, he came to the house of Mary the mother of John, whose surname was Mark,*[35] *where many were gathered together praying.*

On his way home, Peter was considering the implications, possibilities, and ramifications of what had just happened.

> 12:13 *And as Peter knocked at the door of the patio, a damsel came to hearken, named Rhoda.*

> 12:14 *And when she recognized Peter's voice, she opened not the gate for gladness, but ran in and told how Peter stood at the gate.*

---

35 Many years later, Peter refers to Mark as "my son" (1 Peter 5:13). Scripture also records that Peter (Cephas) was married and traveled in ministry together with his wife (1 Corinthians 9:5). Could this house be where Peter's family was staying?

12:15 *And they said unto her, Thou art mad. But she constantly affirmed that it was even so. Then they said, It is his angel.*

"Rhoda" means "a rose." Rhoda may not have been very old when this happened. The adults in the house, who were apparently praying for Peter in the middle of the night, first thought that Rhoda was insane, and when she insisted that she had heard Peter speaking, they assumed that the voice must have been that of Peter's angel.

What were they thinking?

Jesus, referring to children, said: *Take heed that ye despise not one of these little ones; for I say unto you, That in the heavens their angels always behold the face of my Father who is in the heavens* (Matthew 18:10). Apparently, some of us may have a heavenly counterpart (or guardian angel) that we don't know very much about. However, if we dwell in the secret place of the Most High, as was the case with Peter, we have the following promise: *He shall give his angels charge over thee to keep thee in all thy ways* (Psalm 91:11).

12:16 *But Peter continued knocking, and when they had opened the door and saw him, they were astonished.*

12:17 *But he, beckoning unto them with the hand to be silent, declared unto them how the Lord had brought him out of the prison. And he said, Go make these things known unto James and to the brethren. And he departed and went to another place.*

This appears to have been a watershed or turning point, after which many of the apostles began to travel forth from Jerusalem in ministry to the Gentiles. In fact, it wouldn't be very long before young John Mark would join Paul and Barnabas on his first missionary journey.

12:18 *Now as soon as it was day, there was no small stir among the soldiers concerning what was become of Peter.*

12:19 *And when Herod had sought for him and found him not, he examined the guards and commanded that they should be taken away. Then he went down from Judaea to Caesarea and abode there.*

Herod "examined" the guards (probably by scourging them without mercy), and when he found out what happened, he commanded that they should be "taken away." The phrase may be a euphemism, since he definitely didn't want the truth to get out.

12:20 *And Herod was highly displeased with those of Tyre and Sidon but they came with one accord to him, and, having bribed Blastus, the king's chamberlain, they asked for peace because their lands were supplied through those of the king's.*

Herod's kingdom, like Satan's, was always prone to division, intrigue, bribes, and interruption of commerce. This is why Jesus said that *every kingdom divided against itself is brought to desolation* (Matthew 12:25).

12:21 *And upon a set day Herod, arrayed in royal apparel, sat upon his throne and made an oration unto them.*

12:22 *And the people gave a shout, saying, It is the voice of god, and not of man.*

12:23 *And immediately the angel of the Lord smote him because he did not give God the glory, and he expired eaten of worms.*

Herod wore royal apparel because he claimed to be the king of the Jews (a title that really belongs to Jesus Christ).

Verse 12:23 contains the last reference to *the angel of the Lord* in Scripture. This scene is really a foreshadowing of what will eventually happen to Satan on *a set day*. After all the wicked things that Herod had done (such as killing John the Baptist, James the brother of John, and countless others), the angel of the Lord finally confronted him when he set himself up to be worshipped as a god.[36]

12:24 *But the word of the Lord grew and multiplied.*

But the word of our God shall stand for ever (Isaiah 40:8). Satan and his followers, however, shall not. God loves to multiply, but he won't multiply anything that's defective or unclean.

12:25 *And Barnabas and Saul returned from Jerusalem, when they had fulfilled their ministry, and took with them John, whose surname was Mark.*

It's quite possible that Luke, the physician (who is believed to have been the inspired writer of this account), also began to travel with Barnabas and Saul.

Acts 13

13:1 *Now there were in the congregation that was at Antioch prophets and teachers: Barnabas and Simeon that was called Niger and Lucius of Cyrene and Manaen, who had been brought up with Herod the tetrarch, and Saul.*

Note that the six prophets and teachers were *in the congregation* (that is, they weren't in authority over the congregation) at Antioch, which means "to nail against" (in other words, it was a good solid place where God could build). So far God

---

36 Herod was unable to stand before the real glory of God, nor will Satan be able to do so (2 Thessalonians 2:8). Herod *expired eaten of worms*, a symbol of the insatiable carnal appetites of the natural man. Regarding the fall of Lucifer (Satan), Scripture states: *Thy pride is brought down to Sheol, and the noise of thy viols: the worm is spread under thee, and the worms cover thee* (Isaiah 14:11).

had Barnabas ("son of consolation" or "son of exhortation"), Simeon ("to hearken") who was called Niger ("black"), Lucius ("of light") of Cyrene ("the control of the bit"), Manaen ("comforter") who had been brought up with King Herod, and Saul ("asked for" or "desired").

Neither apostles, evangelists, pastors, nor elders are mentioned, but these would undoubtedly be added as God saw fit.

13:2 *As they ministered to the Lord and fasted, the Holy Spirit said, Separate me Barnabas and Saul for the work unto which I have called them.*

13:3 *And when they had fasted and prayed and laid their hands on them, they released them.*

It wasn't the congregation at Antioch who sent Barnabas and Saul out as missionaries; it was the Holy Spirit. Those of Antioch didn't name a missions committee or develop a human strategy to evangelize the world. The congregation there didn't formulate an approved curriculum of study or confer human credentials. They didn't even promise to support the missionaries financially. God would take care of all of that. The congregation ministered to the Lord (that is, they were focused on pleasing God) and fasted (not feeding their own lives), and the Holy Spirit told them what to do.

13:4 *So they, being sent forth by the Holy Spirit, departed unto Seleucia, and from there they sailed to Cyprus.*

This is the first apostolic missionary journey of Barnabas and Saul. They were first sent by the Holy Spirit to the port of Seleucia ("white light"), and then they sailed (by the power of the wind – a symbol of the Spirit) to Cyprus (meaning "love" or "a flower"[37]), arriving at the port of Salamis ("large wave"

---

37 The flower represents the gifts of the Spirit, and love is a fruit of the Spirit. The seed, of course, is in the fruit.

or "breaker"). God was sending them as the first part of a great spiritual wave that would soon turn the world upside down.

13:5 And when they arrived at Salamis, they preached the word of God in the synagogues of the Jews, and they also had John as an attendant.

13:6 And when they had gone through the isle unto Paphos, they found a certain wise man, a false prophet, a Jew whose name was Barjesus,

13:7 who was with the proconsul, Sergius Paulus, a prudent man, who called for Barnabas and Saul and desired to hear the word of God.

13:8 But Elymas[38] the wise man (for so is his name by interpretation) withstood them, seeking to turn away the proconsul from the faith.

At Paphos (meaning "hot" or "boiling"), the capital city of Cyprus, a *wise man* named Barjesus ("son of Jesus") withstood them as the devil attempted to stop the Roman proconsul from hearing and believing the gospel.

13:9 Then Saul (who also is Paul), filled with the Holy Spirit, set his eyes on him

13:10 and said, O full of all deception and all licentiousness, thou son of the devil, thou enemy of all righteousness, wilt thou not cease to pervert the right ways of the Lord?

13:11 And now, behold, the hand of the Lord is against thee, and thou shalt be blind, not seeing the sun for a season. And immediately there fell on him a mist and a darkness, and he went about seeking some to lead him by the hand.

38 "Elymas" can also mean "sorcerer."

13:12 *Then the proconsul, when he saw what was done, believed, being astonished at the doctrine of the Lord.*

At the doctrine (or word) of the Lord flowing through Saul, the sorcerer was struck blind, the proconsul named Sergius Paulus (or "small Sergius"[39]) believed the gospel, and Saul's name was changed to Paul ("small" or "little"). No wonder the proconsul was *astonished at the doctrine of the Lord!*

13:13 *Now when Paul and his company sailed from Paphos, they came to Perga in Pamphylia; then John, departing from them, returned to Jerusalem.*

They left the "hot" situation over in Paphos with the proconsul on fire for God, and they came to another enemy fortress. "Perga" means "a tower," and "Pamphylia" means "every tribe." It was here that young John Mark decided to turn around and go home.

13:14 *But when they departed from Perga, they came to Antioch in Pisidia and went into the synagogue on the sabbath day and sat down.*

13:15 *And after the reading of the law and the prophets the princes of the synagogue sent unto them, saying, Ye men and brethren, if ye have any word of exhortation for the people, speak.*

Before anyone can understand the message, God must do a work in their heart – we are convinced of this. Even understanding the message and receiving it with joy isn't enough. In order for the gospel message to be completed in us, our lives must be brought into compliance with the Word of God. Only the Holy Spirit can accomplish this.

When Peter was in prison, unable to escape, he knew he was about to be killed. Indeed, all of us are, in a certain sense,

---

39 "Sergius" can mean "born as a marvel" (i.e., born again).

condemned to death. Sooner or later, we will die; there's no other way out of here. While we're here, however, we can respond to the offer sent to us by the Lord and decide whether to reject that offer or to accept it. If we accept it, we consider ourselves dead with Christ and we allow God to accomplish whatever he desires with us.

If we follow Jesus in the way of the cross, it might not be long before someone kills us, as King Herod did with John the Baptist or with James the brother of John. On the other hand, we might follow in the footsteps of Peter, Paul, and John, and have a long life of dangerous service to the Lord.

Peter followed the angel of the Lord out of the prison into another dimension of ministry. At first he thought he might be having a vision, and there was a moment when even some of his close friends wondered if he were an angel. Paul, too, entered into another dimension of ministry, but in his case it happened when his name changed from Saul (meaning "asked for" or "desired") to Paul ("little" or "small," reflecting that he was, as he often called himself, the least of the apostles).

When Saul became Paul, the demons began to tremble; *for we wrestle not against flesh and blood, but against principalities, against powers, against the lords of this age, rulers of this dark-ness, against spiritual wickedness in the heavens* (Ephesians 6:12).

Human teachers have spent many centuries attempting to distill the New Testament into logical doctrines, precepts, and values that can be learned and applied by man even while dif-ferent schools of thought compete against one another. The New Testament, however, is not law. It is grace. Grace operates by the power of God through the Holy Spirit, and the New Testament is a record of God's unique responses to unique situations.

The Roman proconsul, Sergius Paulus, *when he saw what was done, believed, being astonished at the doctrine of the Lord.* It's high time for us to repent of any preconceived ideas that we may have and return to *the doctrine of the Lord*, for it's only as the grace and presence and doctrine of the Lord are displayed in and through us that the powers of spiritual darkness in the heavens will be displaced.

Many seem to think that we must wait for the physical return of our Lord Jesus Christ before we have victory, and it's undeniable that his return in victory will be extremely important. However, if the Lord hasn't yet returned, it's partly because there's still work to be done in his name according to his will, and also because the number of those who will lose their own lives *because of the word of God and for the testimony which they held* is not yet complete (Revelation 6:9-11).

Let Us Pray

Lord, We ask that you might lead us out of our prison, out of being useless hostages bound by the chains of the system of this world.

May we trust you completely and be at peace, whether we live or die, as we allow you to order our lives and choose our fate.

We ask that you may sovereignly intervene in our nation, just as you did in Israel in the days of the early apostles. May you open great opportunity to those who, like Saul of Tarsus, are mistaken and who will respond favorably to your dealings, even to the point of replacing those whom they have killed, persecuted, or slandered in your service. May you resolve the doubts of those who genuinely desire to have faith, and at the same time may you judge those who, like old King Herod, continue to harm your servants and are evil to the core.

Above all, may we be your worthy representatives according to the desires of your heart. Amen.

Chapter 5

Paul Stands Up and Helps Others to Stand

Acts 13

13:13 *Now when Paul and his company sailed from Paphos, they came to Perga in Pamphylia; then John, departing from them, returned to Jerusalem.*

When the Holy Spirit sent Saul of Tarsus out from Antioch, the apostle was still named Saul ("desired"). Now, his name has been changed to Paul ("small"), and this remains his name throughout the rest of the New Testament. Paul maintained a low profile and a humble attitude, working with his hands as a tentmaker to sustain his ministry financially. Despite the success of his work for the Lord, he didn't become proud and arrogant.

13:14 *But when they departed from Perga, they came to Antioch in Pisidia[40] and went into the synagogue on the sabbath day and sat down.*

In the synagogue, those who were deemed important and those

---

40 Antioch in Pisidia is in Asia Minor; it's not the Antioch of Syria where Paul and Barnabas began their journey.

who had the potential to teach sat down, just as kings and rulers in ancient culture sat on their thrones and made declarations or pronounced judgment.

> 13:15 *And after the reading of the law and the prophets the princes of the synagogue sent unto them, saying, Ye men and brethren, if ye have any word of exhortation for the people, speak.*

> 13:16 *Then Paul stood up, and beckoning with his hand said, Men of Israel and ye that fear God hearken.*

Paul stood up to speak (in an apparent break with tradition), and ever since that time, it has been the custom of Christian ministers to speak standing up, out of respect for the Lord (who is present when those who are clean congregate in his name) and for the congregation.

> 13:17 *The God of this people of Israel chose our fathers and exalted the people when they dwelt as strangers in the land of Egypt, and with a high arm he brought them out of it.*

> 13:18 *And for the time of about forty years, he suffered their manners in the wilderness.*

> 13:19 *And when he had destroyed seven nations in the land of Canaan, he divided their land to them by lot.*

> 13:20 *And after that he gave unto them judges about the space of four hundred and fifty years, until Samuel the prophet.*

> 13:21 *And afterward they asked for a king, and God gave unto them Saul the son of Cis, a man of the tribe of Benjamin, for forty years.*

This is a very clear and interesting summary of the history of

Israel from the Exodus until the beginning of the reign of King David. We know that David began to reign at approximately age thirty, and he would therefore have been born ten years into King Saul's reign. This would have been about five hundred years (40+450+10) after the coming out of Egypt.[41] Scripture also states that King Saul more or less did well for the first few years of his kingdom, while he still considered himself small in his own eyes. As soon as Saul disqualified himself, however, God had Samuel anoint David, even though David was only a boy (possibly twelve years old or less).

> 13:22 *And when he had removed him, he raised up unto them David to be their king, to whom also he gave testimony, saying, I have found David, the son of Jesse, a man after my own heart, who shall fulfil all my will.*

Many years passed between David being anointed as a boy and his receiving the kingdom at age thirty. After David killed the giant Goliath, King Saul persecuted the younger man without mercy and made repeated attempts to kill him until David was forced to flee into the wilderness and take refuge in the land of the Philistines, whom God eventually used to remove Saul. David reigned for forty years and accomplished all the objectives that God raised him up to fulfill.

> 13:23 *Of this man's seed has God according to his promise raised up Jesus as Saviour unto Israel:*

---

41 Ussher dates the Exodus at 1491 BC (*Annals of the World*, 1658), and if that is the case, then according to the above scripture, David would have been born in 991 BC (1491 minus 500). Ussher, however, dates the beginning of the reign of Saul at 1095 BC, and therefore the birth of David, according to him, would have been 1085 BC. This points to an apparent 94-year discrepancy between the 480 years mentioned in I Kings 6:1 and the above account in Acts, possibly due to 1 Kings 6:1 not counting some years in which God sold or delivered the children of Israel into the hands of their enemies (Judges 2:14; 3:8, 11; 4:2; 6:1; 10:7; 13:1). My preferred date for the Exodus is 1488 BC, and if this is correct, then according to the above scripture in Acts 13, King David would have been anointed by Samuel about the year 1000 BC, assuming David was about twelve years old at that time.

13:24 *John, having first proclaimed before his coming, the baptism of repentance to all the people of Israel.*

Under the law of Moses, there were many ways in which a person could become unclean, and in order to be cleansed, washing with water was required. The Jews expected the Messiah to find the entire nation unclean, and therefore the ministry of John the Baptist was expected and understood by many. Even though the concept of ceremonial washing was ingrained into Jewish culture, John emphasized that his ministry was to conduct the baptism of (or into) repentance.

13:25 *And as John fulfilled his course, he said, Whom think ye that I am? I am not he. But, behold, there comes one after me, whose shoes of his feet I am not worthy to loose.*

As mentioned earlier, shoes represent preparation (getting ready to cross the hot sand and razor-sharp rocks of the desert). The Father sent Jesus Christ to earth with a heavenly purpose and a heavenly preparation that no one in this world is worthy to touch or modify.

13:26 *Men and brethren, sons of the lineage of Abraham, and whosoever among you fears God, unto you is this word of saving health sent.*

Paul's message is first to the Jews (of the lineage of Abraham) and then to the Gentiles (those among them who fear God).

13:27 *For those that dwell at Jerusalem and their princes, because they knew him not nor yet the voices of the prophets who are read every sabbath day, they have fulfilled them in condemning him.*

13:28 *And without finding cause of death in him, yet they asked Pilate that he should be slain.*

13:29 And when they had fulfilled all that was written of him, they took him down from the tree and laid him in a sepulchre.

13:30 But God raised him from the dead,

13:31 and he was seen many days by those who came up with him from Galilee to Jerusalem, who until now are his witnesses[42] unto the people.

Jesus's resurrection from the dead is fundamental to the gospel, as is our hope of coming forth in resurrection unto eternal life at his return.

13:32 And we declare unto you the gospel of the promise which was made unto the fathers,

This is *the gospel of the promise which was made unto the fathers.*

13:33 which God has fulfilled unto us their children, in that he has raised up Jesus again; as it is also written in the second psalm, Thou art my Son, this day have I begotten thee.

13:34 And as concerning that he raised him up from the dead, now no more to return to corruption, he said this, I will give you the sure mercies promised to David.

13:35 Therefore he also says in another place, Thou shalt not suffer thy Holy One to see corruption.

13:36 For David, after he had served his own generation by the will of God, fell asleep and was gathered unto his fathers and saw corruption;

13:37 but he, whom God raised again, saw no corruption.

---

42 The word translated "witness" is the same as the word for "martyr."

13:38 Be it known unto you, therefore, men and brethren, that through this one is preached unto you the remission of sins;

13:39 and in him all that believe are justified from all the things from which ye could not be justified by the law of Moses.

This proclamation of the gospel was short, simple, and extremely effective. Paul simply told them, in effect, that all the animals they had sacrificed to expiate their sin and guilt were only symbols, and that they (the Jews), in their ignorance of God's purposes (even though they had been reading the law and the prophets every Sabbath day in their synagogues for hundreds of years), had unwittingly fulfilled the prophecies by killing Jesus and thus making the unique sacrifice that is valid forever. Paul's presentation of the gospel also came with a very strong warning: ignorance is one thing, but willful rejection of the gospel is quite another.

13:40 Beware, therefore, lest what is spoken of in the prophets come upon you:

13:41 Behold, ye despisers, and wonder and perish, for I do a work in your days, a work which ye would in no wise believe, if one should declare it unto you.

This appears to be a quote from Habakkuk 1:5 and may also refer to Isaiah 53:1 (the entire chapter is messianic and is prophetic of Jesus's death and resurrection and the promised reward). Even today, there are many who refuse to believe our report when we share the wonderful things that God is doing and the fact that Jesus Christ is about to return in victory and bring down the entire system of this world.

13:42 And when they were gone out of the synagogue of

*the Jews, the Gentiles besought that these words might
be spoken to them the next sabbath.*

Notice that the synagogue is labeled "the synagogue of the Jews";
that is, it belongs not to God, but to the Jewish people. In the
Old Testament, God gives no directive whatsoever about the
setting up of institutional synagogues.

*13:43 Now when the synagogue was dismissed, many
of the Jews and religious proselytes followed Paul and
Barnabas, who, speaking to them, persuaded them to
remain in the grace of God.*

Where was the grace of God? In the dead letter of Jewish tradition taught at the synagogue? Hardly!

*13:44 And the next sabbath day almost the whole city
came together to hear the word of God.*

After going home, many people must have spent the week telling their friends and neighbors about the gospel.

*13:45 But when the Jews saw the multitudes, they were
filled with envy and spoke against that which Paul said,
contradicting and blaspheming.*

*13:46 Then Paul and Barnabas speaking with freedom,
said, It was necessary indeed that the word of God
should first have been spoken to you; but seeing ye put
it from you and judge yourselves unworthy of eternal
life, behold, we turn to the Gentiles.*

The Jews were filled with envy when they saw the multitudes of
Gentiles who were drinking in the word of the gospel. This envy
caused them to contradict Paul and blaspheme (misrepresent
God). Paul and Barnabas spoke with freedom, however, for
where the Spirit of the Lord is, there is liberty.[43] They told these
rebellious Jews that by rejecting the gospel, they had adjudged

43 2 Corinthians 3:17.

themselves unworthy of eternal life. Paul and Barnabas made it plain that by refusing to turn from their blind and arrogant envy, these Jews had caused them to pivot exclusively to the Gentiles.

Many today, consumed with the same jealous envy, defend their own synagogue (or church), contradicting those whom God sends and blaspheming against the true gospel by refusing to cooperate with them. Those who are unconverted and outside the church find it more difficult to enter the kingdom of God when such bad religious testimony abounds.[44]

Paul and Barnabas, however, continued speaking with liberty outside the synagogue of the Jews.

13:47 *For so has the Lord commanded us, saying, I have set thee to be a light of the Gentiles that thou should be for saving health unto the ends of the earth.*

13:48 *And when the Gentiles heard this, they were glad and glorified the word of the Lord, and as many as were ordained[45] to eternal life believed.*

Eternal life doesn't mean that our natural earthly life will go on forever, full of wrong, envious desires for the things of this world. Eternal life is the very life of God, with his desires, goals, and purposes imparted into us. It's a wholly different quality of life, and because it is his life, it will never end.

When Paul and Barnabas told the people that the hope of eternal life was linked to faith in Jesus Christ rather than to the dry religious legalism of the synagogue of the Jews, the Gentiles were glad, and those who were ordained (or disposed)

---

44 See Matthew 23.

45 The Greek word *tasso*, translated here as "ordained," can also mean "to have arranged things or disposed." It seems obvious that God arranges things, but it's also true that we must be disposed to trust and follow him. The word *tasso* seems to cover both sides of the equation.

to eternal life believed and followed Paul and Barnabas out of the synagogue.

13:49 *And the word of the Lord was published throughout all the region.*

God blessed the ministry of Paul and Barnabas.

13:50 *But the Jews stirred up the devout and honourable women and the principals of the city and raised up persecution against Paul and Barnabas and expelled them out of their borders.*

13:51 *But they shook off the dust of their feet against them and came unto Iconium.*

13:52 *And the disciples were filled with joy and with the Holy Spirit.*

It didn't take the devil very long to raise up persecution, but even though Paul and Barnabas were expelled from the region, the new disciples *were filled with joy and with the Holy Spirit.*

There had been some Gentile proselytes in the synagogue of the Jews when Paul and Barnabas arrived, but when the two men departed from the area, they left behind them not proselytes, but disciples. Proselytes are created by religious ritual and indoctrination. Disciples, on the other hand, are willing to let go of everything and follow Jesus Christ. A disciple is someone who has made a change of course and no longer loves the things of this world because Jesus is now in first place in his life. Disciples use whatever worldly treasure, influence, or position they have for the purposes of the Lord. Verse 52 tells us that the disciples were filled with joy and with the Holy Spirit. True joy only comes by the Spirit of God, and even though Paul and Barnabas were unable to stay and follow up, the Holy Spirit would lead the new believers into all truth.

Acts 14

14:1 And it came to pass in Iconium that they went both together into the synagogue of the Jews and so spoke, that a great multitude both of the Jews and also of the Greeks believed.

"Iconium" means "like an icon" or "like an image." The place was a great pagan center where there was also a *synagogue of the Jews.*

What did Paul and Barnabas say, and how did they say it, to achieve such wonderful results? They gave God all the glory and didn't become puffed up or arrogant. Paul continued to live up to his new name ("small").

14:2 But the disobedient Jews stirred up the Gentiles and corrupted their desire against the brethren.

Brethren of whom?

Of Jesus Christ.

14:3 With all this, they abode there a long time speaking with freedom in the Lord, who gave testimony unto the word of his grace and granted that signs and wonders be done by their hands.

Signs and wonders follow the true word of the Lord and the true apostles whom he sends (Mark 16:20).

14:4 But the multitude of the city was divided, and part held with the Jews, and part with the apostles.[46]

14:5 And when there was an assault made both of the Gentiles and also of the Jews with their princes, to insult them and to stone them,

Persecution is also a sign that ministry is true and on track (Matthew 5:10-12). It didn't take long for the opposition among

---

46 The use of the plural word "apostles" means that both Paul and Barnabas were considered apostles of Christ.

both Gentiles and Jews to increase to a level where they weren't content just to insult Paul and Barnabas, but they actually attempted to kill them.

> 14:6 *they were aware of it and fled unto Lystra and Derbe, cities of Lycaonia, and unto the region that lies round about.*

> 14:7 *And there they preached the gospel.*

"Lycaonia" means "land of wolves."

> Jesus said: *Behold, I send you forth as sheep in the midst of wolves; be ye therefore prudent as serpents and innocent as doves. But keep yourselves from men, for they will deliver you up in councils, and they will scourge you in their synagogues; and ye shall even be brought before princes and kings for my sake, for testimony unto them and to the Gentiles* (Matthew 10:16-18).

> *And ye shall be hated of all men for my name, but he that endures to the end shall be saved. But when they persecute you in this city, flee ye into another, for verily I say unto you, Ye shall not have gone over the cities of Israel until the Son of man be come* (Matthew 10:22-23).

Here we are almost two thousand years later, and there still appear to be cities of "Israel" that the messengers of God haven't confronted with the true gospel. Israel is the people of God, and now both Jews and Gentiles congregate in his name, but those who have their own synagogues (and churches) still abound.

> 14:8 *And a certain man sat at Lystra, impotent in his feet, being a cripple from his mother's womb, who never had walked;*

"Lystra" means "rescuing." This *certain man* represents many Gentiles living in the "land of wolves" who had never had a chance to walk uprightly in a moral and spiritual sense due to factors beyond their control, and thus may be deemed to need rescuing.

14:9 *this man heard Paul speak, who steadfastly beholding him and perceiving that he had faith to be healed,*

14:10 *said with a loud voice, Stand upright on thy feet. And he leaped and walked.*

The gospel was being preached to the Gentiles with the power, anointing, and conviction of the Holy Spirit, and God confirmed his word with a powerful sign.

The miracle was triggered when Paul locked in on the man and perceived that he had faith to be healed. This is also representative of all those who have faith to be saved.

In the face of this great victory, the devil responded with a new tactic. Instead of opposing them, he decided to follow the principle of "If you can't beat them, join them." Over the next couple hundred years, Satan would hone this approach to the point where he was able to mix humanism and paganism with Christianity. This type of thing eventually helped usher in the Dark Ages.

14:11 *And when the people saw what Paul had done, they lifted up their voices, saying in the speech of Lycaonia, The gods are come down to us in the likeness of men.*

14:12 *And they called Barnabas, Jupiter; and Paul, Mercurius because he was the chief speaker.*

This attempt to rename the apostles is rather ironic, given that centuries later, pagan statues and shrines all across the

Roman kingdom would be renamed after Christian heroes like Barnabas and Paul.

14:13 Then the priest of Jupiter, who was before their city, brought bulls and garlands unto the gates and would have done sacrifice unto them with the people.

14:14 Which when the apostles, Barnabas[47] and Paul, heard of it, they rent their clothes and ran in among the people, crying out

14:15 and saying, Sirs, why do ye these things? We also are men of like passions with you and preach unto you that ye should turn from these vanities unto the living God, who made the heaven and the earth and the sea and all the things that are therein,

14:16 who in generations past suffered all the Gentiles to walk in their own ways.

14:17 Nevertheless he did not leave himself without witness, in that he did good and gave us rain from heaven and fruitful seasons, filling our hearts with food and gladness.

14:18 And with these words they scarcely restrained the people, that they not sacrifice unto them.

When the devil saw that even though the apostles made an all-out effort, *they scarcely restrained the people, that they not sacrifice unto them*, he went back to frontal opposition and made another attempt to have Paul killed.

Let Us Pray

Lord, We ask that there may be many more disciples

---

47 Here is another reference making it clear that both Barnabas and Paul were apostles, and at this point Barnabas was mentioned first as the senior of the two.

everywhere – true disciples who belong to you, not proselytes of a religious sect. And we ask that your disciples will be full of joy and of the Holy Spirit, ready to do your will under every circumstance no matter what type of difficulties they face. Amen.

Chapter 6

The Jerusalem Council

In ancient history, when King Saul was anointed and began to reign over Israel successfully, he considered himself small in his own eyes. Soon, however, thoughts of splendor and of having a grand reputation took root, and these began to flourish and spread to such a point that the Holy Spirit left him. Tragically, Saul didn't even notice. He ended up consulting a witch, and he died on his own sword. King Saul began well, but pride and arrogance led to his downfall.

Saul of Tarsus did the exact opposite. As God granted him grace and authority, he became humbler and humbler, so that all the glory for his good works would go to God. Saul, now Paul, considered himself the least of the apostles, and this attitude set the stage for God to move and turn the world upside down.

Satan was now beside himself. He even tried to get the people to worship Barnabas and Paul by having them refer to Barnabas as Jupiter and Paul as Mercurius, hoping that the apostles would succumb to the pagans' flattery and the lure of prosperity. When this failed, Satan sent in rebellious Jews with murder in their hearts.

It was becoming increasingly clear that the entire religious system of the Jews was going down. God was definitely doing something new.

Acts 14

14:19 *And certain Jews from Antioch and Iconium came there, who persuaded the people, and, having stoned Paul, drew him out of the city, supposing he was dead.*

The Jews normally did a pretty thorough job of stoning people. If they *drew him out of the city, supposing he was dead*, Paul may have really been dead. I wonder if this is when he had the experience of being caught up to the third heaven and hearing *unspeakable words, which it is not lawful for a man to utter* (2 Corinthians 12:2-4).

14:20 *But as the disciples stood round about him, he rose up and came into the city, and the next day he departed with Barnabas to Derbe.*

When someone is called and sent forth by God and is clean and in the center of the will of God, then the time of his death won't be decided by the Enemy. As the disciples stood round about him, Paul rose up and went back on another tour through the "land of wolves."

14:21 *And when they had preached the gospel to that city and had taught many, they returned again to Lystra and to Iconium and Antioch,*

14:22 *confirming the souls of the disciples and exhorting them to remain in the faith, and that we must through much tribulation enter into the kingdom of God.*

How did they "confirm the souls" of the new disciples?

Did they have a confirmation class and make sure everyone

could recite the Ten Commandments, the Beatitudes, the Lord's Prayer, and the Apostles' Creed?

Not in the least! Baptism in water isn't even mentioned here, nor is any other religious rite or ritual.

With regard to the new disciples, I think that what Barnabas and Paul were primarily concerned about was making sure that they were all really tracking with the Holy Spirit. By *exhorting them to remain in the faith*, the apostles were encouraging them to stay under the anointing and direction of the Holy Spirit even in the midst of *much tribulation*, because entering into the kingdom of God is seldom easy.

> 14:23 *And having ordained elders[48] for them in every congregation and having prayed with fasting, they commended them to the Lord on whom they believed.*

The word "elder" has to do with maturity (the same word is also translated as "perfection"). Here *having ordained elders* is paired with *having prayed with fasting*. Thus, ordaining elders doesn't necessarily appear to have been directly ordered by God. In this book of Acts and under the grace of God, human initiative in these matters is not stifled.[49] Time would tell whether all of these new "elders" were truly mature in the faith. Later on in his ministry, Paul seems to be less inclined to ordain elders swiftly in each new congregation, instead preferring to wait prudently until mature godly character was clearly developed in each potential elder.[50] Therefore, in several cases, when he wrote to men like Timothy or Titus to discuss the selection of elders, he was writing many years after certain congregations had been founded.

---

48 See Appendix A, number 161 (use of the word *elders* in Scripture).

49 Two more examples of this are: 1) In the first chapter, Peter and the other disciples cast lots and chose Matthias to replace Judas. 2) In the tenth chapter, Peter commanded those of the household of Cornelius to be water baptized.

50 Also bear in mind that during this first apostolic missionary journey, Barnabas was evidently the senior apostle.

Even so, note that Paul and Barnabas didn't commend the new disciples to the elders, but rather *they commended them to the Lord on whom they believed.*

14:24 *And after they had passed throughout Pisidia, they came to Pamphylia.*

14:25 *And when they had preached the word in Perga, they went down into Attalia*

14:26 *and from there sailed to Antioch, where they had been recommended to the grace of God for the work which they fulfilled.*

"Pisidia" means "of tar," which can also mean "to seal." "Pamphylia" means "of each tribe," "Perga" means "a tower," "Attalia" means "the appointed time of the LORD," and "Antioch" means "something to nail onto." Here we have a beautiful word picture of those from "every tribe" who are seen and protected from God's strong "tower" (so strong that it can be "nailed onto") and "sealed" at "the appointed time of the LORD." Paul and Barnabas then sailed back to Antioch, which was the base from which the Holy Spirit had sent them out and was also *where they had been recommended to the grace of God for the work which they fulfilled.*

14:27 *And when they were come and had gathered the congregation together, they related what great things God had done with them and how he had opened the door of faith unto the Gentiles.*

14:28 *And there they abode a long time with the disciples.*

Disciples are those who are willing to leave everything to follow the Lord Jesus. Barnabas and Paul had been preaching the gospel, and those who believed became disciples.

Acts 15

15:1 Then certain men who came down from Judaea taught the brethren and said, Except ye be circumcised after the manner of Moses, ye cannot be saved.

15:2 When therefore Paul and Barnabas had no small dissension and disputation with them, they determined that Paul and Barnabas and certain other of them should go up to Jerusalem unto the apostles and elders[51] about this question.

The *certain men* who came down from Judaea determined that Paul and Barnabas, as well as certain others, should go to Jerusalem. This was not, however, a direct initiative of the Holy Spirit.

15:3 And they, being accompanied by some from the congregation, passed through Phenice and Samaria, declaring the conversion of the Gentiles, and they caused great joy unto all the brethren.

The news of the conversion of the Gentiles caused great joy to all the brethren, even though Barnabas and Paul hadn't been circumcising these converts after the manner of Moses.[52] True joy is a fruit of the Holy Spirit.

15:4 And when they were come to Jerusalem, they were received by the congregation and by the apostles and elders,[53] and they declared all the things that God had done with them.

---

51 This is only the second scriptural mention of the existence of "elders" among the congregation of believers in Jerusalem. The first mention is in Acts 11:30. It seems that it took a number of years for disciples to reach maturity and to be established as elders. Also note that we are not told who ordained these elders. However, the behavior of the congregation and the context would imply that they were ordained of God. See Appendix A, number 162 (use of the word *elders* in Scripture).

52 In fact, Scripture doesn't even record any water baptisms during their entire missionary journey.

53 See Appendix A, number 163 (use of the word *elders* in Scripture).

15:5 *But there rose up certain of the sect of the Pharisees who had believed, saying, That it was needful to circumcise them and to command them to keep the law of Moses.*

When someone becomes a believer, God can change their heart and quickly remove bitterness and resentment, replacing those negative emotions with forgiveness. However, it's not at all easy to change a cultural mindset or its respective worldview, nor does this type of change tend to take place quickly. The Pharisees, for example, had been brought up in strict legalism. Even after believing in Jesus Christ and having a profound change of heart, it was still unthinkable to many of them that circumcision and letter-of-the-law compliance to Mosaic law weren't obligatory for the salvation of the Gentiles.

15:6 *And the apostles and elders[54] came together to consider of this matter.*

15:7 *And when there had been much disputing, Peter rose up and said unto them, Men and brethren, ye know how that a good while ago God chose that the Gentiles by my mouth should hear the word of the gospel and believe.*

15:8 *And God, who knows the hearts, bore them witness, giving them the Holy Spirit, even as he did unto us,*

15:9 *and put no difference between us and them, purifying their hearts by faith.*

God gave the Holy Spirit to Gentiles without first requiring either circumcision or water baptism. Here Peter makes it plain that God purifies hearts by faith and not by any type of religious works.

---

54   See Appendix A, number 164 (use of the word *elders* in Scripture).

15:10 Now therefore why tempt ye God, putting a yoke upon the neck of the disciples, which neither our fathers nor we were able to bear?

15:11 For we believe that through the grace of the Lord Jesus Christ we shall be saved, even as they.

God had been putting up with quite a bit of human input, but now Peter wanted to draw a line. It's one thing for us to have an opinion in good conscience, but it's quite another to tempt God by *putting a yoke upon the neck of the disciples* when fifteen hundred years of tragic history have proven that this particular yoke is one that no one can bear. Peter made it very clear to the Jews that the basis for salvation is the same for everyone: it is *through the grace of the Lord Jesus Christ.*

15:12 Then all the multitude kept silence and gave audience to Barnabas and Paul, declaring what great miracles and wonders God had wrought among the Gentiles by them.

It was extremely important for Barnabas and Paul to be present at that meeting. They had fresh testimony of all the *great miracles and wonders God had wrought among the Gentiles by them*, and furthermore, they could testify that all of these amazing things happened without them having to circumcise anyone or submit them to any Jewish ceremonies or rituals.

15:13 And after they had become silent, James answered,[55] saying, Men and brethren, hearken unto me:

15:14 Simeon has declared how God first visited the Gentiles, to take out of them a people for his name.

---

55 This is James the Lesser, who was half-brother to Jesus and who wrote the epistle of James. James the brother of John was killed by Herod.

15:15 *And to this agree the words of the prophets; as it is written,*

15:16 *After this I will return and will restore the tabernacle of David, which is fallen down; and I will repair its ruins, and I will set it up again,*

15:17 *that the men that are left might seek after the Lord, and all the Gentiles, upon whom my name is called, saith the Lord, who does all these things.*

The *words of the prophets* that James is referencing form Amos 9:8-10:

Behold, the eyes of the Lord GOD are against the sinful kingdom, and I will destroy it from off the face of the earth saving that I will not utterly destroy the house of Jacob, said the LORD. For, behold, I will command, and I will cause the house of Israel to be sifted among all the Gentiles like as the grain is sifted in a sieve, yet shall not the least grain fall to the earth. All the sinners of my people shall die by the sword, who say, For our sake the evil shall not come near nor overtake us.

It was now evident to James and the other apostles, by the Spirit, that Jerusalem and the sinful kingdom surrounding her were about to be destroyed and that God was going to *cause the house of Israel to be sifted among all the Gentiles* until the times (the two thousand years) of the Gentiles were fulfilled (and this is very close to now).[56]

Amos continues: *In that day I will raise up the tabernacle of David that is fallen and close up its breaches; and I will raise up its ruins, and I will build it as in the days of old* (Amos 9:11).

What is the tabernacle of David?[57]

---

56 See Luke 21:24.
57 See *What About the Church?*, Russell M. Stendal, Life Sentence Publishing, 2013.

This refers to the time when King David brought the ark of the covenant back to Jerusalem and pitched a tent for it in his backyard (2 Samuel 6:17), thus enabling him to go into the tent and enjoy the presence of the Lord without any religious ritual or intermediary priesthood. Therefore, the tabernacle of David refers to the concept of coming back to God in the realm of the Holy of Holies without any religious rigmarole whatsoever. Under the law of Moses, only the high priest could come into the direct presence of God as symbolized by the ark of the covenant, and even he could only do so once a year, on the Day of Atonement; even then, if the rituals weren't carried out properly and if everything wasn't deemed clean, he could die when he stepped behind the veil. With the tabernacle of David, King David had unlimited access to the presence of God at any time. He could step inside whenever he and/or God desired.

Why does *the tabernacle of David that is fallen* need to be raised up and have its breaches closed?

According to Amos 9:12, this had to be done in order *that those who are called by my name may possess the remnant of Edom and all the Gentiles, said the LORD that does this.*

Those who are called by my name are the people of God; that is, those in Israel and the church who are true (obviously this doesn't include the tares).

And whom may they possess?

The remnant of Edom (of those who build their own kingdoms) and all the Gentiles (all who are not in a proper covenant with God).

> *Behold, the days come, saith the LORD, that the plowman shall catch up with the reaper, and the treader of grapes with him that sows seed; and the mountains shall drop new wine, and all the hills shall melt* (Amos 9:13).

When God reaps what appears to us to be the end-time harvest, the plowman shall catch up with the reaper and immediately plant a new crop (and this time Satan and his cohorts will be locked up in the abyss and unable to plant tares). The treader of grapes will come right behind, causing the mountains (of God) to continuously drop the new wine of the life of Christ. Then all the "hills" that represent all the obstacles shall melt.

And I will turn the captivity of my people of Israel, and they shall build the waste cities and inhabit them; and they shall plant vineyards and drink the wine thereof; they shall also make gardens and eat the fruit of them (Amos 9:14).

For I will plant them upon their land, and they shall no more be pulled up out of their land which I have given them, said the LORD thy God (Amos 9:15).

This time, the land that the Lord has given us isn't just the portion of the Middle East; it's the entire earth (for *the meek . . . shall inherit the earth*).

Let us continue with the words of James as recorded in Acts:

Acts 15

15:18 *Known unto God are all his works from the beginning of the world.*

God's plan was in place from the beginning of Satan's rebellion (when Satan started the world system, based on lies and leading to sin and death).

15:19 *Therefore my sentence is that those from among the Gentiles who are converted to God not be troubled,*

15:20 *but that we write unto them that they abstain*

from pollutions of idols and from fornication and from things strangled and from blood.

15:21 *For Moses of old time has in every city those that preach him, being read in the synagogues every sabbath day.*

James doubled down on what Peter had said and gave what he referred to as *my sentence.* This sentence or judgment mentions only four things to abstain from: pollutions of idols, fornication, things strangled, and blood. Pretty simple.[58]

15:22 *Then it pleased the apostles and elders,[59] with the whole congregation, to send chosen men of their own company to Antioch with Paul and Barnabas; namely, Judas surnamed Barsabas and Silas, principal men among the brethren;*

15:23 *and they wrote letters by them after this manner: The apostles and elders[60] and brethren send greeting unto the brethren who are of the Gentiles in Antioch and Syria and Cilicia;*

15:24 *forasmuch as we have heard that certain ones who went out from us have troubled you with words, subverting your souls, saying, Ye must be circumcised and keep the law, to whom we gave no such commandment,*

15:25 *it seemed good unto us, being assembled with one*

---

58   Even so, there are many places in the world today where large segments of the church are polluted with one form of idolatry or another (for some, even their doctrines are idols), where fornication (spiritual and otherwise) is rampant, where the breath of the Holy Spirit is quenched and strangled, and where virtually everyone, one way or another, has blood on their hands (for in cultures where the literal killing of enemies isn't in vogue, killing their reputation will do).

59   See Appendix A, number 165 (use of the word *elders* in Scripture).

60   See Appendix A, number 166 (use of the word *elders* in Scripture).

accord, to send chosen men unto you with our beloved Barnabas and Paul,

15:26 *men that have hazarded their lives for the name of our Lord Jesus Christ.*

15:27 *We have sent therefore Judas and Silas, who shall also tell you the same things by mouth.*

15:28 *For it seemed good to the Holy Spirit and to us to lay upon you no greater burden than these necessary things:*

15:29 *that ye abstain from foods sacrificed to idols and from blood and from things strangled and from fornication; from which if ye keep yourselves, ye shall do well. Fare ye well.*

Here the four items are slightly rephrased: *pollution of idols* is tweaked to *things sacrificed to idols*. This directive is prefaced by the statement that *it seemed good to the Holy Spirit and to us to lay upon you no greater burden than these necessary things.*

More than three hundred and fifty years later, in the midst of much spiritual confusion and apostasy, the Apostles' Creed (with which I wholeheartedly agree) became prevalent, and it exists to this day as a theological mainstay of many important denominations. Yet here is the original creed sent forth by the Holy Spirit through the apostles, elders, and congregation at Jerusalem. Sadly, many who today proudly recite the Apostles' Creed don't seem to place much relevance or importance on this original and extremely practical creed to *abstain from foods sacrificed to idols and from blood and from things strangled and from fornication* in either a natural or a spiritual sense.

15:30 *So when they were dismissed, they came to*

Antioch; and when they had gathered the multitude together, they delivered the epistle,

15:31 *which when they had read, they rejoiced for the consolation.*

When Barnabas and Paul got back to Antioch, the Gentile disciples delivered the message sent by the apostles and elders at Jerusalem, and the multitude rejoiced for the consolation that epistle brought them. They felt the joy of the Comforter (the Holy Spirit). Today when the people stand up on Sunday morning in church and recite the Creed, do they *rejoice for consolation* or is something missing?

15:32 *And Judas and Silas, being prophets also themselves, exhorted the brethren with many words and confirmed them.*

Judas and Silas, by the Holy Spirit, were able to give the people a continual fresh word that exhorted and confirmed the brethren. Another and quite wonderful aspect of replacing the Mosaic circumcision of the flesh with Jesus's circumcision of the heart is that it opened the way for everyone, male and female, to enter into direct covenant with God through the circumcision of Christ. Incidentally, when Scripture says that Judas and Silas exhorted *the brethren*, this term doesn't refer to gender. Under Jewish order, the role of women was limited, but later, Paul would go on to write that *there is neither male nor female* in Christ[61] (Galatians 3:28).

15:33 *And after they had tarried there a space, they were let go in peace from the brethren unto the apostles.*

---

61 *Christ*, means, the anointing, or the Anointed One. Anything accomplished, *in Christ*, means that the person is being moved by the Holy Spirit and not according to any whim or desire of their own. The Holy Spirit may move anyone, male or female, to do and say whatever God wants them to do or say. This, however, does not annul or abrogate our roles and responsibilities as male, or female, or as a husband, or as a wife, or as a child as defined in passages such as Ephesians:5:21-6:4.

15:34 *Notwithstanding it pleased Silas to abide there still.*

When *it pleased Silas to abide there still*, no one said, "Wait a minute. If you're going to stay here, you have to get permission from the apostles and elders in Jerusalem, and then they'll place you under the elders here at Antioch." No, there was complete freedom in the Spirit for Silas to do what he felt led to do.

15:35 *Paul also and Barnabas continued in Antioch, teaching the word of the Lord and announcing the gospel, with many others also.*

15:36 *And some days after, Paul said unto Barnabas, Let us go again and visit our brethren in every city where we have preached the word of the Lord and see how they do.*

15:37 *And Barnabas determined to take with them John, whose surname was Mark.*

15:38 *But Paul thought it not good to take him with them, who departed from them from Pamphylia and did not go with them to the work.*

15:39 *And the contention was so sharp between them that they departed asunder one from the other, and so Barnabas took Mark and sailed unto Cyprus;*

15:40 *and Paul chose Silas and departed, being recommended by the brethren unto the grace of God.*

15:41 *And he went through Syria and Cilicia, confirming the congregations.*

Paul didn't think that John Mark should go with them, even though Barnabas was determined to take him. So Barnabas took Mark and Paul chose Silas, and they went their separate ways.

Years later, Paul changed his opinion about Mark and wrote to Timothy from prison, saying, *Take Mark and bring him with thee, for he is profitable to me for the ministry* (2 Timothy 4:11).

When the Holy Spirit enters our lives, he doesn't annul our personality or our capacity to make decisions and to take action. However, the more we're led by the Spirit (if it's the real Holy Spirit), the less we'll desire to do radical things on our own.

It takes a while, under the instruction of the Holy Spirit and the discipline and correction of our Heavenly Father, to be confirmed in the fullness of God's will and to begin to produce good fruit. The seed is in the fruit, and the person who fails to yield the fruit of the Spirit doesn't have any viable incorruptible seed to plant. This situation cannot be remedied unless this person changes and allows God to order his or her life. It can't be remedied just by giving the person a seminar or course of intellectual study. To send such a person forth to carry out the Lord's work is to court unmitigated disaster.

The Holy Spirit separated out Barnabas and Paul for the work of the ministry precisely because they were developing godly character, and the fruit was evident. This is what qualified them to plant the life of God in others.

Let's return for a moment to the prophecy of Amos: *Behold, the days come, saith the LORD, that the plowman shall catch up with the reaper* (Amos 9:13).

This has both a near and a far application. The immediate application in the time of Paul was that God was reaping from among the Jews a godly remnant who were faithful in the midst of all the religious mixture that was going on in the synagogues as the age of the law was closing. God sent men like Paul and Barnabas to reap this harvest, and their message filled with joy the hearts of those who were true, and it brought them out of the religion contaminated by man. They were set free in the liberty of the Spirit, and at the same time they were commissioned by God to go forth and plow and plant a new crop in the territories of the Gentiles. Soon those who were plowing new territory and planting God's Word caught up with those who were reaping the godly remnant of Jews.

This portion of Scripture, however, has another fulfillment at the time of the end, because the tabernacle of David wasn't fully restored at the time of the early Christians when James quoted the prophecy of Amos. This is similar to the situation when Peter quoted the prophecy of Joel in Acts 2:16, for it was the down payment or earnest of the Spirit, not the fullness, that was poured out on the day of Pentecost (Ephesians 1:14).

Why wasn't the tabernacle of David fully restored?

For the most part, the elders who were ordained in the new Gentile congregations must have come from among those who were harvested out of the synagogues. Like the Pharisees who were converted in Jerusalem, they had their cultural concepts of leadership, with an undue emphasis on human authority. Church history proves that not only did this not die out, but it gathered strength over the centuries until religious ritual and human intermediary clergy became once again the order of the day.

And yes, throughout church history, the odd individual here or there, or even the occasional group of believers, has discovered the wonders of the "tabernacle of David" and has enjoyed intimate and direct fellowship with God.

The fullness of the prophecies, however, has still not been fulfilled. The fullness of the life of Christ has not yet begun to flow, and all the hills (and obstacles) have not yet melted (Amos 9:13).

God has declared that when the fullness happens, *I will turn the captivity of my people of Israel, and they shall build the waste cities and inhabit them; and they shall plant vineyards and drink the wine thereof; they shall also make gardens and eat the fruit of them. For I will plant them upon their land, and they shall no more be pulled up out of their land which I have given them, said the LORD thy God* (Amos 9:14-15).

Let Us Pray

Lord, May we learn the lessons of history. May we understand that the revelation of the New Testament is not law that we should attempt to replicate in our own strength, and that the wonderful examples of what you accomplished in and through people like Barnabas and Paul and Timothy can only be duplicated as the same Holy Spirit moves us.

May we understand that the security, the future, and the salvation of those around us depend on your initiative. May we be found at your side, doing your will. At your return, may we not be found doing something different from your will or attempting to convince you to do our will. Amen.

Chapter 7

The Man of Macedonia

Paul left Antioch on his second missionary journey, this time accompanied by Silas, and *went through Syria and Cilicia, confirming the congregations* (Acts 15:41).

Acts 16

16:1 Then he came to Derbe and Lystra; and, behold, a certain disciple was there named Timothy, the son of a Jewish woman, who was faithful, but his father was a Gentile,

16:2 of whom the brethren that were at Lystra and Iconium gave good witness.

"Timothy" means "honoring God." Timothy had a faithful Jewish mother named Eunice ("victorious"), and Scripture even mentions the faith of his godly grandmother, Lois[62] (2 Timothy 1:5).

16:3 Paul desired to have him go forth with him and took and circumcised him because of the Jews who were

---

62 The name Lois is of uncertain meaning, possibly from the Greek *loion* ("most desired").

*in those quarters, for they all knew that his father was
a Greek.*

*16:4 And as they went through the cities, they asked
them to keep the decrees that had been determined by
the apostles and elders[63] who were at Jerusalem.*

One of the decrees that had been agreed upon by the apostles
and elders who were at Jerusalem (and in accord with the Holy
Spirit) was not to circumcise Gentile believers or impose Jewish
law on them. So after having his controversial policy of not
circumcising Gentile converts confirmed by the apostles and
elders at Jerusalem, why would Paul now circumcise Timothy?

There are several good reasons: 1) Since time immemorial,
Jewish citizenship has been defined by the mother even more
so than by the father, and Timothy's mother was Jewish. 2)
As we will see later in this book, Paul was planning to have
Timothy accompany him in ministry to places like Corinth,
where the believers were still meeting in the Jewish synagogue
under Jewish order, and therefore Timothy would need to be
circumcised in order to be received and allowed to minister. 3)
Every time we think we've discovered a set formula, God may
decide to make exceptions.

*16:5 And so the congregations were established in the
faith and increased in number daily.*

The number of congregations increased and the number of
people in the congregations increased daily. This verse isn't
describing an institutional church, but rather individual congregations that are all part of the universal body of Christ of
which the Lord Jesus is the head.

16:6 Now passing through Phrygia and the region of

---

63   See Appendix A, number 167 (use of the word *elders* in Scripture).

*Galatia, they were forbidden by the Holy Spirit to
preach the word in Asia;*

*16:7 after they were come to Mysia, they assayed to go
into Bithynia, but the Spirit suffered them not.*

The elders and apostles back at Jerusalem weren't calling the
shots about where and when Paul and Silas should minister.
This was being decided directly by the Holy Spirit on a con-
tinuous basis.

"Phrygia" means "dry" or "desert," "Galatia" means "colonized
by Gauls" (who were people of power), and "Asia" means "east"
or "eastern." "Mysia" means "land of fir trees," and "Bithynia"
means "a violent encounter."

16:8 And they passing by Mysia came down to Troas.[64]

*16:9 And a vision was shown to Paul in the night: There
stood a man of Macedonia, asking him, saying, Come
over into Macedonia and help us.*

"Macedonia" means "ample land" or "extended land," and it
was a man of this country who appeared to Paul in a night
vision, asking for help. When God decides where to send forth
ministry, he tends to give priority to those who desire to receive
his messengers.

*16:10 And after he had seen the vision, immediately we
endeavoured to go into Macedonia, assuredly gathering
that the Lord had called us to preach the gospel unto
them.*

The narration moves into the first person – *immediately **we**
endeavoured to go into Macedonia, assuredly gathering that the
Lord had called **us** to preach the gospel unto them* – indicating

---

64 The meaning of "Troas" is uncertain, but it could mean "penetrated."

that the writer of the book of Acts (probably Luke) is traveling with Paul and Silas.[65]

16:11 *Therefore loosing from Troas, we came with a straight course to Samothracia, and the next day to Neapolis,*

16:12 *and from there to Philippi, which is the chief city of that part of Macedonia, and a colony; and we were in that city abiding certain days.*

"Samothracia" means "a sign with flags," and "Neapolis" means "a new city." "Philippi," meaning "lover of horses," was named after Philip of Macedon.

16:13 *And on one of the sabbaths we went out of the city by a river side, where it was customary to pray; and we sat down and spoke unto the women who gathered there.*

16:14 *Then a certain woman named Lydia, a seller of purple, of the city of Thyatira, who feared God, heard us, whose heart the Lord opened that she attended unto the things which were spoken by Paul.*

"Lydia" means "from Lud" (a North African people to the west of Egypt), and "Thyatira"[66] means "the aroma of persecution" or "the aroma of tribulation." She was a woman who feared God, and the Lord opened her heart to the message given by Paul.

16:15 *And when she was baptized, with her household, she besought us, saying, If ye have judged me to*

65　It is worth noting that the writer of the book of Acts chose to join Paul and Silas instead of traveling with other worthy men such as Barnabas and John Mark. The wisdom of this discernment was borne out by the fact that it was Paul who later wrote such an important part of the New Testament.

66　Some years later, Jesus dictated an important letter to the angel of the congregation at Thyatira. Lydia may have had a role in establishing the congregation in her hometown.

*be faithful to the Lord, come into my house and abide
there. And she constrained us.*

This verse simply records that *she was baptized, with her household*, and doesn't specify whether she was baptized in water or
in the Holy Spirit or both. However, her subsequent desire to
invite Paul and his companions into her house is evidence that
the Holy Spirit was active in her heart.

16:16 *And it came to pass, as we went to prayer, a
certain damsel possessed with a Pythian spirit met us,
which brought her masters much gain by divination:*

A Pythian[67] spirit is basically an unclean spirit specializing in
divination (a form of prophecy).

16:17 *she followed Paul and us and cried out, saying,
These men are the slaves of the most high God, who
announce unto us the way of deliverance.*

16:18 *And she did this for many days. But Paul, being
grieved, turned and said to the spirit, I command thee
in the name of Jesus Christ to come out of her. And he
came out the same hour.*

Jesus also cast out many unclean spirits that cried out and
properly identified him as the Christ.

16:19 *And when her masters saw that the hope of their
gains was gone, they caught Paul and Silas and drew
them into the marketplace unto the rulers*

16:20 *and brought them to the magistrates, saying,
These men, being Jews, do exceedingly trouble our city*

16:21 *and teach rites which are not lawful for us to
receive neither to observe, being Romans.*

---

67   In paganism, this is related to Apollo (the Greek and Roman god of music and
prophecy) as patron of Delphi and the oracle that was located there.

Divination and fortunetelling were obviously big business in Philippi,[68] and the masters of the girl who was delivered had a considerable amount of power and connections. After all, the multitude had been paying to have their fortune told or to receive divination regarding what decisions to make towards the future. Now, the girl's masters' hope of gains was gone, as was the hope of those of the multitude who wished to have seemingly wise supernatural (yet actually demonic) counsel.

16:22 *And the multitude rose up together against them, and the magistrates rent off their clothes and commanded to beat them.*

16:23 *And when they had laid many stripes upon them, they cast them into prison, charging the jailor to keep them safely,*

16:24 *who, having received such a charge, thrust them into the inner prison and made their feet fast in the stocks.*

Paul and Silas got into quite a bit of trouble for casting out an unclean Pythian spirit. Obviously, the Holy Spirit had his reasons for forbidding them to preach in Asia and not even allowing them to go into Bithynia. It would seem that there was a huge battle going on in the spiritual realm. Evil principalities and powers of wickedness in high places were evidently not taking kindly to having their kingdoms evangelized. They wanted to keep the people imprisoned in darkness.

16:25 *But at midnight as Paul and Silas prayed and sang praises unto God, and the prisoners heard them,*

16:26 *then suddenly there was a great earthquake, so*

---

68 In Scripture, horses can represent the power of the flesh. Philippi, meaning "lover of horses," could also symbolically mean "lover of doing things according to the flesh."

that the foundations of the prison were shaken; and immediately all the doors were opened, and every one's bands were loosed.

If the foundations of Paul and Silas's natural prison were shaken, what about the foundations of the spiritual prison that was holding the other prisoners? Scripture tells us that immediately all the doors were opened and everyone's bands were loosed. When Satan attempts to mistreat, scourge, and imprison those who are clean, everything may backfire on him and he may lose some or even all of his hostages as they suddenly perceive the way to spiritual freedom.

16:27 And the keeper of the prison, awaking out of his sleep and seeing the prison doors open, he drew out his sword and would have killed himself, supposing that the prisoners had fled.

Who was the man of Macedonia who appeared to Paul in his nighttime vision, asking for help? Could it have been someone like the keeper of this prison? There are numerous useful idiots who help the powers of darkness keep as many as possible locked up in spiritual dungeons of darkness – not because such people actively wish to keep others spiritually imprisoned, but simply because they, like so many people, are spiritually asleep. Should they awaken to their spiritual danger, as the prison guard awakened to the danger he faced if the captives escaped, they may well urgently ask for help.

16:28 But Paul cried with a loud voice, saying, Do thyself no harm, for we are all here.

16:29 Then he called for a light and came inside and fell down trembling before Paul and Silas

16:30 and brought them out and said, Sirs, what must I do to be saved?

The Philippian jailer knew beyond a shadow of a doubt that he needed to be saved. He knew that he needed help, and it only took him an instant to recognize that help had arrived. When we are sent by God to evangelize, it really helps when people start asking the right questions.

> 16:31 *And they said, Believe on the Lord Jesus Christ, and thou shalt be saved, and thy house.*

> 16:32 *And they spoke unto him the word of the Lord, and to all that were in his house.*

> 16:33 *And he took them the same hour of the night and washed their stripes and was baptized, he and all his, straightway.*

The earthquake struck at midnight, and the jailer almost immediately began asking about how to be saved. He was told to believe on the Lord Jesus Christ and was promised that his house (family) would also be saved. Then, in very short order, even before they would have had time to go to his house, Scripture tells us that he and everyone who were his were baptized. Again there is no mention made of the baptism being in water. It appears that the Holy Spirit fell upon the jailer's entire household and baptized all of them.

> 16:34 *And when he had brought them into his house, he set food before them and rejoiced, believing in God with all his house.*

The keeper's willingness to take Paul and Silas into his house and the joy he displayed at his new relationship with God were all signs of the presence of the Holy Spirit.

The devil had undoubtedly been doing everything possible to keep the man of Macedonia in the dark in his role as the keeper of the prison. However, when the evil demonic forces began to taunt Paul and Silas relentlessly through the Pythian spirit by exposing who they really were, something was triggered that even Satan didn't expect. By stirring up the people against the gospel and having the evangelists beaten and imprisoned, the devil unwittingly set the stage for the keeper of the prison and his entire family to be filled with the Holy Spirit.

> 16:35 *And when it was day, the magistrates sent the sergeants, saying, Let those men go.*

> 16:36 *And the keeper of the prison made these words known unto Paul, The magistrates have sent to let you go; now therefore depart and go in peace.*

The magistrates sent word as soon as it was day, but they were too late. God had already freed the prisoners (including the jailer), starting at midnight. This particular prison and its jailor would never be the same. Even the other prisoners would never forget the testimony of the events that took place that night as they were given a glimpse of what spiritual freedom is like, for *where that Spirit of the Lord is, there is liberty* (2 Corinthians 3:17).

> 16:37 *But Paul said unto them, They have beaten us openly uncondemned, being Romans, and have cast us into prison; and now do they thrust us out in secret? no indeed; but let them come themselves and fetch us out.*

> 16:38 *And the sergeants returned and told these words unto the magistrates; and they feared when they heard that they were Romans.*

> 16:39 *And they came and besought them, and bringing them out, asked them to depart out of the city.*

> 16:40 *And leaving the prison, they entered into the house of Lydia; and when they had seen the brethren, they comforted them and departed.*

This is how the gospel came to Philippi. After only a few days in town, Paul left two entire households filled with the power and presence of God, and these households soon grew into a number of thriving congregations.

Let Us Pray

Lord, Thank you for including us in your plans and for allowing us to walk by your side. May we continue to claim new territory for you and to impregnate each place with entire families filled with your power and presence. Amen.

Chapter 8

The Unknown God

The pagan world in general and the religious Jews in particular were, for the most part, extremely hostile to the gospel. Even under the specific guidance of the Holy Spirit with corresponding conviction after each anointed message, confirmed by astounding signs and wonders, there weren't many places where Paul and Silas were able to stay for any considerable length of time. It was the infilling (or baptism) of the Holy Spirit that caused these early believers not only to persevere and remain on course, but to multiply exceedingly.

Acts 17

17:1 *Now when they had passed through Amphipolis and Apollonia, they came to Thessalonica, where the synagogue of the Jews was.*

"Amphipolis" means "city surrounded by the sea" (the sea is symbolic of pagan Gentiles), and "Apollonia" means "place of Apollo" (the pagan god of prophecy and music). "Thessalonica" means "victory of the false." It appears that Paul and Silas were heading into a perfect storm, not least because *the synagogue of the Jews* turned out to have a very significant component of *disobedient Jews* (Acts 17:5), as had been the case in Iconium (Acts 14:1). As was also the case when describing the situation in Iconium (Acts 14:2), Scripture describes the synagogue as being *of the Jews* to stress the fact that it was theirs.

> 17:2 *And Paul, as his manner was, went in unto them, and three sabbath days reasoned with them out of the scriptures,*

> 17:3 *declaring openly and proposing that it behooved the Christ to have suffered and risen again from the dead and that this Jesus, whom I preach unto you, is the Christ.*

> 17:4 *And some of them believed and consorted with Paul and Silas; and of the devout Greeks a great multitude, and of the noble women not a few.*

This is similar to what happened in many other places. Anyone with a heart for God responded to the messages delivered by Paul.

> 17:5 *But the disobedient Jews, moved with envy, took unto them certain lewd fellows of the baser sort and gathered a company and set all the city on an uproar and assaulted the house of Jason and sought to bring them out to the people.*

> 17:6 *And when they did not find them, they brought Jason*[69] *and certain brethren unto the rulers of the city, crying, These that have turned the world upside down have come here also,*

> 17:7 *whom Jason has received, and these all do contrary to the decrees of Caesar, saying that there is another king, one Jesus.*

---

69 "Jason" means "to heal."

17:8 *And they troubled the people and the rulers of the city when they heard these things.*

Even the enemies of Paul and Silas acknowledged that the world was being turned upside down by the gospel. The accusation that *these all do contrary to the decrees of Caesar, saying that there is another king,* would continue to fester against the believers, however, and over the next hundred and fifty years or so, pagan Rome would kill an estimated seven million Christians (many of them were tortured or fed to the lions in cruel sport at the coliseum).

17:9 *And when they had taken security of Jason and of the others, they let them go.*

The ministry of Paul, Silas, and Timothy had only been going on in Thessalonica over the space of *three sabbath days.* Therefore, Jason and the others had only known Paul for a couple of weeks. The love, trust, and affection shown to Paul by the believers in Thessalonica came from the bond of the Holy Spirit that unites the body of Christ. Even though Paul wasn't able to stay very long in Thessalonica, the congregation that he planted became one of the most successful anywhere and soon multiplied all over the entire area.[70] An important factor behind this astounding success was the fact that Paul taught the Thessalonians to personally hear the voice of the Lord (1 Thessalonians 2:13).

17:10 *And the brethren immediately sent Paul and Silas away by night unto Berea,[71] who when they got there went into the synagogue of the Jews.*

No amount of persecution was able to stop Paul and Silas. Even when they had to flee by night, they showed up at the next synagogue of the Jews and kept on preaching, and their perseverance really paid off.

---

70   See *Preparing for the End of the World*, Russell M. Stendal, ANEKO Press.
71   "Berea" means "beyond."

17:11 *These were more noble than those in Thessalonica, in that they received the word with all diligence and searched the scriptures daily, whether those things were so.*

17:12 *Therefore many of them believed, also of honourable women who were Greeks and of men, not a few.*

God was pouring out the Spirit on women as well as on men.

17:13 *But when the Jews of Thessalonica had knowledge that the word of God was preached by Paul at Berea, they came there also and stirred up the people.*

17:14 *And then immediately the brethren sent Paul to go away towards the sea, but Silas and Timothy abode there still.*

Paul was obviously more controversial than any of the other believers, because he had an anointed message, a classical Jewish intellectual capacity and background, and authority from God – a combination that enabled him to pierce through Jewish legalism and clearly present the gospel that Jesus is the Messiah.

17:15 *And those that conducted Paul brought him unto Athens; and receiving an order from him unto Silas and Timothy to come unto him as soon as possible, they departed.*

17:16 *Now while Paul waited for them at Athens, his spirit was stirred in him when he saw the city completely given over to idolatry.*

Athens is the plural of Athene (the pagan goddess of wisdom). Rome was the political and military capital of the empire, but Athens was the cultural capital. Greek was spoken not only in Athens, but was dominant in most of the known world, and the pagan Greek gods all had their Roman equivalents. Not only was Paul concerned, but also *his spirit was stirred.*

17:17 Therefore he disputed in the synagogue with the Jews and with the devout persons and in the market daily with those that he met with.

17:18 Then certain philosophers of the Epicureans and of the Stoics encountered him. And some said, What will this babbler say? others, He seems to be a setter forth of new gods, because he preached unto them Jesus and the resurrection.

17:19 And they took him and brought him unto the Areopagus, saying, May we know what this new doctrine is, of which thou speakest?

17:20 For thou bringest certain new things to our ears; we desire, therefore, to know what these things mean.

17:21 (For all the Athenians and strangers who were there spent their time in nothing else, but either to tell or to hear some new thing.)

Sounds similar to what's happening today, doesn't it?

17:22 Then Paul stood in the midst of the Areopagus,[72] and said, Ye men of Athens, I perceive that in all things ye are too superstitious.

They were too superstitious in *all* things? What is superstition?

Superstition has to do with tightly held beliefs that coincide only imperfectly with logic or science. Much of this pagan residue continues even in our modern world. People are irrationally afraid of breaking mirrors, walking under ladders, seeing black cats cross their paths, or staying on the thirteenth floor (in fact, many hotels, apartment blocks, and public buildings

---

72 Mars Hill.

don't even have a thirteenth floor), and any number of strange home remedies are still used today and can even be found on the Internet, along with their respective fables and old wives' tales.

Superstition is one thing, but faith is another. Faith means believing and trusting God even though there are many things past, present, and future that we don't fully understand. When we place our trust and confidence in the Lord Jesus Christ, he'll send us the Holy Spirit to lead us into all truth and to comfort and console us even in the midst of serious trials and tribulations.

17:23 For as I passed by and beheld your sanctuaries, I found an altar with this inscription, TO THE UNKNOWN GOD. Whom therefore ye ignorantly worship, him I declare unto you.

Sometime in the history of Athens, someone must have had some doubts about all the pagan gods and wondered if somehow God – the real God – might still be unknown to them. In order to cover all the bases, therefore, this altar had been erected. Now the Holy Spirit moved Paul to use this as the starting point for his message.

17:24 The God that made the world and all the things therein, seeing that he is Lord of heaven and earth, does not dwell in temples made with hands;

17:25 neither is worshipped with men's hands, as though he needed any thing, seeing he gives to all life and breath and all things

17:26 and has made of one blood all the lineage of men to dwell on all the face of the earth and has determined the seasons[73] (which he has limited) and the bounds of their habitation;

---

73 What are the seasons that God has determined (and limited)? He determined a season for the Jews, which was ending, and another season for the Gentiles, which was beginning (and now, almost two thousand years later, is ending).

17:27 that they should seek the Lord, if in any manner they might reach out to touch him and find him though he is not far from each one of us;

17:28 for in him we live and move and have our being; as certain also of your own poets have said, For we are also of his lineage.

This message is straight and simple and begins by defining God as he actually is. The Athenian concept of their pagan gods was quite different, in that they believed that all these gods must be appeased. They endowed their gods with the same defects and problems that humans have, but they also took the view that the gods were supernaturally powerful. Greek mythology doesn't describe the gods as being very benign toward humans. These were gods who fought among themselves, betrayed one another, and then took revenge. The Greek gods were really demons, yet over in one small corner, someone had built an altar with an inscription: *TO THE UNKNOWN GOD.*

Unlike all the pagan deities, the real God doesn't need to be appeased. He's the one who made us, and he gives us life and He desires for us to seek him because we are of his lineage and he wants to restore us into his image. (The pagans, on the other hand, were up to their ears in a demonic attempt to recreate gods in the image of fallen man.)

17:29 Being therefore of the lineage of God, we ought not to think that which is Divine is like unto gold or silver or stone, bearing the mark of art and man's imagination.

17:30 For the times of this ignorance God overlooked, but he now commands all men everywhere to repent

---

What are the bounds of their habitation? The Jews were under law; the Gentiles are under grace. Both were given the opportunity to reach out and touch God. After this will come the judgment (see verse 31).

17:31 *because he has appointed a day, in which he will judge the world in righteousness by that man whom he has ordained; of whom he has given assurance unto all men in that he has raised him from the dead.*

Paul trumpeted this important proclamation of the impending judgment day in the midst of the Areopagus!

God has never closed the door to anyone. He has always been close by. Even in the times of ignorance, people could always seek the truth and recognize that there is a creator and that we all ought to be thankful and grateful to him (Romans 1:20-32). From the time of the apostle Paul forward, however, God *commands all men everywhere to repent.* And yes, on the day of judgment, when each of us will stand before Jesus Christ, we will all be held accountable in light of the truth that was available to us (Revelation 11:18, 20:11-15).

17:32 *And when they heard of the resurrection of the dead, some mocked; and others said, We will hear thee again of this matter.*

17:33 *So Paul departed from among them.*

17:34 *But certain men believed and joined themselves with him, among whom was Dionysius of the Areopagus and a woman named Damaris and others with them.*

"Dionysius" means "belonging to Dionysus" (Bacchus, the reveler), and "Damaris" means "gentle." Here Paul had great results among pagans who had no background whatsoever in Judaism. Those who believed *joined themselves with him,* which is the bond of the Holy Spirit.

Many today don't seem to believe that God *now commands all men everywhere to repent because he has appointed a day, in which he will judge the world in righteousness,* but one day they will find themselves sadly mistaken. God will not only hold those accountable who pertain to Israel and the church, but he will hold the entire world accountable for their words and deeds.

Let Us Pray

Lord, We ask that you open our minds that we might understand the Scriptures and realize our need for the infilling of the Holy Spirit. May we understand the time and season in which we are living. May we be found keeping the faith and depending upon you and upon your life as this present age comes to an end. Amen.

Chapter 9

Being Helpful Through Grace

Acts 18

18:1 *After these things Paul departed from Athens and came to Corinth*

18:2 *and found a certain Jew named Aquila, born in Pontus, lately come from Italy, with his wife Priscilla (for Claudius[74] had commanded all Jews to depart from Rome) and came unto them.*

"C orinth" means "filled," "Aquila" means "an eagle," "Pontus" means "belonging to the sea," and "Italy" means "like a calf." "Priscilla" is the diminutive of "Prisca" ("ancient").

18:3 *And because he was of the same craft, he abode with them and worked, for by their occupation they were tentmakers.*

18:4 *And he reasoned in the synagogue every sabbath and persuaded Jews and Greeks.*

18:5 *And when Silas and Timothy were come from*

---

74 Claudius succeeded Caligula as Roman emperor (AD 41-54). The name means "lame" or "crippled."

*Macedonia, Paul was impressed by the Spirit and testi-
fied to the Jews that Jesus was the Christ.*

Paul reasoned in the synagogue every Sabbath, but he waited
until Silas and Timothy joined him before testifying that Jesus
was the Christ, because every matter of life or death requires two
or three witnesses under the law (Numbers 35:30; Deuteronomy
17:6). Paul considered his message and testimony to be of life-
or-death importance, because he knew that dire consequences
awaited those who rejected the gospel.

18:6 *And when they opposed themselves and blas-
phemed, he shook his raiment and said unto them,
Your blood be upon your own heads; I am clean; from
now on I will go unto the Gentiles.*

18:7 *And he departed from there and entered into a
certain man's house, named Titus[75] the Just, one that
feared God, whose house was next to the synagogue.*

18:8 *And Crispus, the chief ruler of the synagogue,
believed on the Lord with all his house; and many of the
Corinthians, hearing, believed and were baptized.*

Here in Corinth, as in many other places, it's evident that the
Holy Spirit was poured out. In fact, many details in the letters
that Paul later wrote to the Corinthians indicate that despite
initial rejection, the congregation of Christ prospered inside
the synagogue. The conversion of Crispus, the chief ruler of the
synagogue, and the faith of many others, such as Titus, turned
the situation around. This would explain some of the Jewish
idiosyncrasies regarding the treatment of women and certain
other points in the epistles to the Corinthians and to Timothy,
who was ministering there.

---

75 "Titus" means "protected."

18:9 *Then the Lord spoke to Paul in the night by a vision, Do not be afraid, but speak and do not be silent,*

18:10 *For I am with thee, and no one shall be able to hurt thee, for I have many people in this city.*

"Corinth" means "filled," and the place turned out to be filled with those who had a heart for God.

18:11 *And he continued there a year and six months, teaching them the word of God.*

18:12 *And when Gallio was the proconsul of Achaia, the Jews rose up with one accord against Paul and brought him to the judgment seat,*

18:13 *saying, This fellow persuades men to honor God contrary to the law.*

18:14 *And when Paul was now about to open his mouth, Gallio said unto the Jews, If it were a matter of wrong or wicked lewdness, O ye Jews, reason would that I should bear with you;*

18:15 *but if it is a question of words and names and of your law, look ye to it, for I will be no judge of such matters.*

18:16 *And he drove them from the judgment seat.*

18:17 *Then all the Greeks took Sosthenes, the chief ruler of the synagogue, and beat him before the judgment seat. And Gallio cared for none of those things.*

"Achaia" means "problems," and "Gallio" means "one who lives on milk" (i.e., someone immature). "Sosthenes" means "savior of his nation."

This time, the opposition of the Jews backfired. Both Crispus and Sosthenes are mentioned as being chief rulers of the synagogue. Crispus was definitely a believer, and Sosthenes was apparently a leader of the uprising against Paul. There were likely multiple "chief rulers," and possibly even more than one synagogue in town. At a bare minimum, we can deduce that there were enough Jewish and Gentile believers to ensure that Paul didn't get run out of town, while at the same time there were also many unbelieving Jews. It's clear in his letters to the Corinthians that Paul was very concerned that the testimony of the believers be exemplary before Jew and Gentile.

18:18 *And Paul after this tarried there yet a good while and then took his leave of the brethren and sailed from there into Syria and with him Priscilla and Aquila, having shorn his head in Cenchrea, for he had a vow.*

Paul was adamant on the policy of not imposing the Jewish law on the Gentile believers. He also knew beyond any doubt that God had commissioned and sent him as the apostle to the Gentiles. Nevertheless, throughout his life and ministry he could never forget about the Jews. He had an inner compulsion to seek a synagogue every Sabbath day and reason with the Jews, and God blessed these efforts in each place, where at least a few and sometimes many of the Jews believed.

The fact that Paul would shave his head in Cenchrea (meaning "cereal grain" or "millet") because he made a vow that would require him to eventually attend purification rites at the temple in Jerusalem[76] seems a bit odd at first glance. What was this vow that Paul made which has been cloaked in mystery for so long?

Bear in mind that as part of his ministry, he felt compelled to seek a synagogue every Sabbath to reason with his fellow Jews there. It seems likely, therefore, that he may have vowed

76 Virtually every vow that could be made unto the Lord required an offering or sacrifice, and all or any of this required the people to present themselves before a priest in the temple at Jerusalem (Leviticus 22:18, 23:37-38, 27:1-8; Numbers 15:1-15, 30:1-2; Deuteronomy 12:5-6).

to return to Jerusalem so that he could attempt to convince the Jewish people and leaders there to believe in Jesus Christ as their Messiah and to repent of the terrible mistake they were making that was about to bring down their nation. The vow, symbolized by the shaven head, would give him a good excuse to go to the temple. Since Paul was apparently unable to attend any synagogue at all without sharing his message and testimony of Jesus Christ, the thought of returning to the temple in Jerusalem and sharing the good news there would be compelling (and it also appears that the Holy Spirit was behind this).

It seems likely that it was while Paul was spending eighteen months or so in Corinth (verse 18:11) that he wrote, or at least began to write, his letter to the Romans.[77] He was given great revelations of the consequences of the Jewish leaders rejecting Jesus Christ, of the gospel being extended to the Gentiles, and of the sovereign will of God regarding election, along with the interaction of the wills of both the obedient and the disobedient. Paul makes it plain that he would be willing to personally pay almost any price to see the Jewish nation redeemed (Romans 9:1-5).

18:19 *And he came to Ephesus[78] and left them there, but he himself entered into the synagogue and reasoned with the Jews.*

18:20 *When they desired him to tarry longer time with them, he consented not,*

18:21 *but bade them farewell, saying, I must by all means keep this feast that comes in Jerusalem, but I*

---

77 Priscilla and Aquila fled Italy after the Emperor Claudius (AD 41-54) expelled the Jews from Rome toward the end of his reign. By the time Paul's epistle was sent to the Romans, however, there were Jewish people back in Rome. Given that it would have taken a few years for them to return after Claudius died, it appears that this letter could have not have been delivered earlier than AD 57 or 58 and might have been delivered in AD 60 or so.

78 "Ephesus" means "permitted."

*will return again unto you, if God wills. And he sailed
from Ephesus.*

Paul was determined to continue to keep the feast of the Lord
in Jerusalem (Leviticus 23:41).

*18:22 And when he had landed at Caesarea and gone
up to Jerusalem and after greeting the congregation, he
went down to Antioch.*

*18:23 And after he had spent some time there, he
departed and went over all the country of Galatia and
Phrygia in order, confirming all the disciples.*

There's no evidence that Paul went about *confirming all the
disciples* by giving them an exam on theology or a seminar on
liturgy, or even questioning them regarding their scriptural
knowledge. He visited these areas to see if the disciples were
still clean and if the Spirit of God was still leading them. Paul
didn't need to set up a detective agency to find out what the
disciples might have been doing when they thought no one was
looking; all he had to do was spend a little time with each one
and receive the witness of the Spirit.

*18:24 And a certain Jew named Apollos, born at
Alexandria, an eloquent man and mighty in the scriptures, came to Ephesus.*

*18:25 This man was instructed in the way of the Lord;
and being fervent in the spirit, he spoke and taught
diligently the things of the Lord, teaching only in the
baptism of John.*

*18:26 And he began to speak boldly in the synagogue,
but when Aquila and Priscilla[79] had heard him, they*

---

79 Note that here the woman Priscilla is taking an active role in expounding the
way of God more perfectly to Apollos. This is, obviously, taking place outside
the synagogue and it is also noteworthy that Aquila and Priscilla were doing
this together as husband and wife. Paul would later write that in Christ, there

*took him unto them and expounded unto him the way
of God more perfectly.*

The "way of God," or simply "the way," was the terminology
used by the early Christians to denote following Jesus Christ
in the power of the Holy Spirit. Apollos, who was eloquent and
mighty in the Scriptures, came to Ephesus teaching only in the
baptism of John (water baptism). So it is today; there are still
some Christians like Apollos, of fervent spirit, eloquent, and
mighty in the Scriptures, but lacking the baptism that only
Jesus can provide. I am confident that what Aquila and Priscilla
expounded to Apollos included the following words of John
the Baptist: *I indeed baptize you in water unto repentance, but
he that comes after me is mightier than I, whose shoes I am not
worthy to bear; he shall baptize you in the Holy Spirit and fire*
(Matthew 3:11).

> 18:27 *And when he was disposed to pass into Achaia,
> the exhorted brethren wrote the disciples to receive him,
> who, when he was come, was very helpful through grace
> unto those who had believed;*

Being *helpful through grace* means that Apollos was now moving in the power of the Holy Spirit by grace.

> 18:28 *for he mightily convinced the Jews in public,
> showing by the scriptures that Jesus was the Christ.*

"Apollos" means "gathering" or "gatherer." Those who are truly
sent by God help to gather the body of Christ together, but those
who are false want to split it into sects or schisms.

---

is no difference between male and female, even though he also wrote to the
Corinthians and to Timothy (who was ministering there in the synagogue) that
they were to respect Jewish order regarding women.

Let Us Pray

Lord, May you grant us the ability to expound the way of God more perfectly. May you send us forth to gather, to unite, and to exhort those who are truly yours.

May we have a place in our heart for those who have been left behind because they do not understand, and may we be helpful through grace unto those who have believed. Amen.

Chapter 10

The Uproar in Ephesus

Acts 19

19:1 And it came to pass that while Apollos was at Corinth, Paul, having passed through the upper coasts, came to Ephesus, and finding certain disciples,

19:2 he said unto them, Have ye received the Holy Spirit since ye believed? And they said unto him, We have not so much as heard whether there is any Holy Spirit.

19:3 And he said unto them, Into what then were ye baptized? And they said, Into John's baptism.

They had been baptized in water as a symbol of repentance (John's baptism), but they had not been baptized or immersed into the Holy Spirit (into the nature of God).

19:4 Then said Paul, John verily baptized with the baptism of repentance, saying unto the people that they should believe on him who should come after him, that is, on Christ, Jesus.

19:5 *When they heard this, they were baptized into the name of the Lord Jesus.*

In Scripture, from the very beginning of Genesis,[80] name has to do with nature. The name of the Lord Jesus is the same nature as the Father and the Holy Spirit. Water baptism has its roots in the ceremonial cleansing described in the law of Moses and is a beautiful symbol of identification with the death and resurrection of Jesus Christ. Without the Holy Spirit, however, it is impossible to be *baptized into the name* [nature] *of the Lord Jesus.*

19:6 *And when Paul had laid his hands upon them, the Holy Spirit came on them, and they spoke in tongues and prophesied.*

In the book of Acts, there are basically two ways that a person could be baptized into the Holy Spirit: 1) On the day of Pentecost, at the house of Cornelius, and possibly on other occasions, the Holy Spirit simply fell on those who were present. 2) On many other occasions, the Holy Spirit came upon the people with the laying on of hands by the apostles.

19:7 *And all the men were about twelve.*

The number twelve is symbolic of divine order.

19:8 *And he went into the synagogue and spoke freely for the space of three months, disputing and persuading the things concerning the kingdom of God.*

In the natural realm, three months is a season. There are times and seasons in God when he grants special opportunities that may not always be available. It behooves us to be found doing what is right with God according to his timetable, instead of trying to get him to bless what we're doing. The plans, projects, and timetables of man have been the bane of much of the institutional church.

---

80   *And God said, Let the earth bring forth the living soul after its nature, beasts and serpents and animals of the earth after its nature; and it was so* (Genesis 1:24).

THE UPROAR IN EPHESUS

19:9 But when some were hardened and disobedient, but cursing the way before the multitude, he departed from them and separated the disciples, disputing daily in the school of one Tyrannus.

Note the reference to *the way. The way* is really Jesus. When those who were hardened and disobedient cursed *the way* in public, Paul decided not only that it was time for him to leave, but also that he should separate the disciples. Incidentally, "Tyrannus" means "tyrant." It seems that Paul moved the disciples to somewhere safe, but he himself continued to go back and dispute daily in *the school of one Tyrannus.*

19:10 And this continued by the space of two years so that all those who dwelt in Asia heard the word of the Lord Jesus, both Jews and Greeks.

In the two and a quarter years or so that Paul spent at Ephesus, he could have written 1 Corinthians. I'm guessing that the time was likely AD 59, give or take a little, which would be roughly twenty-two years after the Holy Spirit was poured out upon the house of Cornelius, and about five or six years before the Roman armies laid siege to cities in Judaea and seriously threatened Jerusalem in AD 64 to 67. Many Christians must have been sensing ever-increasing urgency in the Spirit that the age of the law was about to come to a terrible end.

19:11 And God wrought special miracles by the hands of Paul

19:12 so that from his body were brought unto the sick handkerchiefs or aprons, and the diseases departed from them, and the evil spirits went out of them.

Note that the anointing of the Holy Spirit upon Paul was increasing, not decreasing.

19:13 Then certain of the vagabond Jews, exorcists, took

upon themselves to invoke over those who had evil spirits the name of the Lord Jesus, saying, We adjure you by Jesus whom Paul preaches.

19:14 (And there were seven sons of one Sceva,[81] a Jew and prince of the priests, who did so.)

19:15 And the evil spirit answered and said, Jesus I know, and Paul I am acquainted with, but who are ye?

The original language seems to indicate that Jesus was very well known in the spiritual realm, where the demons existed. The demons also had a pretty good idea of who Paul was, but they had no reason at all to fear this so-called Sceva ("left-handed") and his seven sons, since to be "left-handed" was to be without power or authority.

19:16 And the man in whom the evil spirit was leaped on them and overcame them and prevailed against them so that they fled out of that house naked and wounded.

19:17 And this was known to all the Jews and Greeks also dwelling at Ephesus; and fear fell on them all, and the name of the Lord Jesus was magnified.

The difference between the true ministers of God and the false ministers suddenly became obvious.

19:18 And many that believed came, confessing and declaring their deeds.

When they believed, the Holy Spirit put them under conviction and brought them to repentance.

---

81 "Sceva" means "left-handed." In Hebrew, the term "left-handed" is used to describe someone who is powerless; that is, metaphorically speaking, someone whose right hand (the hand of power and authority) is incapacitated. The word *sceva* is not of Greek origin. Some think it is Latin, but Sceva, the prince of the priests, was definitely a Hebrew.

19:19 *In the same manner many who had practiced vain arts brought their books together and burned them before everyone, and they counted the price of them and found it fifty thousand pieces of silver.*

This was a substantial amount of money. How much do people spend on materials related to *vain arts* today? What type of *vain arts*[82] are practiced? How much of what is taught in our schools and universities would be classified as *vain arts* if placed under the spotlight of the Holy Spirit?

19:20 *So the word of God grew mightily and prevailed.*

19:21 *After these things were ended, Paul purposed by the Spirit to go to Jerusalem, after he had passed through Macedonia and Achaia, saying, After I have been there, it behooves me to see Rome also.*

This is the same desire expressed in Romans 1:11-13 and 15:22-25.

19:22 *So he sent into Macedonia two of those that ministered unto him, Timothy and Erastus,*[83] *but he himself stayed in Asia for a season.*

19:23 *And the same time there arose no small stir about the way.*

Here we have a second reference to "the way."

19:24 *For a certain man named Demetrius,*[84] *a silversmith who made silver shrines for Diana,*[85] *brought no small gain unto the craftsmen,*

---

82 "Vain arts" in this context has to do with the manipulation of people, things, or circumstances in a way that is useless or even counterproductive. These vain arts could be linked to the occult.

83 "Erastus" means "beloved."

84 "Demetrius" means "belonging to Demeter" (or Ceres), the goddess of grain and agriculture.

85 "Diana" is the Roman name for Artemis, the Greek goddess of the hunt, childbirth, and virginity. Some, including the Arcadians, believed that Diana was the daughter of Demeter and twin sister to Apollo.

19:25 *whom he called together with the workmen of like occupation and said, Sirs, ye know that by this gain we have our wealth.*

19:26 *Moreover ye see and hear, that not alone at Ephesus, but almost throughout all Asia, this Paul has persuaded and turned away many people, saying that they are not gods which are made with hands*

19:27 *so that not only this our craft is in danger to be set at nought, but also that the temple of the great goddess Diana should be despised, and her magnificence should be destroyed, whom all Asia and the world worship.*

Here we see the magnitude of the success of the gospel (now referred to as "the way"). That the craft of those who made the silver shrines for Diana was now *in danger to be set at nought,* that her temple *should be despised,* and that there was concern that *her magnificence should be destroyed* even though she had been one of the most worshipped deities *in all Asia and the world,* all meant that Paul had been extremely successful in his work and ministry for the Lord.

19:28 *And when they heard these sayings, they were full of wrath and cried out, saying, Great is Diana of the Ephesians.*

19:29 *And the whole city was filled with confusion, and having caught Gaius[86] and Aristarchus,[87] men of Macedonia, Paul's companions in travel, they rushed with one accord into the theatre.*

19:30 *And when Paul would have entered in unto the people, the disciples suffered him not.*

---

86 "Gaius," if of Latin origin, probably means "to rejoice." This is likely the same Gaius who hosted Paul in Corinth while he wrote the book of Romans (Romans 16:23).

87 "Aristarchus" means "best ruler."

> 19:31 *And certain of the chief persons of Asia, who were his friends, sent unto him, asking him that he not present himself in the theatre.*

Many important people had become believers and were Paul's friends. Erastus (verse 22), for example, was the chamberlain of the city of Corinth (Romans 16:23). The obvious reason for Paul's noble friends asking him not to present himself in the theater was that they were afraid Demetrius and his cohorts would use the mob to lynch him. Up until now, the main opposition to Paul's ministry had come from the Jews. Now, Demetrius and all the silversmiths were wild with fury about the negative economic effects of Paul's ministry on their shrine-making and idol-making throughout Asia Minor, and this was a harbinger of more serious pagan and government opposition to come. Christianity was beginning to threaten the pagan and Roman way of life.

> 19:32 *Some therefore cried one thing, and some another, for the assembly was confused; and most of them did not know why they were come together.*

> 19:33 *And they drew Alexander out of the multitude, the Jews putting him forward. And Alexander beckoned with the hand and would have made his defense unto the people.*

> 19:34 *But when they knew that he was a Jew, all with one voice about the space of two hours cried out, Great is Diana of the Ephesians.*

There was quite a bit of unrest growing in the Roman Empire, not just about the Christians, but also about the Jews. Here it appears that the Jews (even those who were against Paul) were concerned about what could happen to them if the mob, mindless and out of control, were to target them. Alexander ("he who defends man") was obviously someone of importance in the area, *but when they knew he was a Jew,* the mob went wild for another two hours. It would not be very many years before Roman armies would destroy Jerusalem and the temple and completely trash Judaea.

19:35 *Then the town scribe, appeasing the people, said, Ye men of Ephesus, what man is there that does not know how the city of the Ephesians is honored of the great goddess Diana and of the image which fell down from Jupiter?*

19:36 *Seeing then that these things cannot be gainsaid, ye ought to be quiet and to do nothing rashly.*

19:37 *For ye have brought here these men, who are neither guilty of sacrilege, nor blasphemers of your goddess.*

19:38 *Therefore if Demetrius and the craftsmen who are with him have a matter against any man, the law is open, and there are proconsuls; let them accuse one another.*

19:39 *But if ye enquire any thing concerning other matters, it shall be determined in a lawful assembly.*

19:40 *For we are in danger of being accused of sedition for this day's uproar, there being no cause by which we may give an account of this concourse.*

19:41 *And when he had thus spoken, he dismissed the assembly.*

The Roman Empire and its corresponding *Pax Romana* (Roman Peace) were held together by the frequent application of brute force anywhere there was even the slightest hint of activity that could be regarded as sedition, and this is what finally caught up with the disobedient, rebellious Jews at Jerusalem.

Let Us Pray

Lord, We ask that the essence of the book of Acts be clarified unto us that we may live to do your will your way. May we be faithful even in the small things. May we pay attention to every detail that your Holy Spirit would impress upon us. May we be in tune with the feelings and desires of your heart. Amen.

Chapter 11

Bound by the Spirit to Jerusalem

Thousands of believers were now being moved by the Holy Spirit, but Paul was unable to remain in Ephesus after being targeted by the silversmiths, whose livelihood was endangered by the success of the gospel (now being called "the way of God" or simply "the way").

Acts 20

20:1 And after the uproar was ceased, Paul called the disciples and embraced them and departed to go into Macedonia.

20:2 And when he had gone over those parts and had exhorted them with much word, he came into Greece

20:3 and there abode three months. And when the Jews laid in wait for him, as he was about to sail into Syria, he took counsel to return through Macedonia.

It was getting harder and harder for Paul to travel anywhere safely or even to stay anywhere safely. The Jews were now seriously trying to ambush him, and it's likely that general orders from Jerusalem had gone out against him virtually everywhere.

20:4 And there accompanied him into Asia Sopater of Berea; and of the Thessalonians, Aristarchus and Secundus; and Gaius of Derbe and Timothy; and of Asia, Tychicus and Trophimus.

20:5 These going before tarried for us at Troas.

20:6 And we sailed away from Philippi after the days of unleavened bread[88] and came unto them to Troas[89] in five days, where we abode seven days.

Having given us the names of Paul's seven special traveling companions, the writer of the book of Acts again appears in person with the addition of personal pronouns such as *These* (the seven companions) *going before us*; and *we sailed away from Philippi.* "Sopater" means "safe father," "Aristarchus" means "best ruler," "Secundus" means "second" (in the sense of a confirmation), "Gaius" possibly means "rejoice," "Timothy" means "honoring God," and "Trophimus" means "nutritious." If the character of these men had any correlation with their names, it seems that Paul was in very good company.

20:7 And the first of the sabbaths,[90] when the disciples

---

88 In order for the dates to correlate (on the Jewish lunar-based calendar) with the concept that Jesus died on Friday, was in the tomb all day Saturday, and rose early Sunday morning, the days would have to align in a way that would have happened only once every seven years. So it's possible, even probable, that church tradition is mistaken. What we know for certain, according to Scripture, is that Jesus died on the afternoon of the thirteenth day of the first month and was resurrected in the early morning of the fifteenth day. The thirteenth was the day of preparation, the fourteenth was the Great Sabbath of the Passover, the fifteenth was the first of the Sabbaths of the Feast of Unleavened Bread (Leviticus 23:5-8), and the day after the seventh Sabbath (counting normal weekly Sabbaths from the fifteenth day of the first month) was the Feast of Pentecost (Leviticus 23:15-16).

89 "Troas" means "a Trojan" or "someone from Troy" (an ancient city that was linked to a Greek god of erotica).

90 This is a direct literal translation of the Greek Received Text (such as was published by Erasmus), and it was translated like this in many early Reformation Bibles. Even the Latin Vulgate has a very similar rendition of the text. This was one of many reasons the high church prelates refused to authorize translations of the Scriptures into the language of the common people: because they feared that it would confuse them and undermine the church calendar for events such as Easter and Sunday worship. Eventually, however, someone came up with the

came together to break bread, Paul preached unto
them, ready to depart the next day, and continued his
word until midnight.

20:8 *And there were many lamps in the upper chamber,*
where they were gathered together.

20:9 *And a certain young man named Eutychus sat in a*
window, being fallen into a deep sleep; and as Paul was
long preaching, he sunk down with sleep and fell down
from the third loft and was taken up dead.

20:10 *And Paul went down and fell on him and,*
embracing him, said, Trouble not yourselves, for his
soul is still in him.

"Eutychus" means "fortunate."

This is very similar to what happened in the ministry of the prophet Elijah and again in the ministry of Elisha (1 Kings 17:17-22; 2 Kings 4:17-35). There appears to be a reverse progression in the number of times a particular action was performed in order for the desired result to be achieved: 1) The boy that Elijah raised from the dead was the son of a Gentile widow, and *Elijah stretched himself upon the child* **three times** *and cried unto the LORD*. 2) In Elisha's case, the woman was a well-connected Israelite with a husband, and Elisha first sent his servant to lay his staff (symbolic of the authority of God) across the face of the child, and then when he arrived, he stretched himself upon the child **two times**, *and the child sneezed seven times*. 3)

---

idea of translating "first of the sabbaths" as "the first day of the week," and this gained widespread approval as soon as the fire of reformation died down and Bible translations had to be approved by the church and/or the state. In making the decision to return to a literal rendition of the text, I'm not pretending to advocate worship on a given day of the week as a magic formula for success. Rather, I'm aiming to return to the unadulterated truth and to let the Holy Spirit lead us in every detail of our personal walk and corporate worship. Truly, we are to worship in spirit and in truth every day and to rest from our own work in order that he may work in and through us.

In Paul's case, the young man, *being fallen into a deep sleep . . . fell down from the third loft and was taken up dead*, and Paul went down and fell on him (**once**) and pronounced him alive.

There are three levels of truth in Scripture that coincide with the three obligatory feasts of Israel and the three courts of the temple (the outer court, Holy Place, and Holy of Holies). The Gentile widow who sustained Elijah was representative of the outer court; the influential married woman who supported Elisha represented the Holy Place (also known as the priesthood of all believers); and Paul was expounding on the deeper truth of our access (through Jesus Christ) into the direct presence of God behind the veil in the realm of the Holy of Holies when the young man sank down with sleep and fell to his death from *the third loft*.

There are, of course, dangers in all three realms, and the answer to all such dangers is obviously resurrection life. It is more difficult to resurrect a "dead" person in the outer court (Elijah had to stretch himself upon the child three times and warm up his flesh). Remember that all of us are dead in trespasses and sin until we come into contact with the life of the Lord. Those who operate in the realm of the Holy Place and spiritually die, or have died, must first come under the direct authority of God (under his staff) again; and when the life of God goes back into them, the seven sneezes symbolize being purged of any or all false spirits that may have been causing the problem.

Regarding the third realm of truth and the direct presence of God behind the veil in the realm of the Holy of Holies, we are all admonished to watch and be vigilant, for we do not know when the Lord will return or when we will be required to stand before him. In the first two realms, it took a while for the child to become sick and die. In the realm of the Holy of Holies, however, all it took was a slight distraction for the young man to sink down with sleep and fall to his death. Nevertheless, the embrace of the apostle Paul immediately brought young Eutychus back to life. We are required to watch and look out for one another in all three realms, but in the realm of the Holy of Holies, even though in one sense the danger is more acute, in another sense it is much easier for us to look out for and cover one another.

Paul was on his way to Jerusalem to celebrate the feast of Pentecost, comfort the brethren, and admonish those who were dead in trespasses and sin in both the first and second courts. This was going to be a very difficult assignment, and God was making it very clear to him that his decision to go forward was voluntary. For many disobedient Jews, this would likely be their last opportunity to be saved.

20:11 *When he therefore was come up again and had broken bread and eaten and talked a long while, even until day break, thus he departed.*

20:12 *And they took the young man home alive and were greatly comforted.*

Paul wasn't sure if he would see any of these people again, so he shared with them everything that was on his heart, and everyone was greatly encouraged by all that happened that night.

20:13 *And we went into the ship and sailed unto Assos, intending to take in Paul there, for so he had determined that he should go by land.*

20:14 *And when he met with us at Assos, we took him in and came to Mitylene.*

20:15 *And we sailed from there and came the next day over against Chios, and the next day we arrived in port*

at Samos; and having rested in Trogyllium, the next
day we came to Miletus.

The route that Paul traveled with his seven chosen companions (the number seven is symbolic of all those whom God
has chosen) on his final trip to Jerusalem appears to typify the
spiritual journey that his ministry historically accomplished.
Sailing from Philippi (meaning "lover of horses," with horses
being a symbol of the strength and ability of the natural man
operating in the flesh) on or near the Passover (the feast that
was instituted when Moses led the children of Israel out of
Egypt, and was fulfilled with the death and resurrection of Jesus
Christ), they passed through many symbolic places on their
way to celebrate the feast of Pentecost in Jerusalem. The Jews
had been celebrating the Passover for fifteen hundred years in
their own strength (in the flesh) before the real Lamb of God,
Jesus Christ, arrived on the scene. The Passover had become
symbolic of the Jews' struggle to fulfill the law of Moses in
the flesh, whereas Pentecost was a symbol of the grace of God
poured out upon all flesh by the Holy Spirit.

The goal of Paul's ministry was to convince as many people
as possible (first the Jews and then the Greeks) not only that
Jesus was the Christ, but also that the gospel was now made
available to all the Gentiles. Immediately after celebrating the
Passover, therefore, they left Philippi by boat for Troas, meaning "from Troy" (Troy is also a Greek god of erotica, symbolizing the Hellenistic Greek Gentiles to whom Paul had been
preaching the gospel). From there they sailed to Assos, meaning
"approximate" (this is symbolic of the number of Gentiles who
will believe), and from there to Mitylene, meaning "shellfish"
(another symbol of the unclean Gentiles living in the sea of
lost humanity).

From Mitylene, they sailed to Chios, meaning "of snow," and

then on to Samos, meaning "height" (symbolizing that there are many cold storms, hardships, and trials along the way, which lies uphill). Soon, however, they arrived at Trogyllium, which means "a cache" or "a hidden store of provision" (for if we seek first the kingdom of God and his righteousness, whatever else we need will be added unto us).

Then they sailed on to Miletus, meaning "pure white wool" (this is a symbol of real, tangible righteousness, which is the character of God).

> 20:16 *For Paul had determined to sail by Ephesus, not to detain himself in Asia, for he hasted to keep the day of Pentecost, if it were possible for him, in Jerusalem.*

> 20:17 *And from Miletus he sent to Ephesus and called the elders*[91] *of the congregation.*

"Ephesus" means "permitted" (and was a center for idolatrous licentiousness). In this symbolic journey, *Paul had determined to sail by Ephesus, not to detain himself in Asia.* When God leads his people out of legalism, he doesn't want them to go to the opposite extreme, which is licentiousness. His people are not to detain themselves in "Asia" (eastern mysticism).

> 20:18 *And when they were come to him, he said unto them, Ye know, from the first day that I came into Asia, after what manner I have been with you at all seasons,*

By this point in his life, Paul had also become somewhat symbolic of the ministry of the Holy Spirit (who works through individuals, not committees or institutions). Thus he was able to say by the Spirit, *I have been with you at all seasons.* This is also a prophetic fulfillment of Jesus's promise never to leave us or forsake us, no matter what "season" we may be going through. Not only will the Holy Spirit be available unto eternity, but

---

91   See Appendix A, number 168 (use of the word *elders* in Scripture).

he will also be palpably with us *at all seasons*, through clean human ministry like that of the apostle Paul.

> 20:19 *serving the Lord with all humility and with many tears and temptations, which have befallen me by the ambushes of the Jews,*

The ambushes by the Jews had been escalating, and it had become increasingly difficult for Paul to find safe haven, yet he never once pulled back from his high calling. Even now, he was headed for the most dangerous place (for him) that anyone could think of.

> 20:20 *and how I kept back nothing that was profitable unto you, but have showed you and have taught you publicly and from house to house,*

> 20:21 *testifying both to the Jews and also to the Gentiles, repentance toward God and faith toward our Lord Jesus Christ.*

There are at least three levels of truth in Scripture: 1) The literal historic facts and truth. 2) The spiritual application of the way of God, which the Holy Spirit transmits to us. 3) The glorious prophecies and promises of God that are yet to be fulfilled.

Paul wrote and ministered on all three levels. He kept back nothing that would be profitable to us. Paul not only taught, but he also *showed* people the truth *publicly and from house to house.*

> 20:22 *And now, behold, I go bound of the Spirit unto Jerusalem, not knowing the things that shall befall me there,*

> 20:23 *except that the Holy Spirit witnesses in every city, saying that prisons and tribulations await me.*

Some think that Paul's worst mistake was continuing his journey to Jerusalem after the Holy Spirit, speaking through prophets in every city along his route, warned him multiple times of prisons and tribulations. I disagree. Yes, it was going to be a difficult assignment, but the Lord was making it clear to Paul that undertaking this mission into the midst of a situation that (from a human perspective) contained such danger, uncertainty, and upheaval was to be a deliberate choice on his part.

> 20:24 *But none of these things move me, neither do I count my life dear unto myself, only that I might finish my course with joy and the ministry, which I have received of the Lord Jesus, to testify the gospel of the grace of God.*

Paul was heading straight into the fire, following the example of Jesus, who also made a fateful final trip to Jerusalem. The way of God is also the way of the cross. Jesus chose to go the way of the cross and fulfill the perfect will of his Father so that we might be redeemed, and Paul chose to follow Jesus along the same path.

From God's point of view, there would be amazing benefits to this decision by Paul. For instance, Paul's arrest would place him into relative safety beyond the hands of the furious Jews, which in turn would give him a platform to preach the gospel without being killed by a mob or at the hands of the Jewish leaders. He would also have time to write, and his prison epistles would form a crucial part of the New Testament. The frosting on the cake would be his unique opportunity to travel to Rome under the protection of the Roman army and witness to various people, including Nero (who prided himself on personally presiding over such trials). There would be fruit for the Lord even from the house of Caesar (Philippians 4:22).

> 20:25 *And now, behold, I know that ye all, among whom I have gone preaching the kingdom of God, shall see my face no more.*

20:26 *Therefore I take you to record this day that I am pure from the blood of everyone.*

20:27 *For I have not refrained from declaring unto you the full counsel of God.*

How many ministers of the gospel today are *pure from the blood of everyone*?

How many can truly state that they have *not refrained from declaring the full counsel of God*?

20:28 *Take heed therefore unto yourselves and to all the flock, in which the Holy Spirit has placed you as bishops to feed the congregation of God, which he has purchased with his own blood.*

Paul now refers to the elders of Ephesus (whom he has summoned) as bishops and points out that their job description is *to feed the congregation of God*; in other words, not to lord it over them.

20:29 *For I know this, that after my departing, grievous wolves shall enter in among you, not sparing the flock.*

20:30 *Also from among your own selves, men shall arise, speaking perverse things to draw away disciples after themselves.*

20:31 *Therefore watch and remember that by the space of three years I ceased not to warn every one night and day with tears.*

The church has had to repeatedly deal with grievous wolves and perverse men over the course of its history, and such incidents continue to accelerate. The bane of the church today is splits that are caused by men *speaking perverse things to draw disciples after themselves*. Paul is seeking to protect disciples, who are true followers of Christ. His warning is not directed at unbelievers.

> 20:32 *And now, brethren, I commend you to God and to the word of his grace, which is powerful to build you up and to give you an inheritance among all those who are sanctified.*

Paul was neither naming someone to replace him nor arming a spiritual hierarchy. Having reminded the elders that they were to be servants and feed the sheep, Paul was not commending them to a head officer within the church, but he was commending them *directly to God and to the word of his grace.*

> 20:33 *I have coveted no one's silver or gold or apparel.*

> 20:34 *Moreover, ye yourselves know that these hands have ministered unto my necessities and to those that were with me.*

> 20:35 *I have showed you in all things how that so labouring, ye ought to support the weak and to remember the words of the Lord Jesus, how he said, It is more blessed to give than to receive.*

In sustaining his own ministry economically, Paul had set everyone an example of how to support the weak and had demonstrated that *it is more blessed to give than to receive.* Today this line is all too often repeated by people who fail to practice what they preach.

> 20:36 *And when he had thus spoken, he knelt down and prayed with them all.*

> 20:37 *Then they all wept sore and fell on Paul's neck and kissed him,*

> 20:38 *sorrowing most of all for the word which he*

*spoke, that they should see his face no more. And they
accompanied him unto the ship.*

As we have seen, Paul's return from his third missionary journey also has a profound and symbolic spiritual significance.
For most of the way they traveled by ship, relying on the wind
to make any progress. The wind, of course, symbolizes the
Holy Spirit. A few times along the way, Paul decided to walk
somewhere, and this is an indication that certain things need
to be "walked out" and actually demonstrated to others. Paul
was a good example in every way.

Acts 21

21:1 *And it came to pass that after we had left them
and had launched, we came with a straight course unto
Coos, and the day following unto Rhodes, and from
there unto Patara;*

"Coos" means "a thorn." "Rhodes" means "a rose" (which is, of
course, a beautiful flower with thorns). "Patara" means "over-
flowing," "spewing forth," or even "cursing."

The meanings of the place names Coos and Rhodes are particularly striking when we recall Paul's famous words: *There is
given to me a thorn in the flesh, a messenger of Satan to buffet
me, lest I should be exalted above measure* (2 Corinthians 12:7).
For centuries, there has been speculation as to what this thorn
might have been. The best explanation I've heard is that Paul's
thorn was the fact that he had originally persecuted, jailed, and
even helped execute Christians. In light of some of his writings,
it seems not only that he was never able to forget this, but also
that Satan continued to use these dreadful memories to buffet
him, presumably hoping that Paul would feel such guilt about
his past that he would stumble in his work (1 Corinthians 15:9).

As Paul was sailing down on the final leg of his last journey to Jerusalem and entered Coos ("a thorn"), it's probable that all of these painful memories came flooding back. Then the boat sailed to Rhodes ("a rose"), and Paul could see that by his grace, God had placed a beautiful flower in the midst of the thorns, inasmuch as he allowed Paul to see that it was his thorn in the flesh that had helped to motivate him and move him to be faithful in ministry against all odds, wherever the Holy Spirit might send him. Satan likely continued his attacks as they sailed into Patara ("spewing forth curses"). As he continued into what he knew by the Spirit would be imprisonment and tribulation, Paul was facing his own Gethsemane.

21:2 *and finding a ship sailing over unto Phenicia, we went aboard and set forth.*

In Patara, they changed ships (both literally and metaphorically) and sailed over to Phenicia, meaning "land of palm trees." The palm tree is a symbol of righteousness.

21:3 *Now when we had sighted Cyprus, we left it on the left hand and sailed into Syria and landed at Tyre, for there the ship was to unload her cargo.*

Sailing forth from that land of palm trees, they soon sighted Cyprus ("love") and passed it on their left (or, since love emanates from God, they were on the right hand of his love, power, and authority). In this way they sailed on to Syria (or Aram), meaning "heights" or "citadel" (a symbol of strength).

The word to Paul about why God hadn't answered his prayer to take away his *thorn in the flesh* was: *My grace is sufficient for thee; for my strength is made perfect in weakness* (2 Corinthians 12:9). To this Paul responded: *Therefore I am content in weaknesses, in reproaches, in necessities, in persecutions, in distress for Christ's sake, for when I am weak, then am I strong* (2

Corinthians 12:10).[92] So, in the strength of the Lord, Paul and his companions sailed into Tyre, meaning "a rock."

21:4 And finding the disciples, we tarried there seven days, who said to Paul through the Spirit that he should not go up to Jerusalem.

21:5 And when we had accomplished those days, we departed; and they all brought us on our way, with wives and children, until we were out of the city; and we knelt down on the shore and prayed.

21:6 And when we had taken our leave one of another, we embarked on the ship, and they returned home again.

21:7 And when we had finished our course from Tyre, we came to Ptolemais and saluted the brethren and abode with them one day.

"Ptolemais" means "warrior" or "to make war," and Paul was now heading directly into the battle. He knew how to fight, not just at the human level, but God's way – the spiritual way. Not too long before, he had written, *Do not be overcome by evil, but overcome evil with good* (Romans 12:21).

21:8 And the next day Paul and those of us that were with him departed and came unto Caesarea; and we entered into the house of Philip the evangelist, who was one of the seven, and abode with him.

Caesarea is named after Caesar and means "to be cut out." "Philip," meaning "lover of horses," is essentially the same Greek word as Philippi (which is the plural of Philip). Now the journey of Paul and his companions had come full circle. Their trip began at Passover when they left Philippi, where

---

92   It's even conceivable that Paul could have been finishing 2 Corinthians at that time, planning to send it back to Corinth with Gaius.

there were many "lovers of horses." (In Scripture, the horse is widely regarded as a symbol of the strength and capability of the natural man in the flesh.) Along with heroic human efforts in culture, philosophy, and world dominance, the Jews were making an all-out attempt to keep the law of Moses in their own strength. While respecting their endeavors, Paul and his companions desired to see the Jews transformed by the gospel of Jesus Christ. Philip the evangelist was one of the seven original deacons, or servants, appointed to wait on the tables (Acts 6:5). He was a "lover of horses" not because he strove in the flesh to fulfill some lofty ideal, but rather, Philip loved "horses" (or humanity) because he was an evangelist.

Note that the number seven, which denotes fullness or completion, shows up repeatedly as this journey nears its end. Having just spent seven days in Tyre, Paul and his seven companions were staying in the house of Philip, who was one of the seven. They had been on a physical journey that symbolized the spiritual journey from Passover to Pentecost. The church has been on a similar journey, spanning from the sacrifice of Jesus, the Lamb of God – and including the pouring out of the earnest of the Spirit in Acts 2 – to the fullness of Pentecost (fullness of the Spirit) as promised for the end of the age.

In order to receive the earnest, or down payment, of the Spirit, it's enough to place our faith and trust in Jesus and to agree sincerely with God's plan and government. In order to receive the fullness of the Spirit (the fullness of our inheritance in Christ), the "old man" must die. We do not, however, have to rely solely on our own strength to kill our carnal selves, for it is by the Spirit that we are to put to death the deeds of the flesh (Romans 8:13).

> 21:9 *And he had four daughters, virgins, who prophesied.*

Four is a number linked to God's heavenly *agape* love that redeems by its very nature.[93] Philip (whose name is close to the Greek word for brotherly love, *phileo*) is the evangelist who has a deep brotherly love for "horses" and longs to put people into contact with the love of God, a love that will redeem them and produce clean heavenly people of God (virgins) who will prophesy (speak God's words instead of their own).

21:10 *And as we tarried there many days, there came down from Judaea a certain prophet, named Agabus.*

Agabus was a well-known prophet who had correctly prophesied a great worldwide famine (Acts 11:28). His name means "bent" or "doubled" (for example, a locust ready to spring and jump over any obstacle).

21:11 *And when he was come unto us, he took Paul's girdle and bound his own hands and feet and said, Thus saith the Holy Spirit, So shall the Jews at Jerusalem bind the man that owns this girdle and shall deliver him into the hands of the Gentiles.*

In the realm of the Spirit, there are many important gifts, ministries, and operations; among them are *word of knowledge* and *word of wisdom* (1 Corinthians 12:8). Agabus gave a word of knowledge regarding what was about to happen, but Paul had a revelatory word of wisdom that encouraged him to carry on in the face of certain risk, hardship, and danger.

21:12 *And when we heard these things, both we and those of that place besought him not to go up to Jerusalem.*

"We" refers to Paul's seven companions and also the writer of the book of Acts (Luke).

21:13 *Then Paul answered, What mean ye to weep*

93 In Genesis 1:14-19, the number four (i.e., "the fourth day") is linked with the heavenly realm.

and to break my heart? For I am ready not only to be bound, but also to die in Jerusalem for the name of the Lord Jesus.

21:14 And when he would not be persuaded, we ceased, saying, Let the will of the Lord be done.

21:15 And after those days we packed our baggage and went up to Jerusalem.

21:16 There went with us also certain of the disciples of Caesarea and brought with them one Mnason of Cyprus, an old disciple, with whom we should lodge.

"Mnason" means "remembering," and "Cyprus," of course, means "love." The meaning of the names associated with this *old disciple* should help us all to *remember* that Jesus said his new commandment is that we are to *love* one another.

21:17 And when we arrived at Jerusalem, the brethren received us gladly.

21:18 And the day following, Paul went in with us to see James,[94] and all the elders[95] were gathered.

21:19 And when he had saluted them, he declared particularly what things God had wrought among the Gentiles by his ministry.

Paul and his companions were also carrying a substantial amount of money, an offering from some of the Gentiles abroad to help the congregation at Jerusalem.

21:20 And when they heard it, they glorified the Lord and said unto him, Thou seest, brother, how many thousands of Jews there are who have believed, and they are all zealous of the law;

---

94 "James" in Greek is the same as "Jacob" in Hebrew.
95 See Appendix A, number 169 (use of the word *elders* in Scripture).

21:21 *and they are informed of thee that thou teachest
all the Jews who are among the Gentiles to forsake
Moses, saying that they ought not to circumcise their
children, neither to walk after the customs.*

The Jewish believers were still deeply attached to all the nuances
of the law of Moses (including blood sacrifices) and the customs
of their forefathers, even after the once-and-for-all sacrifice of
Jesus Christ and the pouring out of the Holy Spirit. Although
they had accepted that the Gentile believers be exempted from
Mosaic law, some of them – particularly those of Pharisee
background – seem to have conceded this reluctantly, and
unfounded rumors that Paul was applying the new liberty to
the Jews as well as the Gentiles had continued to trickle in.
James and the elders were glad to receive Paul and the good
report that he brought. They also knew that the whole multitude of the congregation would want to hear from him, so they
proposed a Solomonic solution in an attempt to avoid further
controversy and division.

21:22 *What is it therefore? The multitude must needs
come together, for they will hear that thou art come.*

21:23 *Do therefore this that we say to thee: We have
four men among us who have a vow on them;*

21:24 *them take, and purify thyself with them, and
pay their expenses, that they may shave their heads,
and all may know that those things, of which they were
informed concerning thee, are nothing, but that thou
thyself dost also walk orderly and keep the law.*

Paul, who was unable to pass by a Jewish synagogue anywhere
without going in there on the Sabbath day to reason with the
Jews and convince them that Jesus Christ was their Messiah,
undoubtedly saw this suggestion as a golden opportunity to

spend a week in the temple (v. 27). (Note that Paul had already made his vow and shaved his head back in Cenchrea.[96]) His presence there would allow the Jews at the temple (those from Jerusalem, as well as those from around the world who had come to celebrate the feast of Pentecost) to observe his behavior and assess his character for themselves. More importantly, it would also give them at least one more chance to hear the gospel and turn to Jesus Christ before the imminent destruction of virtually everything and everyone remaining in Jerusalem.

> 21:25 *As touching the Gentiles who believe, we have written and concluded that they observe no such thing, except only that they keep themselves from things offered to idols and from blood and from that which has been strangled and from fornication.*

James and the elders also made it clear that their previous agreement regarding the Gentile believers, bonded by the Holy Spirit, was firm.

> 21:26 *Then Paul took the men and the next day, purifying himself with them, entered into the temple to signify the accomplishment of the days of purification until an offering should be offered for each one of them.*

> 21:27 *And when the seven days were almost ended,*

---

96 The exact type of vow that Paul made has been a matter of controversy over the centuries. The fact that Paul shaved his head in Cenchrea (apparently marking the beginning of a time period) and then spent seven days being purified in the temple does not seem to fit with a Nazarite vow, which would have required that his head be shaved at the temple and the hair burned under the caldron in which the peace offerings were boiled according to the Law of the Nazarite (Numbers 6:13-21). Under normal conditions, this law does not require the person to remain seven days inside the temple, as was the case with Paul and his companions (Acts 21:27). It is the purification of priests that requires the obligatory seven days inside the temple (Exodus 29:30-46; Leviticus 8:33-36). Paul's situation here appears to be an anomaly (although Jewish tradition may be the explanation). Remember, however, that David set a precedent of being prophet, priest, and king by putting the ark of the covenant into a tent in his backyard and communing with God on a regular basis. This is the tabernacle of David that James said was being restored. Paul may have also been setting a precedent.

the Jews, who were of Asia, when they saw him in the temple, stirred up all the people and laid hands on him,

21:28 *crying out, Men of Israel, help; this is the man that teaches everyone everywhere against the people and the law and this place and further brought Greeks also into the temple and has polluted this holy place.*

21:29 *(For before this they had seen Trophimus,[97] an Ephesian, with him in the city, whom they supposed that Paul had brought into the temple.)*

21:30 *So that all the city was moved, and the people ran together; and they took Paul and drew him out of the temple, and immediately the doors were shut.*

Paul almost made it through the seven days of purification without incident.

21:31 *And as they went about to kill him, tidings came unto the tribunal[98] of the company that all Jerusalem was in an uproar*

21:32 *who immediately took soldiers and centurions and ran down unto them; and when they saw the tribunal and the soldiers, they left off beating Paul.*

21:33 *Then the tribunal came near and took him and commanded him to be bound with two chains and demanded to know who he was and what he had done.*

21:34 *And some cried one thing, some another, among the multitude; and when he could not know the*

---

97 Remember that Trophimus from Ephesus was one of Paul's seven travelling companions (Acts 20:4).

98 The use of the word "tribunal" here refers to a single commanding officer who also had judicial power.

*certainty for the tumult, he commanded him to be car-
ried into the fortress.*

21:35 *And when he came upon the stairs, so it was that
he was borne of the soldiers because of the violence of
the people.*

21:36 *For the multitude of the people followed after, crying, Away with him.*

After the uproar in Ephesus, the town scribe was very concerned
lest the city be accused of sedition (Acts 19:40). In fact, when
he raised this possibility, it immediately sobered up the mob
and he was able to dismiss them. None of them wanted to give
the Romans an excuse to come and level their city.

You will recall that before the death sentence on Jesus was
pronounced, the priests and scribes had to go to a great deal of
trouble to turn the people against him and to rile up the mob
so they would demand that Pilate allow his execution. Now,
more than twenty-five years after his death (and resurrection),
it appears that the atmosphere in Jerusalem was much more
volatile. The mob, representing the vast majority of the city,
rose up against Paul in spontaneous combustion. It appears
that uproars like this were becoming increasingly frequent in
Jerusalem and that the Roman garrison had been strengthened
as a result. In fact, it's likely that by this time, the Romans were
seriously considering contingency plans to intervene with
overwhelming force should the Jewish situation continue to
spiral out of control.

21:37 *And as Paul was to be led into the fortress, he said
unto the tribunal, May I speak unto thee? Who said,
Canst thou speak Greek?*

21:38 *Art not thou that Egyptian, who before these days*

*made an uproar and led four thousand men out into
the wilderness that were murderers?*

It appears that just a few days earlier, the tribunal had finished
dealing with a major rebellion, and this gave him reason to be
very uneasy. Even with heightened Roman security, he knew
that he wouldn't be able to contain a full-fledged Jewish revolt.

*21:39 But Paul said, I am certainly a Jew, a citizen of
Tarsus, a city known in Cilicia; and, I beseech thee, suffer me to speak unto the people.*

*21:40 And when he had given him license, Paul stood
on the stairs and beckoned with the hand unto the people. And when there was made a great silence, he spoke
unto them in the Hebrew tongue, saying;*

The Lord doesn't ask us to do things that he wouldn't do himself.
He came to save us of his own free will, and Paul volunteered
for this mission of his own free will. Jesus loves to overcome
evil with good; that is, after all, how he redeemed us. The Jews'
rejection of Christ's message helped open the way to send the
gospel to the Gentiles, and their rejection of the apostle Paul
now opened the way for God to use him to present the gospel
one last time to the entire city of Jerusalem.[99]

---

99 Many modern historians date this event as being AD 58 or 59. With greater
certainty, virtually all historians have placed the Jewish Wars as beginning in
AD 64, with the revolt of the Jews (which had been festering for several years)
coming to a head in AD 66 and with Vespasian having the responsibility that
same year to deal with the situation. The destruction of Jerusalem and the temple
is placed at AD 70 and took place under Titus (son of Vespasian, who was the
Roman emperor from AD 69 to 79).

I'm inclined to think that if Aquila and Priscilla left Italy because Claudius
Caesar (who reigned from AD 41 to 54) expelled the Jews toward the end of his
reign (Acts 18:1), and if (as appears to be the case) by the time Paul wrote the
book of Romans from the house of Gaius in Corinth (Romans 16:23) there were
numerous Jews (and Jewish believers) back in Rome, then the book of Romans
would have been written no earlier than AD 57 and probably later. The date of
Paul's arrest in Jerusalem could therefore have been later than many suppose,
since it was up to three or so years after the writing of Romans. I think that
Paul's arrest could have been as early as AD 60, but more likely took place in
the spring of AD 61 or even 62. In his pre-modernist *Commentary* (published

Let Us Pray

Lord, May we be able to see above and beyond the concerns of this life and of the world around us, and may we understand and view things from your eternal perspective. Amen.

in 1850), Joseph Benson dates Paul's arrest in AD 60 (which is the date given by Ussher).

Chapter 12

The Lord Stands by Paul

Standing on the steps leading into the Roman fortress in Jerusalem, Paul was allowed to make his defense in Hebrew to the violent mob that had just tried to lynch him.

Acts 22

22:1 *Men, brethren, and fathers, hear ye my defense which I make now unto you.*

Paul solidly identified himself with the Jews.

22:2 *(And when they heard that he spoke in the Hebrew tongue to them, they kept the more silence, and he said,)*

22:3 *I am indeed a Jew, born in Tarsus, a city in Cilicia, yet brought up in this city at the feet of Gamaliel and taught according to the truth of the law of the fathers, zealous toward God, as ye all are this day.*

"Gamaliel" means "benefit of God" or "God is recompenser." A Pharisee and a well-known doctor of the law, Gamaliel was on record as advising the Sanhedrin not to harm the apostles

(Acts 5:34-39). By the time of Paul's speech, however, he was almost certainly deceased.

22:4 And I persecuted this way unto the death, binding and delivering into prisons both men and women.

22:5 As also the prince of the priests bears me witness, and all the estate of the elders,[100] from whom also I received letters unto the brethren, and went to Damascus to bring those who were bound there unto Jerusalem to be punished.[101]

"Damascus" means "the weaver of sackcloth is silent" (i.e., repentance is lacking).

22:6 And it came to pass that, as I made my journey and was come near unto Damascus about noon, suddenly there shone from heaven a great light round about me.

Paul, when he was Saul, had been a Pharisee who zealously persecuted Christians. He had almost reached "Damascus" (almost passed beyond the point of possible repentance) when God intervened. Now it was Paul's desperate hope that everyone in the crowd who was still capable of repentance would receive his testimony and believe on the Lord Jesus Christ.

22:7 And I fell unto the ground and heard a voice saying unto me, Saul, Saul, why dost thou persecute me?

22:8 And I answered, Who art thou, Lord? And he said unto me, I Am Jesus of Nazareth, whom thou dost persecute.

Nazareth, meaning "branch" or "shoot," links Jesus to a

---

100 See Appendix A, number 170 (use of the word *elders* in Scripture).

101 If Paul was converted in AD 37 or so, then his persecution of those who followed "this way" would have happened approximately twenty-three to twenty-five years prior to this powerful discourse.

well-known prophecy referring to the Messiah (Isaiah 11:1). The phrase "I Am Jesus" also links Jesus to the sacred name of God (YHWH, or literally, "I Am"). This would have caused consternation in most of the Sadducees and Pharisees, as they would have considered it to be blasphemy. Paul, however, didn't beat around the bush, nor did he mince words.

> 22:9 *And those that were with me saw indeed the light and were afraid, but they did not hear the voice of him that spoke to me.*

> 22:10 *And I said, What shall I do, Lord? And the Lord said unto me, Arise and go into Damascus, and there it shall be told thee of all things which are appointed for thee to do.*

Paul had now made it plain to his Jewish audience, beyond the shadow of a doubt, that Jesus, their Messiah, had appeared to him in the midst of a blinding light. He said nothing ambiguous and left nothing open to interpretation. His listeners were left with only two choices: to accept his witness or to reject it.

> 22:11 *And when I could not see for the clarity of that light, being led by the hand of those that were with me, I came into Damascus.*

> 22:12 *And one Ananias, a devout man according to the law, having a good witness of all the Jews who dwelt there,*

"Ananias" means "the LORD is a cloud" (of protection).

> 22:13 *came unto me and stood and said unto me, Brother Saul, receive thy sight. And the same hour I looked up upon him.*

> 22:14 *And he said, The God of our fathers has chosen*

*thee that thou should know his will and see that Just
One and should hear the voice of his mouth.*

Ananias provided a crucial second witness that Paul really had
seen and heard the Just One (the Messiah).

22:15 *For thou shalt be his witness unto all men of what
thou hast seen and heard.*

22:16 *And now why tarriest thou? Arise and be baptized and wash away thy sins, calling on the name of
the Lord.*

Calling on the name (nature) of the Lord brought Paul to baptism in the Holy Spirit (of which water is a symbol).

22:17 *And it came to pass that, when I was come again
to Jerusalem, even while I prayed in the temple, I was in
a rapture of understanding*

Only the Holy Spirit can bring about such *a rapture of understanding* that a person can have direct two-way communication
with the Lord, without intermediaries.

22:18 *and saw him saying unto me, Make haste and go
quickly out of Jerusalem, for they will not receive thy
testimony concerning me.*

22:19 *And I said, Lord, they know that I imprisoned
and in every synagogue beat those that believed on thee;*

22:20 *and when the blood of thy martyr Stephen was
shed, I also was standing by and consenting unto his
death and kept the raiment of those that slew him.*

22:21 *And he said unto me, Depart, for I will send thee
far from here unto the Gentiles.*

The tension had been building ever since the "I Am Jesus" quote.
Now Paul described a conversation that he had with the Lord

at the temple in which he was told that the Jews would reject his testimony about Jesus. He talked of *the blood of the martyr Stephen* (a name that means "crowned"). He announced that Jesus had ordered him to take his testimony to the Gentiles. His listeners promptly erupted into a sustained and histrionic demonstration of unreasonable rage.

> 22:22 *And they gave him audience unto this word and then lifted up their voices and said, Away with such a fellow from the earth, for it is not fit that he should live.*

> 22:23 *And as they cried out and cast off their clothes and threw dust into the air,*

> 22:24 *the tribunal commanded him to be brought into the fortress and bade that he should be examined by scourging that he might know why they cried out so against him.*

> 22:25 *And as they bound him with thongs, Paul said unto the centurion that stood by, Is it lawful for you to scourge a man that is a Roman and uncondemned?*

> 22:26 *When the centurion heard that, he went and told the tribunal, saying, Take heed what thou doest, for this man is a Roman.*

> 22:27 *Then the tribunal came and said unto him, Tell me, art thou a Roman? He said, Yes.*

> 22:28 *And the tribunal answered, With a great sum I obtained this freedom. And Paul said, But I was free born.*

Paul was born a Jew in the free Roman city of Tarsus, and thus had Roman citizenship by birth. It is also possible that one or both of his parents were Roman citizens. Romans had special privileges and could not be beaten or tortured. They had a right to a legal trial and could even appeal directly to Caesar.

22:29 *Then straightway those who should have tormented him departed from him, and the tribunal was also afraid, after he knew that he was a Roman and because he had bound him.*

22:30 *On the next day, because he wanted to know of certainty the cause for which he was accused of the Jews, he loosed him from his bands and commanded the princes of the priests and all their council to appear and brought Paul down and set him before them.*

Although Paul was freeborn in earthly terms, in spiritual terms he was a servant. He had come to this place, *bound of the Spirit unto Jerusalem* (Acts 20:22), because God wanted to present a final witness to the Jewish people and authorities. Jesus wages war in righteousness. When those whom he sends are received, he is received, and when he is received, the Father who sent him is received. God the Father sends forth his witnesses, *and if anyone desires to hurt them, fire proceeds out of their mouth and devours their enemies; and if anyone desires to hurt them, he must in this manner be killed* (Revelation 11:5). Today we're entering into the close of the world age of the Gentiles, a time when Jesus is about to return and the fullness of the Scriptures will be fulfilled.

Acts 23

23:1 *Then Paul, earnestly beholding the council, said, Men and brethren, I have lived in all good conscience before God until this day.*

23:2 *And the prince of the priests, Ananias,*

*commanded those that stood by him to smite him on
the mouth.*

Paul was only able to utter a single phrase before they laid
into him.

*23:3 Then Paul said unto him, God shall smite thee,
thou whitewashed wall, for dost thou sit to judge me
after the law and command me to be smitten contrary
to the law?*

*23:4 And those that stood by said, Dost thou revile
God's high priest?*

*23:5 Then Paul said, I did not know, brethren, that he
was the prince of the priests, for it is written, Thou shalt
not speak evil of the ruler of thy people.*

As followers of Jesus, we're required to be respectful and behave
decently according to the rules, even when our enemies don't.

*23:6 But when Paul perceived that the one part were
Sadducees and the other Pharisees, he cried out in the
council, Men and brethren, I am a Pharisee, the son of
a Pharisee, and of the hope and resurrection of the dead
I am called in question.*

*23:7 And when he had so said, there arose a dissension
between the Pharisees and the Sadducees, and the multitude was divided.*

23:8 For the Sadducees[102] say that there is no

---

102 Of the more recent intellectual "Sadducees," Dr. James Strong (1822-1894) has
had quite an influence on evangelical theology. His popular concordance, con-
taining a humanly brilliant numbering system to identify each Hebrew or Greek
word, defines angels such as cherubim as "imaginary figures" (Strong's #3742),
and he doesn't appear to believe in a literal devil or a literal hell. Almost a third
of his definitions of proper names in Scripture lead the reader around in circles,
are flipped 180 degrees from their true meaning (which is easy to do in Hebrew,
especially with names that are used only once or twice), or don't agree with Dr.

resurrection, neither angel, nor spirit; but the Pharisees confess both.

23:9 And there arose a great cry; and the scribes that were of the Pharisees' part arose and strove, saying, We find no evil in this man, but if a spirit or an angel has spoken to him, let us not fight against God.

Paul's mission turned out to be very worthwhile. There were those who did their best to defend him against his accusers. We know that some of the Pharisees had already become believers, and on this occasion, others undoubtedly joined them. However, it was now obvious that the Sadducees were his mortal enemies and that the high priest favored the Sadducees.

23:10 And when there arose a great dissension, the tribunal, fearing lest Paul should have been pulled in pieces by them, commanded the soldiers to go down and to take him by force from among them and to bring him into the fortress.

23:11 And the night following the Lord stood by him and said, Be of good cheer, Paul, for as thou hast testified of me in Jerusalem, so must thou also bear witness at Rome.

This wasn't a dream or even a night vision. The Lord came and stood by Paul to encourage him and to confirm in his own words that Paul would bear witness at Rome. Those who think

---

Young's concordance or Webster's dictionary, to cite just two other well-known sources that don't make wild guesses and pass them off as scholarship.

Dr. Strong is also one of a great number of modern theologians who tend to define the Greek terminology of the New Testament in the light of pagan Greek roots, rather than tracing key words through the Hebrew of the Old Testament and letting them be defined by the way they're introduced and used by God throughout Scripture. As this type of "modern" intellectual thinking permeates Bible schools and theological seminaries, it tends to weaken, if not eliminate, the fear of the Lord from among Christian leaders in this Laodicean hour. Left unchecked, this type of human thinking will undermine the veracity of the Scriptures until its proponents no longer even believe in the literal existence of God.

that Paul made a big mistake going to Jerusalem in the face of so many dire warnings fail to take this verse into account. If what we do is pleasing to the Lord, that's all that really matters.

Jesus didn't even mention the fact that Paul had spoken harshly to the high priest by telling him that God would smite him and calling him a whitewashed wall. Paul had already acknowledged that it was wrong of him to *speak evil of the ruler of thy people*, but Jesus is the real ruler of God's people. Many of the Jews may have thought that they were judging Paul according to the law, when in reality, God was using Paul's voluntary obedience to judge them.

> 23:12 *And when it was day, certain of the Jews banded together and they vowed under a curse, saying that they would neither eat nor drink until they had killed Paul.*

> 23:13 *And they were more than forty who had made this conspiracy.*

> 23:14 *And they came to the princes of the priests and the elders[103] and said, We have made a vow of anathema that we will eat nothing until we have slain Paul.*

Under the law, vows were an extremely serious matter. Jesus had said, *Again, ye have heard that it was said to the ancients, Thou shalt not perjure thyself, but shalt perform unto the Lord thine oaths; but I say unto you, Swear not at all* (Matthew 5:33-34). Forty is a number linked to trials and tests. The Jews who desired to kill Paul overreached themselves. Operating under the mistaken assumption that God wanted Paul dead, their vow included a curse that they would eat or drink nothing until they had slain him.

> 23:15 *Now therefore ye with the council signify to the tribunal that he bring him down unto you tomorrow,*

---

103 See Appendix A, number 171 (use of the word *elders* in Scripture).

*as though ye would enquire something more certain
concerning him, and we, before he arrives, are ready to
kill him.*

*23:16 And when Paul's sister's son heard of their
ambush, he went and entered into the fortress and told
Paul.*

God was giving Paul grace with the Romans. The Jews' desire
to kill him was so intense that the safest possible place for Paul
virtually anywhere in the world was under the guard of the
Roman army. God also had his hand on Paul's nephew so that
he was at the right place at the right time to hear the enemy plan.

*23:17 Then Paul called one of the centurions unto him
and said, Bring this young man unto the tribunal, for
he has a certain thing to tell him.*

*23:18 So he took him and brought him to the tribunal
and said, Paul the prisoner called me unto him and
asked me to bring this young man unto thee, who has
something to say unto thee.*

*23:19 Then the tribunal took him by the hand and went
with him aside privately and asked him, What is that
thou hast to tell me?*

The tribunal first took an interest in Paul out of what appears
to have been honest curiosity, as well as dedication to his duty
to keep the city safe. Now, however, it appears that the tribunal
(who was obviously the commander of all the Roman soldiers
in Jerusalem) was genuinely befriending him.

*23:20 And he said, The Jews have agreed to ask thee
that thou would bring down Paul tomorrow into the
council, as though they would enquire something more
certain of him.*

23:21 *But do not believe them, for more than forty of them lie in wait to ambush him, who have vowed under a curse that they will neither eat nor drink until they have killed him, and now they are ready, looking for a promise from thee.*

23:22 *So the tribunal then let the young man depart and charged him, See thou tell no one that thou hast showed these things to me.*

God's grace and favor upon Paul continued to multiply.

23:23 *And he called unto him two centurions, saying, Make ready two hundred soldiers to go to Caesarea and seventy horsemen and two hundred spearmen, at the third hour of the night*

23:24 *and provide them beasts that they may set Paul on and bring him safe unto Felix the governor.*

Paul was sent to Caesarea riding on horseback like royalty, with a powerful escort. Even so, for added security this adventure would begin *at the third hour of the night* (approximately 9:00 p.m.). It would appear that the forty Jews who had vowed to kill Paul were going to have to either die of hunger and thirst or else come under the anathema curse that they themselves had invoked. In fact, everyone who agreed with them would likely come under that curse.

23:25 *And he wrote a letter after this manner:*

23:26 *Claudius Lysias unto the most excellent governor Felix sends greeting.*

23:27 *This man was taken of the Jews and should have been killed by them; then I came with an army and rescued him, having understood that he was a Roman.*

23:28 And when I desired to know the cause of why they accused him, I brought him forth into their council,

23:29 whom I found to be accused of questions of their law, but to have nothing laid to his charge worthy of death or of bonds.

23:30 And when it was told me how the Jews lay in wait to ambush the man, I sent straightway to thee and gave commandment to his accusers also to say before thee what they had against him. Farewell.

"Claudius" means "crippled" and "Lysias" means "he who releases." Although he was "crippled" in the sense that he couldn't totally exonerate Paul, the tribunal was able to "release" him from the hands – and the ambush – of the Jews and deliver him to Governor Felix (whose name means "happy"), along with an honest report.

23:31 Then the soldiers, as it was commanded them, took Paul and brought him by night to Antipatris.

"Antipatris" means "like a father," and certainly the hand of Father God was upon Paul.

23:32 On the next day they left the horsemen to go with him and returned to the fortress,

23:33 who, when they came to Caesarea and delivered the epistle to the governor, presented Paul also before him.

23:34 And when the governor had read the letter, he asked of what province he was. And when he understood that he was of Cilicia,

23:35 I will hear thee, said he, when thine accusers

are also come. And he commanded him to be kept in Herod's judgment hall.

Governor Felix was apparently fond of Cilicia, the province where Paul was born (in Tarsus, the capital city). Herod's "judgment hall" was a praetorium, or palace, on the edge of the sea. Paul was not only being treated like royalty, but he was now in a position to witness to the king and queen and to their court, when they arrived.

Let Us Pray

Lord, May we have discernment from the heart, and may we perceive the desires of your heart so that we can see things from your point of view. Help us to see the open doors that you would place before us. Help us to take all opportunities to fulfill your plan and purpose instead of our own. May we be willing to trust you completely and follow your wishes, one step at a time. Amen.

Chapter 13

A Conscience Void of Offense

It took Paul's accusers a few days to obtain the modern equivalent of a high-powered lawyer and hustle down to Caesarea so that they could accuse Paul before Felix, the governor.

Acts 24

24:1 *And after five days Ananias, the prince of the priests, descended with the elders[104] and with a certain orator named Tertullus, who informed the governor against Paul.*

"Tertullus" means "triple hardened." Even though they claimed to represent God upon the earth, the high priest, the elders, and their "lawyer" were hardened against the truth.

24:2 *And when he was called forth, Tertullus began to accuse him, saying, Seeing that by thee we enjoy great peace and that very worthy deeds are done unto this nation by thy prudence,*

24:3 *we accept it always and in all places, most noble Felix, with all thankfulness.*

---

104 See Appendix A, number 172 (use of the word *elders* in Scripture).

Contrary to the flattering picture painted by Tertullus, the relationship between the Jews and the Romans was undoubtedly becoming increasingly strained. The Romans were getting greedier and greedier and the Jews more and more rebellious.

24:4 *Notwithstanding, that I be not further tedious unto thee, I pray thee that thou would hear us of thy clemency a few words.*

24:5 *For we have found this man a pestilent fellow and a mover of sedition among all the Jews throughout the world and prince[105] of the seditious sect of the Nazarenes,*

24:6 *who also has gone about to profane the temple, whom we took and would have judged according to our law.*

Sedition, or rising up against Rome, was a very serious crime. Tertullus's accusation against Paul and the Christians was groundless at this time, but very soon virtually the entire Jewish nation would rise up against Rome. Sadly, this uprising would not only fail, but it would bring wrath and destruction upon Jerusalem, Judaea, and Jews all over the world.

24:7 *But the tribunal Lysias came upon us, and with great violence took him away out of our hands,*

24:8 *commanding his accusers to come unto thee; by examining of whom thou may take knowledge of all these things, of which we accuse him.*

24:9 *And the Jews also assented, saying that these things were so.*

Making these deceptive declarations before Felix, the Roman

---

105 A colossal blunder on the part of the Jews was to think that Paul was the "prince" or head of the Christians, when the real prince, Jesus Christ, is seated at the right hand of the Father with all power and authority.

governor, would be equivalent to giving false testimony under oath today.

> *24:10 Then Paul, after the governor had beckoned unto him to speak, answered, Forasmuch as I know that thou hast been of many years a judge unto this nation, I do the more cheerfully answer for myself;*

> *24:11 because thou art able to understand that there have been but twelve days since I went up to Jerusalem to worship.*

> *24:12 And they neither found me in the temple disputing with any man, neither raising up the people, neither in the synagogues, nor in the city,*

> *24:13 neither can they prove the things of which they now accuse me.*

Tertullus, Ananias, and the Jewish elders didn't bring any witnesses or hard evidence against Paul. They apparently wanted Felix to hand Paul over to them so that they could take him back to Jerusalem and do to him what they had previously done to Jesus Christ and many of his followers. They were used to relying on false witnesses and an enraged mob (which they might be hard pressed to come up with in the Roman town of Caesarea).

Paul went on:

> *24:14 But this I confess unto thee, that after the way which they call a sect, so worship I the God of my fathers, believing all things which are written in the law and in the prophets,*

> *24:15 and have hope toward God, which they themselves also allow, that there shall be a resurrection of the dead, both of the just and unjust.*

Once again, Paul refers to Christianity as "the way."

24:16 And for this reason do I exercise myself to have always a conscience void of offense toward God and toward men.

To *have always a conscience void of offense toward God and toward men* is the key to living in spiritual victory.

24:17 Now after many years I came to bring alms to my nation and offerings.

Paul had brought a substantial offering from the Gentile believers, as orchestrated by the Holy Spirit. Believers had already begun an orderly exodus out of Jerusalem, and the alms brought by Paul and his companions would enable many Christians to leave the area well before the Roman armies fulfilled Jesus's prophecy by besieging Jerusalem. Paul had undoubtedly left the funds with James and the elders before he entered the temple with the four men who had made vows (Acts 21:23-24).

24:18 Whereupon certain Jews from Asia found me purified in the temple, neither with multitude, nor with tumult,

24:19 who ought to have been here before thee and object if they had anything against me.

24:20 Or else let these same here say if they have found any evil doing in me, while I stood before the council,

24:21 except it be for this one voice, that I cried out standing among them, Touching the resurrection of the dead, I am called in question by you this day.

Since it was the theme of the resurrection of the dead that split the Pharisees and the Sadducees when Paul brought it up at the council, those of his accusers who accompanied Tertullus and Ananias to Caesarea must have been mostly Sadducees.

24:22 And when Felix heard these things, he deferred

them, saying, I shall have more information regarding
that way, when Lysias the tribunal shall come down,
Then I will know the uttermost of your matter.

Now Felix wanted to investigate the Christian movement more deeply, referring to it as "that way," and as the first step in that investigation, he intended to obtain evidence from Lysias, the tribunal, on whom Paul had undoubtedly made quite an impression.

24:23 And he commanded a centurion to keep Paul and
to let him have liberty, and that he should forbid none
of his own to minister or come unto him.

Paul was thus comfortably installed in Herod's judgment hall[106] (or palace) and had his own centurion (an officer over a hundred soldiers), who had orders to let him have liberty and unlimited access to visitors. This situation went on for two years, providing Paul with optimal conditions for ministry in the area, along with maximum comfort and protection. The palace was also a handy location for Paul to be able to collect or borrow Old Testament scrolls that would be of help with his writings.

24:24 And after certain days when Felix came with his
wife Drusilla,[107] who was a Jewess, he sent for Paul and
heard of him the faith which is in Christ.

24:25 And as he reasoned of righteousness, temperance,
and judgment to come, Felix trembled and answered,
Go away for this time; when I have a convenient season,
I will call for thee.

24:26 He hoped also that money should have been given
him from Paul, that he might loose him; therefore he
sent for him many times and communed with him.

---

106 The ruins of Herod's praetorium at Caesarea are massive and even include a freshwater swimming pool next to the ocean.

107 "Drusilla" means "showered with dew." Herod Agrippa II was her brother.

Felix trembled when Paul reasoned with him about righteousness (same word as "justice" in the original), temperance (keeping all appetites under control), and judgment to come. However, he was unwilling to give up using his position and authority for personal gain. There are still many people like Felix, who cover their doubts about their way of life with an outward show of happiness.

24:27 *But after two years Felix received Porcius Festus*[108] *as successor; and Felix, wanting to win the grace of the Jews, left Paul bound.*

Acts 25

25:1 *Now when Festus was come into the province, after three days he ascended from Caesarea to Jerusalem.*

25:2 *Then the prince of the priests and the principals of the Jews informed him against Paul and besought him,*

25:3 *asking for grace against him, that he would send for him to Jerusalem, they placing an ambush in the way to kill him.*

The Jews who had made the vow (with a curse) to kill Paul were obviously still active and still had plenty of friends. Now they are asking for "grace" against him so they can resurrect their plan for an ambush.

25:4 *But Festus answered that Paul should be kept at Caesarea and that he himself would depart shortly there.*

God kept his hand on the situation, and Paul was saved from another ambush.

25:5 *Let them, therefore, said he, who among you are*

---

108 "Porcius Festus" means "swinish festival."

able, go down with me and accuse this man, if there is
anything in him.

25:6 And when he had tarried among them no more
than ten days, he went down unto Caesarea and the
next day, sitting on the judgment seat, commanded
Paul to be brought.

Paul's time in the palace at Caesarea would soon be over, and
time was running out for the Jews.[109]

25:7 And when he was come, the Jews who came down
from Jerusalem stood round about and laid many and
grievous complaints against Paul, which they could not
prove.

The fact that there were no Pharisee believers left to witness
on Paul's behalf, as some had done at the council in Jerusalem
two years previously, may be another indicator of the lateness
of the hour, as the Holy Spirit continued to lead the believers
to safe havens all over the world. As on many other occasions,
Paul made his defense alone.

25:8 While he answered for himself, Neither against
the law of the Jews, neither against the temple, nor yet
against Caesar have I sinned in anything at all.

25:9 But Festus, willing to ingratiate himself with
the Jews, answered Paul and said, Wilt thou go up to
Jerusalem, and there be judged of these things before me?

Festus had obviously been sent to attempt to put a lid on the
explosive situation that was developing in Jerusalem. He was
willing to sacrifice Paul if that would *ingratiate himself with*

---

109 Conybeare and Howson (1905), in *The Life and Epistles of Saint Paul*, place the
change from Felix to Festus at AD 60. Many modern scholars say a year or two
earlier, but the *Commentary* of Joseph Benson (1850) dates this change at AD
62. If certain details mentioned earlier in this treatise are taken into account, it
could have been even later.

the Jews. There was something, however, that neither Festus nor the Jews knew about. Jesus himself had visited Paul in the Roman fortress at Jerusalem and had said, *Be of good cheer, Paul, for as thou hast testified of me in Jerusalem, so must thou also bear witness at Rome* (Acts 23:11). It's likely that the Holy Spirit now prompted Paul to play his trump card.

25:10 *Then said Paul, I stand at Caesar's judgment seat, where I ought to be judged; to the Jews I have done no wrong, as thou very well knowest.*

25:11 *For if I am an offender or have committed anything worthy of death, I do not refuse to die; but if there are none of these things of which these accuse me, no one may deliver me unto them. I appeal unto Caesar.*

25:12 *Then Festus, when he had conferred with the council, answered, Hast thou appealed unto Caesar? unto Caesar shalt thou go.*

Every freeborn Roman citizen had the right to appeal directly to Caesar should the need arise. Festus, who was doing what he could to develop a rapport with the Jews, now decided that if he couldn't put Paul on trial in Jerusalem, then the next best thing was to send him to Rome in chains. There was only one problem with this plan: there were no charges against Paul that would be serious enough, under Roman law, to warrant sending him to Caesar. Festus needed help.

25:13 *And after certain days King Agrippa and Bernice*[110] *came unto Caesarea to salute Festus.*

It's possible, even probable, that King Agrippa and Bernice had heard about Paul from their sister, Drusilla. They may also have

---

110 Bernice, whose name means "victory," was the sister of King Agrippa ("tamer of wild horses") and also the sister of Drusilla, Felix's wife.

visited Felix in the past and had come into contact with Paul there in Herod's praetorium.

25:14 *And when they had been there many days, Festus declared Paul's cause unto the king, saying, There is a certain man left in bonds by Felix,*

25:15 *about whom, when I was at Jerusalem, the princes of the priests and the elders*[111] *of the Jews informed me, desiring to have vengeance against him.*

25:16 *To whom I answered, It is not the manner of the Romans to deliver any man to die, before the one who is accused is face to face with his accusers and is given license to answer for himself concerning the crime laid against him.*

25:17 *Therefore, when they were come here, without any delay on the next day I sat on the judgment seat and commanded the man to be brought forth.*

25:18 *Against whom when the accusers stood up, they brought no accusation of such things as I supposed,*

25:19 *but had certain questions against him of their own superstition, and of one Jesus, who was dead, whom Paul affirmed to be alive.*

25:20 *And because I doubted of such manner of questions, I asked him whether he would go to Jerusalem and there be judged of these matters.*

25:21 *But when Paul had appealed to be reserved unto the hearing of Augustus,*[112] *I commanded him to be kept until I might send him to Caesar.*

---

111 See Appendix A, number 173 (use of the word *elders* in Scripture).

112 Augustus, meaning "great" or "venerable," is the title given to the first Roman

> 25:22 *Then Agrippa said unto Festus, I would also hear the man myself. Tomorrow, said he, thou shalt hear him.*

Agrippa seemed to have a genuine interest in hearing Paul, perhaps even a secret desire or curiosity to hear more about Jesus and "the way." Agrippa and Bernice would also have known the high priest, Ananias, and the Jewish elders in Jerusalem, and may have even been influential in appointing Ananias.

> 25:23 *And the next day when Agrippa was come and Bernice, with great pomp, and was entered into the place of hearing, with the tribunals and principal men of the city, at Festus' commandment, Paul was brought forth.*

Ruling elites seem to love pomp and ceremony. Paul would now be the main attraction of the hearing, and every important person from miles around would have the opportunity to hear his witness for Jesus Christ.

> 25:24 *Then Festus said, King Agrippa, and all men who are here present with us, ye see this man, about whom all the multitude of the Jews have dealt with me, both at Jerusalem and also here, crying that he ought not to live any longer.*

> 25:25 *But when I found that he had committed nothing worthy of death and that he himself has appealed to Augustus, I have determined to send him.*

> 25:26 *Of whom I have no certain thing to write unto my lord. Therefore I have brought him forth before you, and specially before thee, O King Agrippa, that, after examination, I might have something to write.*

---

emperor, Octavian, who began the Julio-Claudian dynasty in 27 BC. Here Festus is referring to Nero, the last Caesar of that line.

25:27 For it seems to me unreasonable to send a prisoner, and not to signify the crimes laid against him.

If all of this was said in the hearing of the crowd, it sounds like quite an exoneration of Paul and a public indictment of *all the multitude of the Jews.* Even though he obviously thought it was politically expedient to send Paul to Rome, the Roman governor frankly admitted that he had no case against him.

Acts 26

26:1 Then Agrippa said unto Paul, Thou art permitted to speak for thyself. Then Paul stretched forth the hand and answered for himself:

Agrippa doesn't seem to have had a bad attitude toward Paul. Maybe he was remembering what happened to one of his relatives thirty years or so before, when a previous King Herod had killed John the Baptist at the insistence of his wife, Herodias (Mark 6:14-29). Then, a couple years later, after despising and mocking Jesus, Herod had made friends with the enemy Roman governor, Pontius Pilate, on the occasion of Jesus being condemned to death (Luke 23:11-12). Several years after that, Herod had ordered the execution of the apostle James (brother of John) because he saw that it pleased the Jews, and he would also have killed Peter if God had not intervened (Acts 12:1-19). Finally, in the midst of splendid pomp and ceremony before the people, *upon a set day Herod, arrayed in royal apparel, sat upon his throne and made an oration unto them. And the people gave a shout, saying, It is the voice of god, and not of man. And immediately the angel of the Lord smote him because he did not give God the glory, and he expired eaten of worms* (Acts 12:21-23).

These past events may have been going through Paul's mind as well, as he made his opening statement.

26:2 I esteem myself blessed, King Agrippa, because I

> *shall answer for myself this day before thee concerning*
> *all the things of which I am accused of the Jews,*

> *26:3 especially because I know thee to be expert in*
> *all customs and questions which are among the Jews;*
> *therefore, I beseech thee to hear me patiently.*

Avoiding any mention of the gory details related to the Herod family, Paul addressed Agrippa as *an expert in all customs and questions which are among the Jews.*

He continued:

> *26:4 My manner of life from my youth, which from the*
> *beginning was among my own nation at Jerusalem, is*
> *known of all the Jews,*

> *26:5 who knew me from the beginning, if they would*
> *testify, that after the most perfect[113] sect of our religion I*
> *lived a Pharisee.*

> *26:6 And now I stand and am judged for the hope of the*
> *promise made of God unto our fathers;*

> *26:7 unto which promise our twelve tribes, constantly*
> *serving God day and night, hope to come. For which*
> *hope's sake, King Agrippa, I am accused of the Jews.*

What is *the hope of the promise* for which Paul says the twelve tribes had been constantly serving God day and night (for over fifteen hundred years) in the hope of attaining? [114]

The *hope of the promise* is fulfilled in Jesus Christ[115] as our only Lord and Savior, and it is inextricably linked to his resurrection from the dead and to the possibility that we may attain

---

113 Remember that the word "perfect" is the same word as "mature" in the original.
114 He goes into more detail in his letters (Ephesians 1:15-18 and Philippians 3:9-14).
115 Remember that "Christ" in Greek means the same thing as "Messiah" in Hebrew (i.e., "anointed one").

unto the first resurrection[116] and reign and rule with Christ if we come under his headship and government (Revelation 20:4).

It is for the sake of this hope, Paul says, that the Jews are accusing him.

> 26:8 *Why should it be thought a thing incredible with you that God should raise the dead?*

Paul places a great deal of emphasis on the resurrection of the dead. It is the *hope of the promise* for those who repent and believe, but the thought of resurrection and final judgment strikes fear and terror into the hearts of the wicked, many of whom react by denying the truth.

> 26:9 *I verily had thought that I ought to do many things contrary to the name of Jesus of Nazareth.*

> 26:10 *Which things I also did in Jerusalem, and I shut up many of the saints in prison, having received authority from the princes of the priests, and when they were put to death, I gave my voice against them.*

> 26:11 *And I punished them often in every synagogue and compelled them to blaspheme; and being exceedingly mad against them, I persecuted them even unto foreign cities.*

In this very critical situation, Paul shares his own testimony of how God brought him to repentance. This gives opportunity for the Holy Spirit to step in and bring conviction to his listeners. For some of them (and even for the entire nation) this could have been their last major opportunity to repent.

> 26:12 *Whereupon as I went to Damascus with authority and commission from the princes of the priests,*

> 26:13 *at midday, O king, I saw in the way a light from*

---

116 In fact, Paul even prophesied that the future restoration of Israel is linked to resurrection *life from the dead* (Romans 11:15).

heaven, above the brightness of the sun, shining round about me and those who journeyed with me.

So abrupt was his turnaround, that in a single sentence Paul went from being a man on a journey to persecute Christians to a man blinded by intense light from heaven.

26:14 *And when we were all fallen to the earth, I heard a voice speaking unto me and saying in the Hebrew tongue, Saul, Saul, why dost thou persecute me? It is hard for thee to kick against the pricks.*

26:15 *And I said, Who art thou, Lord? And he said, I am Jesus whom thou dost persecute.*

26:16 *But rise and stand upon thy feet, for I have appeared unto thee for this purpose, to make thee a minister and a witness both of these things which thou hast seen and of those things in which I will appear unto thee;*

On the Damascus road, Jesus had promised Paul that he would continue to appear unto him in the future. He had fulfilled that promise two years before, at the Roman fortress in Jerusalem, when he stood by Paul to encourage him and to tell him that he would be a witness in Rome.

26:17 *delivering thee from the people and from the Gentiles, unto whom now I send thee*

26:18 *to open their eyes and to turn them from darkness to light and from the power of Satan unto God, that they may receive remission of sins and inheritance among those who are sanctified by the faith that is in me.*

At the time when Paul heard these words from Jesus, he had literally been blinded by Jesus's glory, and someone had to lead him into the city. This was the way in which Jesus personally appeared to Paul in order to raise him up as a minister and a witness even to the Gentiles, to open their eyes. After three days, God sent someone to open Paul's natural eyes, but his spiritual eyes had already been opened.[117] Jesus opened his understanding so he could see that the gospel isn't just about receiving remission of sins, but it is also about receiving an inheritance among those who are sanctified by the faith that is in Jesus.

This is the *hope of the promise* that Paul mentioned earlier. For over fifteen hundred years, the twelve tribes had been striving night and day under the law of Moses, and now, suddenly, in a moment of time, God bestowed the hope of the promise that the Jews had been working so hard for upon Paul (Saul) by grace. This is the real, though unacknowledged, reason that the Jews were accusing Paul. Without doing any work, he had been given a down payment (he called it the earnest[118]) of the resurrection life of Jesus, and this down payment had rekindled his hope for the fullness of the promise (or high calling[119]).

We can be certain that by now Paul had the full attention of King Agrippa, Bernice, and many others, and the conviction of the Holy Spirit had surely begun penetrating hearts and consciences. Many of those present would never forget Paul's witness and testimony.

---

117 Jesus mentioned *those who are sanctified by the faith that is in me*. By persecuting the Christians, Paul had been doing the opposite of placing his faith in Jesus Christ, right up until Jesus appeared to him. To be sanctified is to be set apart for the exclusive use of the Lord. Nothing that we can do or contrive on our own can make this happen (the Jews found this out the hard way). It isn't a question of Paul making a great effort to have faith in Jesus despite a flurry of Jewish doubts. Jesus was saying that from now on, his faith was going to flow in and through Paul. The faith of Jesus would sanctify Paul and those to whom he was being sent to minister; and yes, it is good and necessary for us to place our faith and trust in Jesus, but Jesus may also decide to place his faith in us, and it is his faith that sanctifies. Jesus overcame by depending totally and unconditionally on his Father. The faith of Jesus, as demonstrated in the life and ministry of the apostle Paul, brought Paul into complete and unconditional dependence upon Jesus by the Spirit.

118 2 Corinthians 1:22; Ephesians 1:14.

119 Philippians 3:11-14.

26:19 *Whereupon, O King Agrippa, I was not disobedient unto the heavenly vision,*

26:20 *but I announced first unto those of Damascus and at Jerusalem and throughout all the coasts of Judaea and then to the Gentiles that they should repent and turn to God, doing works worthy of repentance.*

Paul told both Jew and Gentile *to repent and turn to God, doing works worthy of repentance,* even while he emphasized that salvation is *by grace* and *through faith,* not of our own works, but that we are *created in Christ Jesus for good works, which God has prepared that we should walk in them* (Ephesians 2:8-10). Paul's message makes no reference to religious rites, ceremonies, or rituals. He doesn't even mention altar calls, prayer meetings, Bible reading, water baptism, confirmation, or communion, let alone circumcision or the nuances of Jewish custom, all of which can be accomplished by human effort and determination.

26:21 *For these causes the Jews caught me in the temple and went about to kill me.*

If we are truly to do *works worthy of repentance,* we must be led and empowered by the Holy Spirit, for *the steps of a good man are ordered by the Lord* (Psalm 37:23).

26:22 *Having, therefore, obtained help of God, I continue unto this day, witnessing both to small and great, saying no other things than those which the prophets and Moses said should come:*

26:23 *that the Christ should suffer and that he should be the first that should rise from the dead and should show light unto this people and to the Gentiles.*

The help of God can come in many different forms. When the Jews caught Paul in the temple and were about to kill him, it

was the Roman tribunal, Claudius Lysias, who came to his aid
with overwhelming military force to save him from the Jews,
allowed him to witness to the multitude and to the Jewish
council, and then safely escorted him to Caesarea.

> 26:24 *And as he spoke these things and answered for
> himself, Festus said with a loud voice, Paul, thou art
> beside thyself; much learning doth make thee mad.*

Paul's testimony was so different and so divergent from what
was accepted as normal life in Roman times, that at first this
message may have seemed insane to Festus. However, then as
now, watching real Christians facing real-life situations will
allow their witness to really sink in.

> 26:25 *But he said, I am not mad, most noble Festus, but
> speak forth words of truth and temperance.*[120]

> 26:26 *For the king knows of these things, before whom I
> also speak freely; for I am persuaded that none of these
> things are hidden from him, for this thing was not done
> in a corner.*

King Agrippa must have been well aware of all that had been
taking place in Jerusalem and Judaea over the past six or more
decades. Others would have told him about any events that he
had not experienced personally.[121] King Agrippa had undoubtedly witnessed the ministry of true men and women of God
and possessed knowledge of the Scriptures.

---

120 Temperance, in the original sense, means self-control. This is the opposite of
the uncontrolled fits of anger that the Jews continually displayed towards Paul
and his message. According to Wikipidea, even Jewish historians such as the
Amoraim (Jewish scholars of the period from about AD 200 to 500, who "said"
or "told over" the teachings of the oral Torah) note that it was the "baseless anger"
(out-of-control fits of anger) by the Jews that led to the wars and confusion that
left Jerusalem in utter ruins by AD 70.

121 Such as the murder in Bethlehem of all the infants under two years of age, as
ordered by his ancestor, Herod the Great, after the visit of the wise men from
the east who were searching for the Christ child (Matthew 2:16).

26:27 King Agrippa, dost thou believe the prophets? I know that thou believest.

26:28 Then Agrippa said unto Paul, Almost thou persuadest me to be a Christian.[122]

How did Paul know that King Agrippa believed the prophets? It's likely that he and Agrippa and Bernice had met before in private, in the same way that Nicodemus had met with Jesus secretly at night. Merely believing in secret, however, is not enough. We must believe in our heart and confess with our mouth (Romans 10:9). Jesus said, *Whosoever therefore shall confess me before men, him will I also confess before my Father who is in the heavens* (Matthew 10:32). Many people today are like King Agrippa. They may be rich and powerful and regarded as "tamers of wild horses," but privately they know in the depths of their hearts that the words of the prophets are true. Sadly, however, they are reluctant to take a public stand for Jesus Christ.

26:29 And Paul said, I desire before God that by little or by much, not only thou, but also all that hear me this day, were such as I am, except these bonds.

26:30 And when he had said these things, the king rose up and the governor and Bernice and those that sat with them;

26:31 and when they were gone aside, they talked between themselves, saying, This man does nothing worthy of death or of bonds.

26:32 Then Agrippa said unto Festus, This man might

---

122 The word "Christian" or "Christians" is only used three times in the Bible, and this is the second usage. The first use of the word is in Acts 11:26, where it refers to the believers in Antioch. King Agrippa's choice of this word is yet another indicator that he had been closely following events involving the early believers.

have been set at liberty if he had not appealed unto
Caesar.

Although they admitted that Paul had done nothing worthy of death or even of bonds, Festus and King Agrippa couldn't bring themselves to do the right thing and release him. Perhaps some paperwork and records had already been sent to Rome and couldn't be retrieved or retracted, but I doubt it. Festus still had to face the problem of what to write to Caesar regarding the nonexistent legal charges. If King Agrippa and Bernice had taken a public stand for Jesus Christ (and it almost happened), this could have had a tremendous impact on the entire region. Instead, Agrippa went down in history as the last king of his family line, as did Emperor Nero of Rome.

Let Us Pray

Lord, May we learn the lessons of the past. May we allow your Holy Spirit to examine our hearts and to purify them so that we may be found doing works worthy of repentance. May your faith come forth in us and sanctify us to serve at your pleasure. Amen.

Chapter 14

A Parable of the End of the Church Age

Paul's journey in chains from Caesarea to Rome is prophetic of events in the church over the course of history. In this parable, Paul represents the Holy Spirit (who, of course, operates in and through individuals).

Acts 27

> 27:1 *But when it was determined that we should sail unto Italy, they delivered Paul and certain other prisoners unto one named Julius, a centurion of the Augustus company.*

Paul wrote to the early believers, *For the Lord is the Spirit, and where that Spirit of the Lord is, there is liberty* (2 Corinthians 3:17). His previous trip, with seven companions, had been toward Jerusalem and toward the greater anointing promised at Pentecost.

Rebellious, disobedient, unbelieving religious Jews interposed themselves just as Paul's time of purification in the temple was being completed. This caused the Romans to intervene, and instead of releasing Paul, they (along with Jewish King Agrippa) sent him in chains to Rome.

Who was it who finally determined they should sail to Italy (which means "like a calf")? Porcius Festus (meaning "swinish festival").

Swine are unclean animals in Jewish culture, and a calf is a symbol of the flesh. Remember how calf worship got the children of Israel into a lot of trouble early in their exodus into the wilderness?

So in this picture of Paul sailing to Italy, we have a spiritual picture of the church making a change of course and heading "west" towards "Italy," with "Paul" and some other prisoners on board.

The authority on board is named Julius, meaning "smooth hair." (Remember that according to 1 Corinthians 11:7-9, the glory of man is woman and is linked to the hair; as noted elsewhere, women are also representative of the congregation.) The initial reason put forward for promoting human authority, which at first would only slightly limit the freedom of the Spirit, was that the congregation would have "smooth hair" and everything would be in order and politically correct. Julius is a Roman centurion of the Augustus company, and "Augustus" means "exalted," "venerable," or "reverend." Julius represents the beginning of a clergy class that is courteous and polite and rules through meekness.

> 27:2 And entering into the ship, Adramyttium, we
> launched, meaning to sail by the coasts of Asia, one
> Aristarchus, a Macedonian of Thessalonica, being with
> us.

"Adramyttium" means "I will remain dead." The early believers knew that if they were to follow "the way," they were to be dead, and Jesus Christ was to be alive in them. Also, Aristarchus (meaning "best governor") was on board and was not one of the prisoners. He was, however, from Macedonia ("extended land") of Thessalonica ("victory of the false").

This is a picture of the early Christians still being on a firm foundation, even though gifted human leadership was gradually beginning to displace the liberty of the Spirit, slowing things down over the centuries and bringing about the victory of things that are false.

> 27:3 *And the next day we touched at Sidon. And Julius courteously entreated Paul and gave him liberty to go unto his friends to refresh himself.*

Having entreated Paul courteously, Julius gave him liberty when they got to Sidon ("fishing"). Those who desire to impose human control over the congregation(s) know enough to grant liberty to people like Paul when there's a possibility of "fishing" for new converts.

> 27:4 *And when we had launched from there, we sailed under Cyprus because the winds were contrary.*

On the previous journey, they had sailed with Cyprus ("love") on their left, placing them symbolically on the right hand (the hand of power and authority) of God's love. Now, with Paul as a prisoner, they are sailing under "Cyprus" with the ship on the left-hand side (symbol of judgment) of God's love and mercy.

> 27:5 *And when we had sailed over the sea of Cilicia and Pamphylia, we came to Myra, a city of Lycia.*

Cilicia was a free Roman province, and "Pamphylia" means "of each tribe." This is symbolic of the church sailing through the sea of lost humanity and coming to Myra, or Myrrh (a symbol of the way of the cross), in Lycia ("land of wolves"). Recall that on the previous journey, Paul had warned the elders of Ephesus *that after my departing, grievous wolves shall enter in among you, not sparing the flock* (Acts 20:29).

27:6 And there the centurion found a ship of Alexandria sailing into Italy, and he put us in it.

Now the centurion, or Roman authority, decided to change ships, and he found one from Alexandria ("he who defends man"). In other words, there is a big switch from the ship of "I will remain in death" to the ship of "he who defends man," or humanism. This ship of Alexandria sailed, of course, to Italy ("like a calf"). Its course was thus towards a destination of pleasing the flesh. This change of "ship" in church history began to take place about the time Emperor Constantine converted to Christianity.

27:7 And when we had sailed slowly many days and scarce were come over against Cnidus, the wind not allowing us, we sailed under Crete, over against Salmone,

27:8 and, passing it with difficulty, came unto a place which is called The Fair Havens, near which was the city of Lasea.

This change of "ship" really messes things up and brings the boat over against Cnidus (meaning "to irritate" or "to provoke"). God is not happy, *and the wind not allowing us, we sailed under Crete* (meaning "of the flesh"). As the church gets more and more into humanism and the flesh, the wind or power of God begins to come around and turn against the "ship." With the wind being contrary, they got under Crete (that is, they came under the control of the flesh) and over against Salmone (meaning "coat" or "covering"). This shows metaphorically how the organized church, guided by very gifted individuals in the flesh, got out from under the covering of the Holy Spirit and got under the covering of humanism.

Note that they passed Salmone *with difficulty* and came unto the Fair Havens near to the city of Lasea (meaning "hairy and rough"). The "Fair Havens" look good on the outside, but this appearance is deceptive, and things will soon become "hairy and rough." The initial purpose of having "smooth hair" through the human control of "Julius" has now come full circle. Even if they achieve their stated objective of going to Italy, their unstated objective is to put Paul on trial.

> 27:9 *Now when much time was spent, and when sailing was now dangerous, because the fast was now already past, Paul admonished them,*

> 27:10 *saying, Sirs, I perceive that this voyage will be with hurt and much damage, not only of the lading and ship, but also of our lives.*

The fast that *was now already past* refers to the Day of Atonement, which was on the tenth day of the seventh month, or towards the end of our September. Thus, the pleasant days of summer sailing have passed, and to sail on into the storms of life against the "wind" and at the end of the "season" is to risk *hurt and much damage, not only of the lading and ship but also of our lives.* This is the true word of the Lord. Sailing is now dangerous because the "fast" is already past. On the previous ship there was no such danger, because the "fast" was the very nature of the ship named "I will remain in death." On the present ship of humanism, there are many who are feeding their own egos.

> 27:11 *Nevertheless the centurion believed the master and the owner of the ship more than those things which were spoken by Paul.*

Who is *the master and the owner of the ship* of humanism?

Man (or at least he thinks he is).

This reeks of the influence of the devil. When he can't get people to worship him openly, he works as an angel of light to deceive mankind into worshipping man instead of God.

It is now clear that the centurion believed the devil more than the inspired words of God from Paul's mouth.

27:12 *And because the haven was not commodious to winter in, many were in agreement to depart from there also, if by any means they might attain to Phenice and winter there, which is a port of Crete and lies toward Africa and the west.*

The "Fair Havens" of humanism (that is, of worshipping man) are not *commodious to winter in.* Winter has to do with tribulation, maybe even great tribulation. Many people on board the ship of Christian humanism in our picture are now starting to realize that Fair Havens aren't the same as Safe Havens (which is where we seem to be today). They want to make a mighty effort to depart from the Fair Havens, if by any means they might attain to Phenice, meaning "a palm tree." Although the palm tree is a symbol of righteousness, this particular "Phenice" or palm tree is a port of "Crete" ("of the flesh") and lies toward "Africa," which at that time could mean "the afflicted" (possibly in reference to the slave trade). So now these people think that their only hope is to sail toward self-righteousness, which is exactly the same thing that got the Jews into so much trouble. In fact, back at Jerusalem, things were rapidly going from bad to worse.

27:13 *And when the south wind blew softly, supposing that they had obtained their purpose, raising sails, they sailed close by Crete.*

In Scripture, the south wind is linked to natural prosperity. Many Jews and Christians have mistakenly thought that economic prosperity and good physical health are signs that God approves of us and of what we are doing, when in reality they are reasons for us to give thanks to God. When *the south wind blew softly,* the humanists supposed *that they had obtained their purpose.* They wanted God to do their will instead of being prepared, like Paul, to do God's will no matter what. Therefore, they sailed close by Crete (that is, close to the flesh). Their desperate attempt to get to Phenice (representing self-righteousness in this parable) would lead them into serious trouble.

> 27:14 *But not long after, there arose against it a tempestuous wind, called Euroclydon.*

Euroclydon[123] is a devastating cold north wind from Europe. In fact, in the world today, there is a substantial amount of trouble emanating out of Europe in the political, economic, and religious realms.

> 27:15 *And when the ship was caught up by it and could not resist against the wind, the ship was taken by the wind and drifted.*

Those who were manning the ship were no longer able to maintain their desired course, and the ship was taken by the wind. Not even the master and owner of the ship could cause it to resist this wind. Over the centuries, humanism and the devil have caused numerous trials, tribulations, and adversities to the people of God. This time, however, I have the distinct impression that God is triggering the tribulation and that even the devil is losing control.

> 27:16 *And running under a certain island which is called Clauda, we had much work to come by the boat,*

"Clauda" means "crippled." This ship and some of the people on board remind me of the prophesied time of Jacob's trouble,

---

123 Today we would call this an extreme cold front capable of spinning off waterspouts.

linked to the end-time day of the Lord (Jeremiah 30:7). When Jacob (representing the chosen people of God) thought his estranged brother, Esau, would kill him and his entire family, he wrestled all night with the angel of the Lord. As time ran out, God touched Jacob's thigh and crippled him, prior to changing his name (nature). Jacob left the encounter with a new name, Israel, and with the blessing of the Lord, but he limped for the rest of his life (Genesis 32).

In our parable, it was all they could do to get the boat to come by and get past the island of Clauda.

> 27:17 *Which when they had taken up, they used helps, undergirding the ship; and, fearing lest they should fall into Syrtis, struck sail and so were driven.*

Now they were being driven directly by God, and whether or not they would fall into Syrtis ("sandbanks" or "shoals") was an open question. Fearing that they would run aground, they struck sail to reduce the ship's momentum, and they shored up the hull lest it be pierced by a rock.

> 27:18 *And we being exceedingly tossed with a tempest, the next day they lightened the ship;*
>
> 27:19 *and the third day with our own hands we cast off the dead works of the ship.*

Each one, with his own hands, had to help *cast off the dead works of the ship* of humanism.

> 27:20 *And when neither sun nor stars in many days appeared and no small tempest lay on us, all hope that we should be saved was then lost.*

Everyone on earth will soon go through a time in which it will become exceedingly clear that we can't be saved through our own effort and works and institutions. Scripture refers to the day of the Lord as a time when the sun and the stars will not shine, but whosoever calls upon the name of the Lord shall be saved (Joel 3:14-16; Acts 2:2, 21).

> 27:21 *Then after long abstinence, Paul stood forth in the midst of them and said, Sirs, ye should have hearkened unto me and not have loosed from Crete to have avoided this harm and loss.*

Paul had apparently not *stood forth in the midst of them* for quite some time, and by this point, almost everyone was ready to hear a fresh word from the Lord.

> 27:22 *And now I exhort you to be of good cheer, for there shall be no loss of any person's life among you, but only of the ship.*

The heart of God is to save people. However, this particular ship will not be saved.

> 27:23 *For the angel of God stood by me this night, whose I am and whom I serve,*

> 27:24 *saying, Fear not, Paul; thou must be brought before Caesar; and, behold, God has given thee all those that sail with thee.*

Everyone on board must have been prey to a tumult of powerful emotions, but nothing would or could interfere with God's plan to bring Paul before Caesar. Since the angel of God appeared to Paul and promised him that none of the passengers would die, we can assume that he had been praying and interceding for everyone on board. The ship was doomed, but the angel assured him that *God has given thee all those that sail with thee.*

If Paul or someone like him hadn't been on that ship, what might have happened to everyone?

> 27:25 *Therefore, sirs, be of good cheer; for I believe God, that it shall be even as it was told me.*

27:26 However we must be cast upon a certain island.

In order to be saved, they must *be cast upon a certain island* (symbolically, this represents the fullness of the kingdom of God).

27:27 And when the fourteenth night[124] was come as we were driven up and down in the Adriatic sea, about midnight the shipmen deemed that they drew near to some country

"Adriatic" means "without wood" (wood being a symbol of the good works of man that will not survive judgment by fire). This was now their fourteenth night in the stormy Adriatic Sea.

27:28 and sounded and found it twenty fathoms; and when they had gone a little further, they sounded again and found it fifteen fathoms.

The situation was growing more and more precarious.

27:29 Then fearing lest we should fall upon rocks, they cast four anchors out of the stern and wished for the day.

Four is a number linked to the heavens (Genesis 1:14-19), and hope is the anchor of our soul (Hebrews 6:19). Thus, *four anchors out of the stern* symbolizes their recognition that God in heaven was their only hope.

27:30 And as the shipmen were about to flee out of the ship, when they had let down the boat into the sea, under colour as though they would have cast anchors out of the foreship,

27:31 Paul said to the centurion and to the soldiers, Except these abide in the ship, ye cannot be saved.

---

124 Remember that with God, it is the evening and the morning that make up a day, and it has been this way since Genesis 1:5.

27:32 Then the soldiers cut off the ropes of the boat and let her fall off.

They were going to need the sailors to maneuver the ship as close as possible to the shore. On Paul's advice, they cut away the lifeboat. There are many religious "sailors" today who have favorite "lifeboat" escapist doctrines. Paul says we need those sailors, but without their lifeboats.

27:33 And while the day was coming on, Paul besought them all to take food, saying, This day is the four-teenth[125] day that ye have waited and continued fasting, having taken nothing.

Even though they had recklessly sailed on this Alexandrian ship after the fast was already over, for the past fourteen days everyone on board had completely lost interest in feeding their own lives.

27:34 Therefore I pray you to take some food, for this is for your salvation and health, for there shall not one hair[126] fall from the head of any of you.

Paul discerned that now was the proper time to offer everyone

---

125 This is the second reference to fourteen in this passage. The number fourteen (two times seven) has to do with bringing the flock of God's people into his rest according to a change of their nature (i.e., as sheep instead of goats). Jacob served Laban fourteen years for Leah and Rachel (Genesis 31:41). When the sons of Israel went to Egypt, we are told that *the sons of Rachel* (meaning "ewe" or "lamb") *who were born to Jacob* numbered *in all, fourteen souls* (Genesis 46:22). After Jacob was converted, God changed his name to Israel (Genesis 32:24-32). This happened in a time of intense crisis for Jacob and his entire family. (Consider Psalm 14.)
The Passover was celebrated on the fourteenth day of the first month, and at that time a lamb was to be sacrificed. The Feast of Tabernacles was celebrated for seven days, and each day, fourteen lambs of the first year were to be sacrificed. An additional seven lambs were to be sacrificed on the eighth day, making a total of 105 lambs (Numbers 29:12-40). One hundred is symbolic of the plan of God, and the number five is associated with his mercy and grace (Psalm 105, or 100+5, sheds light on this).

126 On this trip, things soon deteriorated under Julius "smooth hair," who picked the wrong ship to sail in the wrong direction at the wrong season into conditions that seemed like Fair Havens, but began to be "hairy and rough" near Lasea. As they came out of the tribulation, Paul promised them that *there shall not one hair fall from the head of any of you.*

"food" for their *salvation and health*. God's plan is to wean us from our own life so that we may partake of his life.

> *27:35 And when he had thus spoken, he took bread and gave thanks to God in presence of them all; and when he had broken it, he began to eat.*

> *27:36 Then they were all of good cheer, and they also took some food.*

> *27:37 And we were in all, in the ship, two hundred and seventy-six souls.*[127]

In addition to physical nourishment, Paul was able to feed them an encouraging word from the Lord.

> *27:38 And when they had eaten enough, they lightened the ship and cast out the grain into the sea.*

Throughout Scripture, grain represents the work of our hands. This is the *fruit of the ground* or the *present* that Cain offered to God when he was rejected (Genesis 4:3-5). Throughout the Old Testament, a present,[128] representing the work of our hands, is only acceptable to God if offered along with a blood sacrifice. This signifies that the work that we do in our own life is not acceptable to God; only the work that's performed after we exchange our life for Christ's life in a blood covenant will be accepted, for only the work that God does in us and through us will have eternal value.

Therefore, as they prepare the ship (representing much of the church at the end of this age) for its final approach toward land, *they lightened the ship and cast out the grain into the sea.* They had already cast off the "dead works," and now, after

---

127 The number 276 is a very significant one. In the Jubilee Bible translation, the word "judgment" occurs 276 times, as does the word "sheep." The judgment will separate the sheep from the goats (Matthew 25:31-46).

128 In many Bible versions, this word "present" is mistranslated as "grain offering."

having been fed a message from God, they cast off the "grain," representing their good works.

> 27:39 *And when it was day, they did not recognize the land, but they discovered a certain gulf with a shore, into which they decided, if it were possible, to thrust in the ship.*

They did not recognize the land because *that which eye has not seen nor ear heard neither has entered into the heart of man is that which God has prepared for those that love him* (1 Corinthians 2:9). However, *they discovered a certain gulf with a shore.* Now they knew where God wanted them *to thrust the ship,* and they went about doing it.

There is still a metaphorical gulf between the church and the shore, and many of today's church leaders and members are in a quandary, because even as some of them catch increasingly clear glimpses of the "shore" of the fullness of the kingdom of God, they also realize that the "ship" in which they have invested so much time and money will most likely be destroyed if they decide to thrust it into the place that God has chosen.

> 27:40 *And when they had taken up the anchors, they committed themselves unto the sea and loosed the rudder bands and hoisted up the mainsail to the wind and made toward shore.*

They had to raise the anchors (remove all resistance to the will of God so that hope can be realized in practice) so that they could *commit themselves unto the sea.*

What sea?

The Adriatic Sea, without wood (without the works of man).

Now they are on course for the fullness of God, and so they must loose *the rudder bands* and hoist *the mainsail to the wind.*

> 27:41 *But falling into a place where two seas met, they*

*ran the ship aground; and the forepart stuck fast and
remained unmovable, but the hinder part was broken
with the violence of the waves.*

What were the two seas?

We know that the sea that they came in on was the Adriatic.
The second sea represents judgment (just like the brazen sea
in the outer court of the temple) that must be passed prior to
reaching the "shore." In this symbolic journey, the first ship,
the Adramyttium ("I must remain in death"), represents how
the church age started out. The second ship, an Alexandrian
(humanistic) vessel, shows what happened later. Now the picture changes to an overall end-time view in which the forepart
of the Adramyttium *stuck fast and remained unmovable.* Our
foundation is in Jesus Christ, and we are to remain there in
death so that he can live in us. The hinder part of the ship (the
Alexandrian part) *was broken with the violence of the waves.*
None of man's plans and programs, even his "good" ideas, will
survive the coming judgment.

27:42 *And the soldiers' counsel was to kill the prisoners,
lest any of them should swim out and escape.*

There were still soldiers on board who wanted to save their own
lives and reputations at the expense of others.

27:43 *But the centurion, desiring to save Paul, frus-
trated this counsel and commanded that those who
could swim should cast themselves first into the sea and
get to land;*

The centurion (representing human authority) knew that he
had to protect Paul.

27:44 *and the rest, some on boards and some on broken
pieces of the ship. And so it came to pass that they were
all saved by making it to land.*

The only part of the ship that *remained unmovable* was the fore-part (indicating that we must be willing to lose our own lives so that Jesus can live in us). This was the only solid place from which those on board could launch themselves into the sea and make it to land. *And so it came to pass that they were all saved.*

Acts 28

> 28:1 *And when they were escaped, then we knew that the island was called Melita.*[129]

Who is the writer referring to as *they*? The master and owner of the ship, the sailors, the centurion, the soldiers, the other prisoners, and anyone else among the 276 souls that God had promised Paul would be physically saved.[130]

"Melita" means "honey," and honey is a symbol of the pure, unadulterated Word of God. This is the "island" representing the haven where God plans to return his people after they go through the end-time storm.

In order for the church to come to a good end, it cannot simply founder like a ship engulfed and overpowered and sunk by the turbulent sea of lost humanity. That's what happened to the disobedient Jews, but the victorious church (the bride without spot or wrinkle representing those like Paul and his companions) must make it safely back to land.

> 28:2 *And the barbarous people showed us no little kindness; for they kindled a great fire and received all of us because of the present rain and because of the cold.*

When God's people are corporately straightened out, we'll

---

129 Or Malta.

130 Does the fact that the 276 souls on board this ship were physically saved because of Paul guarantee that in the end, everyone "on board" the church will be spiritually saved? No, but this parable shows what the people need to do to be saved, even while the institutions of man fail. The number 276 is linked to sheep, not goats.

receive a great reception from many "barbarous people" out in the world where the "weather" is miserable.

Remember, this is just one example of what happened with one ship. There are untold thousands of religious sects, denominations, and congregations that will all face the judgment that begins in the house of the Lord as we enter the day of the Lord, and some of these "ships" may sink like a rock with everyone on board (Revelation 18:21). Our example, however, shows that as long as a given ship still has passengers on board who, like Paul, are in communion with God, it's possible for all the souls on that ship to be saved, even though the vessel itself (that is, the institution), however useful it may have been for a certain time and season, does not survive.

28:3 *And when Paul had gathered a bundle of sticks and laid them on the fire, a viper came out of the heat and fastened on his hand.*

The fire of judgment (2 Peter 3:7) and the brightness and clarity of the return of Jesus Christ with and for his saints will expose the serpent, or Wicked one (2 Thessalonians 2:8), who will be in the midst of making one last attempt to kill God's elect, as represented by Paul.

28:4 *And when the barbarians saw the venomous beast hang on his hand, they said among themselves, No doubt this man is a murderer, whom, though he has escaped the sea, yet vengeance does not suffer him to live.*

28:5 *And he shook off the beast into the fire and felt no harm.*

The venomous beast hung on Paul's hand for long enough that the barbarians were able to comment to one another about it. Then Paul *shook off the beast into the fire.* To call it a *beast* is a very interesting choice of words. Compare this episode with Revelation 19:20.

> 28:6 *But they were waiting to see when he should have swollen or fallen down dead suddenly; but after they had waited a great while and saw no harm come to him, they changed their minds and said that he was a god.*

The Greek literally says that *they changed their minds and said that he was God.*[131] Jesus said to his disciples, *He that has seen me has seen the Father* (John 14:9). Now it appears that the barbarians could see Jesus in Paul (and Jesus is God). This is the result of the resurrection life of Jesus, which Paul repeatedly said is the *hope of the promise.*

> 28:7 *In the same quarters were possessions of a principal man of the island, whose name was Publius, who received us and lodged us three days courteously.*

"Publius" means "popular" or "common" (even "public").

> 28:8 *And it came to pass that the father of Publius lay sick of a fever and of dysentery, to whom Paul entered in and prayed and laid his hands on him and healed him.*

Who is the "father" of Publius? And why does he lie *sick of a fever and of dysentery*?

The natural father of the sick and fallen human race is Adam. Only the resurrection life of Jesus Christ, the hope of the promise, can heal mankind's condition.

> 28:9 *So when this was done, others also, who had diseases in the island, came and were healed,*

> 28:10 *who also honoured us with many gifts; and when*

---

131 It's interesting that in this instance, Paul did not dispute this title with them as he did when the people of Lystra attempted to worship him and Barnabas, calling them Mercury and Jupiter (Acts 14:8-18).

we departed, they laded us with such things as were necessary.

The Voyage to Rome is Resumed

28:11 *And after three months we departed in a ship of Alexandria, which had wintered in the isle, whose ensign was Castor and Pollux.*[132]

This ship is also of Alexandria. In fact, this is likely what the voyage would have been like if not for the terrible storm. This "ship" represents a situation in which humanism is now mixed with paganism.

28:12 *And landing at Syracuse, we tarried there three days.*

The meaning of Syracuse is uncertain. It could mean "to hear as a Syrian" (that is, in Aramaic). If so, this would indicate a degradation of the spiritual capacity to hear on the way to "Rome."

28:13 *And having gone around, we came to Rhegium, and after one day the south wind blew, and we came the next day to Puteoli,*

"Rhegium" means "breach," and "Puteoli" means "sulfur springs" or "brimstone springs."[133] These are two indicators of impending judgment from God.

28:14 *where we found brethren, who asked us to tarry with them seven days, and so we went toward Rome.*

The road to Rome ("fortress") has some warning signs along the way. Yes, there are brethren in unexpected places. God loves to infiltrate the enemy forces with those who are his.

28:15 *And from there, when the brethren heard of us,*

---

132 Castor and Pollux were the twins Dioscuri, and were the patron gods of sailors.

133 In Scripture, brimstone is always associated with the righteous judgments of God against the wicked.

*they came to meet us as far as Appii Forum and The
Three Taverns whom when Paul saw, he thanked God
and took courage.*

I doubt that Paul was thrilled with the *Appii Forum* and *The
Three Taverns*. It was the brethren who came to meet him and
his companions *whom when Paul saw, he thanked God and
took courage.*

28:16 *And when we came to Rome, the centurion delivered the prisoners to the praetorian prefect, but Paul
was allowed to dwell by himself with a soldier that kept
him.*

The *praetorian prefect* was a very high-ranking Roman offi-
cial, likely in charge of the personal guard of the emperor and
responsible for the administration of justice. Once again, Paul
found grace and favor at the hands of his captors.

28:17 *And it came to pass, that after three days Paul
called the principals of the Jews together, and when
they were come together, he said unto them, Men and
brethren, though I have committed nothing against the
people or customs of our fathers, yet was I delivered
prisoner from Jerusalem into the hands of the Romans,*

28:18 *who, when they had examined me, would have let
me go because there was no cause of death in me.*

28:19 *But when the Jews spoke against it, I was constrained to appeal unto Caesar, not that I had anything
to accuse my nation of.*

The Jews had treated Paul most horribly and had made constant
attempts on his life, yet he chose not to accuse them before
Caesar. He was content to leave this issue in the hands of God.

He made his appeal to Caesar because Jesus wanted him to be a witness there.

28:20 For this cause therefore I have called for you, to see you and to speak with you: because for the hope of Israel I am bound with this chain.

There are only three references to *the hope of Israel* in Scripture. This is one, and the others are in Jeremiah 14:8[134] and 17:13.[135] In previous defenses, Paul had referred to *the hope and resurrection of the dead* (Acts 23:6) and *the hope of the promise* (Acts 26:6).

28:21 And they said unto him, We neither received letters out of Judaea concerning thee, neither any of the brethren that came showed or spoke any harm of thee.[136]

28:22 But we desire to hear of thee what thou thinkest; for as concerning this sect, we know that everywhere it is spoken against.

This is further evidence that things continued to deteriorate rapidly back in Judaea and Jerusalem, and it's likely that the time line was more advanced than most modern commentators and historians are willing to admit. If the high priest and elders (who hated Paul more than they hated almost anyone else) had been unwilling or unable to send accusatory letters about him to the Jews in Rome, it's highly likely that they were

---

134 *O the hope of Israel, the Keeper thereof in time of trouble, why should thou be as a stranger in the land and as a wayfaring man that turns aside to tarry for a night?*

135 *O hope of Israel! LORD, all that forsake thee shall be ashamed; and those that depart from me shall be written in the dust because they have forsaken the LORD, the fountain of living waters.*

136 Most pre-modern historians and commentators date this at AD 63, some likely derived from Ussher's *Annals of the World*, (1658). If this is true or if it happened even slightly later, the fire of AD 64 (which reportedly started between July 18 and 19 of that year and burned for days) would have been a major factor in explaining why Paul dwelt two whole years in his own hired house while the Roman government was in confusion. The *Commentary* of Joseph Benson (1850) also dates this at AD 63. It's possible that it could even have been the late spring of AD 64, with the fire following in a matter of weeks.

in a mess of ever-increasing trouble of their own. This would suggest that by this time, the Jewish Wars were either imminent or underway (which could point to at least AD 64).

> 28:23 *And when they had appointed him a day, many came to him into his lodging, to whom he expounded and testified the kingdom of God, procuring to persuade them of that concerning Jesus, the Christ, out of the law of Moses and out of the prophets, from morning until evening.*

> 28:24 *And some believed the things which were spoken, and some did not believe.*

The Word of God does not return void (Isaiah 55:11). Each time Paul had an opportunity to speak and reason with the Jews, God gave him results. If God sends us and commissions us to speak on his behalf, we can expect no less. In order for this to happen, however, we – like Jesus and Paul – must be willing to lay our own lives on the line.

> 28:25 *And when they did not agree among themselves, they departed, after Paul had spoken this word, Well spoke the Holy Spirit by Isaiah the prophet unto our fathers,*

> 28:26 *saying, Go unto this people, and say, Hearing ye shall hear and shall not understand; and seeing ye shall see and not perceive;*

> 28:27 *for the heart of this people is waxed gross, and their ears are dull of hearing, and their eyes have they closed; lest they should see with their eyes and hear with their ears and understand with their heart and should be converted and I should heal them.*[137]

---

137 This Old Testament prophecy (Isaiah 6:9-10) is quoted by Jesus in the Gospels

A person's ability to hear or to see in the spiritual realm is linked to the state of his heart. Are there entire corporate groups today in which their heart *is waxed gross*?

> 28:28 *Be it known, therefore, unto you that this saving health of God is sent unto the Gentiles and that they will hear it.*

> 28:29 *And when he had said these words, the Jews departed and had a great dispute among themselves.*

What is this *saving health of God* that the Jews rejected and that is *sent unto the Gentiles*?

The kingdom of God.[138]

> 28:30 *And Paul dwelt two whole years in his own hired house and received all that came in unto him,*

> 28:31 *preaching the kingdom of God[139] and teaching those things which concern the Lord Jesus Christ, with all liberty, without hindrance.*

Let Us Pray

Lord, We ask not only that we may have your light, your revelation, and your grace, but that we may also have the capacity to follow you against all odds, against the system of this world.

May our faith be joined with your faith that we may overcome and bring forth fruits worthy of your kingdom. Amen.

(Matthew 13:14-15; Mark 4:12; Luke 8:10) and is referred to by Paul in one of his epistles (Romans 11:8).

138 *Therefore I say unto you, The kingdom of God shall be taken from you and given to a people bringing forth the fruits thereof* (Matthew 21:43).

139 Note that here in his own hired house, Paul preaches *the kingdom of God* to the Roman Gentiles, and in verse 23 he *expounded and testified the kingdom of God* to the Jews.

Epilogue

Some think that Paul was released from prison in Rome and continued his missionary journeys, as indicated by the verses listed below.

> *At my first answer no one stood with me, but all men forsook me: let it not be imputed unto them. But the Lord stood with me and strengthened me, that by me the preaching might be fully known and that all the Gentiles might hear, and I was delivered out of the mouth of the lion. And the Lord shall deliver me from every evil work and will save me for his heavenly kingdom, to whom be glory for ever and ever. Amen* (2 Timothy 4:16-18).

> *When I shall send Artemas unto thee or Tychicus, procure to come unto me to Nicopolis; for I have determined to winter there* (Titus 3:12).

Prior to arriving as a prisoner in Rome, Paul was not known to have travelled to Nicopolis. Therefore, this would have happened after the *two whole years in his own hired house* in Rome.

It is likely that Hebrews[140] was the last of Paul's writings.

---

140 Yes, I know that some modern scholars claim Paul didn't write Hebrews because his name isn't included in any of the verses. However, his name is always in the title on the old manuscripts. These scholars also claim to have analyzed the style

Know ye that our brother Timothy is set at liberty; with whom, if he comes shortly, I will see you (Hebrews 13:23).

There is no record in Scripture of the death of Paul or of his place of burial.[141] Paul's counterpart in the Old Testament is Moses. The death of Moses is recorded, but the place where he was buried is not (Deuteronomy 34:6). At the end of the book of Acts, according to my calculations, Paul would have only been in his early 60s. Maybe he was finally able to travel to Spain and to parts unknown, according to the desires of his heart. Maybe he outlasted Nero and Agrippa, who were each near the end of their respective dynasties. Maybe he lived to see the demise of the rebellious Jews of Jerusalem. God knows.

---

and found it to be different. It's likely that Hebrews was originally written in Hebrew and later translated to Greek; this could account for the difference in style. (My books differ in style depending on whether I originally wrote them in English or in Spanish.) Also, Paul liked to include others, and perhaps there were some (like Priscilla and Aquila) who helped with this but didn't want to have their names listed for some reason. At any rate, throughout history the book of Hebrews has traditionally been labeled as coming from Paul or authorized by him.

141 Ussher states that Paul was beheaded at Rome on the twenty-ninth day of June in AD 67, under Nero, and that there are records of both the eastern and western church to confirm this. Modern historians date this event as early as AD 63. Regarding the death of Paul (unconfirmed in Scripture), I think we need to take the proclamations of all the historians with a grain of salt. Centuries after the fact, the powerful forces who desired to concentrate religious power in Rome would no doubt have wanted the tombs of Paul and Peter to be at or near that city and may well have applied pressure toward this end. I believe that Paul continued to travel in ministry as long as God wanted him to do so.

Appendix

Use of the Word "Elders" in the Jubilee Bible

I don't think this book, *The Unquenchable Life*, would be complete without a study of the word "elders." In the Jubilee Bible translation, there are 192 Scripture references to elders.[142] Those who marvel at the spiritual health and dynamic of the early Christians and yearn to see similar vigor and vitality restored to the body of Christ today will do well to carefully consider the Scriptural definition and trajectory of what godly elders are and are not.

The Hebrew word *gadowl*, translated "elder" (singular), is completely different from the word *zaqen*, translated as "elders" (plural). *Gadowl* means "great" or "older," whereas *zaqen* comes from a root word meaning "old" or "aged" (i.e., mature), but in the plural. Hebrew uses the plural for emphasis, and in this case, elders (plural) also gives the connotation of government.[143]

It seems that every faction, tribe, nation, or denomination of human society has leadership in the form of elders, and this was also true of the nation of Israel and the early Christians.

142 Note that 192 is 24 (symbolic of the corporate people of God who have come to maturity in divine order) multiplied by 8 (eight is symbolic of new beginnings).
143 Five references to godly elders in the first part of the book of Ezra use the word *siyb*, which is of Chaldean origin.

There is, however, a great divide between earthly elders and spiritual elders. Those of the world come to maturity (as elders) in the fallen corrupt earthy life of Adam, while believers are encouraged to come to maturity in the incorruptible heavenly life of Jesus Christ (1 Corinthians 15:47-49).

A close examination of the following Scriptures will shed light on the biblical concept of maturity. At the time of the harvest, the wheat and the tares both come to maturity, but with diametrically opposed results and consequences. Jesus said the "good seed" represents the sons of the kingdom, and the "tares" are the sons of the wicked (Matthew 13:38). At the time of the end, both could be considered "elders" according to the use of this word in Scripture.

The topic of elders invariably comes up wherever believers gather together in fellowship and worship. There is a widespread tendency to name as elders those who are very talented, even while they are still spiritually immature. Those who do this, however, may fail to differentiate between the wheat and the tares, because in immature form, the two are almost indistinguishable (Matthew 13:24-30).

Here are the scriptures in question, including the number of times that the word "elders" has appeared at this point:

(1, 2) Genesis 50

*50:7 Then Joseph went up to bury his father, and with him went up all the slaves of Pharaoh, the **elders** of his house, and all the **elders** of the land of Egypt.*

In the first two instances of this word in Scripture, there are clear indications that it has to do with government. Exactly how these elders came to be appointed isn't spelled out, but common sense would tell us that they were the oldest and most respected patriarchs.

(3, 4) Exodus 3

3:15 *And God said moreover unto Moses, Thus shalt thou say unto the sons of Israel: The LORD God of your fathers, the God of Abraham, the God of Isaac, and the God of Jacob, has sent me unto you. This is my name for ever, and this is my memorial unto all ages.*

3:16 *Go and gather the **elders** of Israel together and say unto them, The LORD God of your fathers, the God of Abraham, of Isaac, and of Jacob, appeared unto me, saying, I have surely visited you and seen that which is done to you in Egypt,*

3:17 *and I have said, I will bring you up out of the affliction of Egypt unto the land of the Canaanite and the Hittite and the Amorite and the Perizzite and the Hivite and the Jebusite unto a land flowing with milk and honey.*

3:18 *And they shall hearken to thy voice, and thou shalt come, thou and the **elders** of Israel, unto the king of Egypt, and ye shall say unto him, The LORD God of the Hebrews has found us; therefore, we shall now go three days' journey into the wilderness that we may sacrifice to the LORD our God.*

Here we have two references to the elders of Israel, each of which refers to the government put in place by the people (even in bondage) that Moses had to deal with and convince. Again, there is no evidence that God appointed them. They are elders by consensus of the people.

(5) Exodus 4

*4:29 And Moses and Aaron went and gathered together all the **elders** of the sons of Israel.*

(6) Exodus 12

*12:21 Then Moses called for all the **elders** of Israel and said unto them, Draw out and take lambs according to your families and sacrifice the passover.*

Here it appears that each family was represented by at least one elder.

(7, 8) Exodus 17

17:4 Then Moses cried unto the LORD, saying, What shall I do with this people? They are almost ready to stone me.

*17:5 And the LORD said unto Moses, Go on before the people and take with thee of the **elders** of Israel and thy rod, with which thou didst smite the river take in thine hand and go.*

*17:6 Behold, I will stand before thee there upon the rock in Horeb, and thou shalt smite the rock, and water shall come out of it that the people may drink. And Moses did so in the sight of the **elders** of Israel.*

The elders of Israel were prone to reflect the will of the people, not necessarily that of God.

(9) Exodus 18

18:12 And Jethro, Moses' father-in-law, took burnt offerings and sacrifices for God; and Aaron came, and all the **elders** of Israel, to eat bread with Moses' father-in-law before God.

The elders of Israel were representatives of the people (somewhat like politicians today).

(10) Exodus 19

19:5 *Now therefore, if ye will give ear to hearken unto my voice and keep my covenant, then ye shall be a special treasure unto me above all peoples; for all the earth is mine.*

19:6 *And ye shall be my kingdom of priests and a holy nation. These are the words which thou shalt speak unto the sons of Israel.*

19:7 *Then Moses came and called for the **elders** of the people and laid before their faces all these words which the LORD commanded him.*

19:8 *And all the people answered together and said, All that the LORD has spoken we will do. And Moses returned the words of the people unto the LORD.*

They didn't have microphones or loudspeakers, so Moses told the elders what God had told him, and the elders in turn told the people.

(11, 12, 13) Exodus 24

24:1 *And he said unto Moses, Come up unto the LORD, thou and Aaron, Nadab, and Abihu and seventy of the **elders** of Israel, and worship afar off.*

24:2 *And Moses alone shall approach the LORD, but they shall not come near; neither shall the people go up with him.*

24:9 *Then Moses and Aaron, Nadab, and Abihu and seventy of the* **elders** *of Israel went up,*

24:10 *and they saw the God of Israel; and there was under his feet as it were a paved work of a sapphire stone like unto the heaven when it is clear.*

24:11 *But he did not lay his hand upon the princes of the sons of Israel, and they saw God and ate and drank.*

Normally the direct presence of God would have destroyed mortal men (and later, God did destroy Nadab and Abihu after they offered "strange fire" that had not been lit by God). These seventy elders, however, were allowed to come and worship afar off (but they and the people could not come near). Note that God chose Moses and Aaron. The people had chosen the seventy elders.

24:13 *And Moses rose up, and his minister Joshua, and Moses went up into the mount of God.*

24:14 *And he said unto the* **elders**, *wait here for us until we come again unto you; and, behold, Aaron and Hur are with you; if anyone has any matters to settle, let him come unto them.*

(14) Leviticus 4

4:13 *And if the whole congregation of Israel sins through ignorance and the thing was hid from the eyes of the assembly and they have done something against any of the commandments of the LORD concerning things which should not be done and are guilty,*

4:14 *when the sin, which they have committed, is understood, then the congregation shall offer a young bullock as the sin and bring it before the tabernacle of the testimony.*

*4:15 And the **elders** of the congregation shall lay their hands upon the head of the bullock before the LORD, and the bullock shall be killed before the LORD.*

If the entire congregation sinned through ignorance, then when the sin was brought to light, it was the responsibility of the elders to deal with it before the people and before the Lord.

(15) Leviticus 9

*9:1 And it came to pass on the eighth day that Moses called Aaron and his sons and the **elders** of Israel.*

(16, 17, 18, 19, 20) Numbers 11

*11:16 Then the LORD said unto Moses, Gather unto me seventy men of the **elders** of Israel, whom thou knowest to be **elders** of the people, and their princes; and bring them unto the tabernacle of the testimony that they may stand there with thee.*

11:17 And I will come down and talk with thee there, and I will take of the spirit which is in thee and will put it upon them, and they shall bear the burden of the people with thee, that thou bear it not thyself alone.

God didn't name the seventy men. Moses got to choose them, with the stipulation that they had to be men whom he knew to be *elders of the people.*

*11:24 And Moses went out and told the people the words of the LORD and gathered the seventy men of the **elders** of the people and set them round about the tabernacle.*

> 11:25 *Then the LORD came down in the cloud and spoke unto him and took of the spirit that was in him and gave it unto the seventy* **elders**, *and it came to pass that when the spirit rested upon them, they prophesied and did not cease.*

The Spirit is God's seal, and he placed it upon the elders of the people who had been chosen by Moses.[144]

> 11:26 *But there remained two of the men in the camp, the name of the one was Eldad and the name of the other Medad, upon whom the spirit also rested; and they were of those that were written, but they had not gone unto the tabernacle; and they began to prophesy in the camp.*

> 11:27 *And a young man ran and told Moses, and said, Eldad and Medad prophesy in the camp.*

> 11:28 *Then Joshua the son of Nun, the minister of Moses, one of his young men, answered and said, My lord Moses, forbid them.*

> 11:29 *And Moses said unto him, Art thou jealous for my sake? It would be good that all the LORD's people were prophets and that the LORD would put his spirit upon them!*

> 11:30 *And Moses withdrew into the camp, he and the* **elders** *of Israel.*

Moses spoke from the heart of God when he desired that all the Lord's people should have the Spirit and be able to prophesy (that is, speak God's words instead of their own words). He wanted all God's people to come to maturity.

---

144 This is a precursor to what happened in the New Testament, when the apostles would choose elders from among the congregation who demonstrated maturity in Christ and had evidence of the fruit of the Holy Spirit.

(21) Numbers 16

16:25 *And Moses rose up and went unto Dathan and Abiram, and the **elders** of Israel followed him.*

Before the elders received the Spirit, Moses had to seek them out on many occasions. Now, with the Spirit upon them, the elders of Israel followed Moses.

(22, 23, 24) Numbers 22

22:4 *And Moab said unto the **elders** of Midian, Now shall this company lick up all that are round about us, as the ox licks up the herbs of the field. And Balak, the son of Zippor, was king of the Moabites at that time.*

22:5 *Therefore he sent messengers unto Balaam, the son of Beor, to Pethor, which is by the river Eufrates in the land of the sons of his people, to call him, saying, Behold, there is a people come out from Egypt; behold, they cover the face of the earth, and they abide over against me.*

22:6 *Come now therefore, I pray thee, curse me this people, for they are too mighty for me; peradventure I shall be able to smite them and drive them out of the land; for I know that he whom thou blessest shall be blessed, and he whom thou cursest shall be cursed.*

22:7 *And the **elders** of Moab and the **elders** of Midian departed with the incantations in their hand; and they came unto Balaam and spoke unto him the words of Balak.*

Midian and Moab (representing spiritual enemies of the people of God) also had elders who formed an important part of their government and who liaised between the people, the king, and Balaam the prophet.

(25) Deuteronomy 5

*5:23 And it came to pass when ye heard the voice out of the midst of the darkness and saw the mountain that burned with fire that ye came near unto me, even all the princes of your tribes and your **elders**;*

5:24 and ye said, Behold, the LORD our God has shown us his glory and his greatness, and we have heard his voice out of the midst of the fire; we have seen this day that God does talk with man, and he lives.

5:25 Now, therefore, why should we die? For this great fire will consume us; if we hear the voice of the LORD our God any more, then we shall die.

The elders helped to broker a deal in which they and the people would no longer personally hear the voice of God. They decided to send Moses to speak with God and Moses would then tell them what God said. They promised to obey God's words, yet for the next fifteen hundred years, in terms of fulfilling their promise, most of them failed miserably. In order to receive the grace necessary to overcome, we must have direct contact with God and personally hear his voice.

(26) Deuteronomy 19

19:11 But when any man hates his neighbour and lies in wait for him and rises up against him and smites him mortally that he dies and flees into one of these cities,

*19:12 then the **elders** of his city shall send and take him* *from there and deliver him into the hand of the avenger* [Hebrew – redeemer] *of blood, and he shall die.*

Here the elders had responsibility as judges.

(27, 28, 29, 30, 31, 32) Deuteronomy 21

21:1 When one is found dead in the land which the LORD thy God gives thee to inherit, lying in the field, and it is not known who has slain him,

*21:2 then thy **elders** and thy judges shall come forth, and they shall measure unto the cities which are round about him that is dead;*

*21:3 and it shall be that the **elders** of the city which is next unto the dead man shall take a heifer, which has not served, and which has not drawn in the yoke;*

*21:4 and the **elders** of that city shall bring down the heifer unto a rough valley, which has neither been plowed nor sown, and shall strike off the heifer's neck there in the valley.*

21:5 And the priests the sons of Levi shall come near; for the LORD thy God has chosen them to minister unto him and to bless in the name of the LORD; and by their word shall every controversy and every stroke be determined.

Note the importance of the priests. We are now in the priesthood of all believers (Hebrews 7:12; 1 Peter 2:5, 9; Revelation 1:6), and the fullness of our responsibility comes with maturity in Christ.

*21:6 And all the **elders** of that closest city next to the dead man shall wash their hands over the heifer that is beheaded in the valley.*

*21:7 And they shall answer and say, Our hands have
not shed this blood, neither have our eyes seen it.*

*21:8 Reconcile thy people Israel, whom thou hast ran-
somed, O LORD, and impute not the innocent blood
shed in the midst of thy people Israel. And the blood
shall be forgiven them.*

*21:9 So shalt thou put away the guilt of innocent blood
from among you, when thou shalt do that which is right
in the sight of the LORD.*

Again, the elders were responsible for making sure that no
innocent blood was spilled, or if this happened anyway, those
located nearest the crime were obligated to deal with the situation and take up the matter before the Lord, along with the
priests. Jesus took this a step further: *Ye have heard that it was
said to the ancients, Thou shalt not commit murder, and whosoever shall commit murder shall be guilty of the judgment; but
I say unto you, That whosoever is angry with his brother out of
control shall be in danger of the judgment, and whosoever shall
insult his brother shall be in danger of the council, but whosoever
shall say, Thou art impious, shall be in danger of hell* (Matthew
5:21-22).

*21:18 When anyone has a stubborn and rebellious son,
who will not obey the voice of his father or the voice of
his mother and when they have chastened him, will not
hearken unto them,*

*21:19 then shall his father and his mother lay hold on
him and bring him out unto the **elders** of his city and
unto the gate of his place;*

*21:20 and they shall say unto the **elders** of his city, This* *our son is stubborn and rebellious; he will not hear our voice; he is a glutton and a drunkard.*

21:21 Then all the men of his city shall stone him with stones, and he shall die; so shalt thou put evil away from among you; and all Israel shall hear and fear.

Here the elders may pronounce judgment if the parents had an impossible situation with a rebellious son. In this case, the line of authority went from the children to the parents to the elders.

(33, 34, 35, 36) Deuteronomy 22

22:13 When any man takes a wife and after having gone in unto her, hates her

22:14 and gives occasions of speech against her and brings up an evil name upon her and says, I took this woman, and when I came to her, I found her not a virgin,

*22:15 then shall the father of the damsel and her mother take and bring forth the tokens of the damsel's virginity unto the **elders** of the city in the gate.*

*22:16 And the damsel's father shall say unto the **elders**, I gave my daughter unto this man to wife, and he hates her;*

*22:17 and, behold, he has given occasions of speech against her, saying, I found not thy daughter a virgin; and yet these are the tokens of my daughter's virginity. And they shall spread the cloth before the **elders** of the city.*

*22:18 Then the **elders** of that city shall take that man and chastise him;*

22:19 *and they shall fine him one hundred shekels of silver and give them unto the father of the damsel because he has brought up an evil name upon a virgin of Israel; and she shall be his wife; he may not put her away all his days.*

At the request of the father of the bride, the elders could take authority and deal with a serious situation in a marriage. The bride and groom were responsible, of course, for their decisions and actions. However, to give or not to give a daughter in marriage was the responsibility of the bride's father. There is also a portion of Scripture to this effect in the New Testament (1 Corinthians 7:36-40).

(37, 38, 39) Deuteronomy 25

25:5 *When brethren dwell together and one of them dies and has no child, the wife of the dead shall not marry outside unto a stranger; her husband's brother shall go in unto her and take her to him to wife and perform the duty of a husband's brother unto her.*

25:6 *And it shall be that the firstborn which she bears shall be raised up in the name of his brother who is dead that his name be not blotted out of Israel.*

25:7 *And if the man does not desire to take his brother's wife, then let his brother's wife go up to the gate unto the **elders** and say, My husband's brother refuses to raise up unto his brother a name in Israel; he will not perform the duty of my husband's brother.*

25:8 *Then the **elders** of his city shall call him and speak unto him, and if he stands and says, I desire not to take her;*

25:9 *then shall his brother's wife come unto him in the presence of the **elders** and loose his shoe from off his foot and spit in his face and shall answer and say, So shall it be done unto that man that will not build up his brother's house.*

25:10 *And his name shall be called in Israel, The house of him that is barefoot.*

This is another example that helps show the type of responsibility vested in the elders.

(40) Deuteronomy 27

27:1 *And Moses with the **elders** of Israel commanded the people, saying, Keep all the commandments which I command you this day.*

Here the elders are a continuation of the government that God vested in Moses.

(41) Deuteronomy 29

29:10 *Ye stand today, all of you, before the LORD your God, your princes of your tribes, your **elders**, and your officers, with all the men of Israel,*

29:11 *your little ones, your wives, and thy strangers that dwell within thy camp, from the hewer of thy wood unto the drawer of thy water,*

29:12 *that thou may enter into covenant with the LORD thy God and into his oath, which the LORD thy God makes with thee today,*

29:13 *to confirm thee today as his people and that he may be unto thee as God, as he has said unto thee, and as he has sworn unto thy fathers, to Abraham, to Isaac, and to Jacob.*

The elders were an integral part of the government of Israel as they entered into covenant with God.

(42, 43) Deuteronomy 31

31:9 *And Moses wrote this law and delivered it unto the priests the sons of Levi, who bore the ark of the covenant of the LORD, and unto all the **elders** of Israel.*

31:24 *And it came to pass when Moses had finished writing the words of this law in the book until they were finished,*

31:25 *that Moses commanded the Levites, who bore the ark of the covenant of the LORD, saying,*

31:26 *Take this book of the law and put it in the side of the ark of the covenant of the LORD your God that it may be there for a witness against thee.*

31:27 *For I know thy rebellion and thy stiff neck; behold, while I am yet alive with you today, ye are rebels against the LORD, and how much more after my death?*

31:28 *Gather unto me all the **elders** of your tribes and your officers, and I shall speak these words in their ears and call the heavens and the earth as witnesses against them.*

31:29 *For I know that after my death ye will utterly corrupt yourselves and turn aside from the way which I have commanded you; and evil will befall you in the latter days because ye will have done evil in the sight of*

*the LORD, to provoke him to anger through the work of
your hands.*

The law of Moses was trusted into the hands of the priests who
bore the ark, and into the hands of all the elders.

(44) Deuteronomy 32

*32:7 Remember the days of old; consider the years of
many generations; ask thy father, and he will show thee;
thy **elders**, and they will tell thee;*

*32:8 when the most High caused the Gentiles to be
inherited, when he separated the sons of men, he set the
bounds of the peoples according to the number of the
sons of Israel.*

The elders were responsible for instructing future generations
regarding the wonderful things that God had done.

We have now examined all forty-four references to elders in
the law of Moses. It is clear that elders formed a very important
part of government, all the way from the local to the national
level. There was no authorization in the law, however, for elders
to meddle in the normal affairs of any individual or family
unless a crime had been committed and a witness came forward. Matters of life or death required two or three witnesses.

(45) Joshua 7

*7:6 Then Joshua rent his clothes and fell to the earth
upon his face before the ark of the LORD until the
evening, he and the **elders** of Israel, putting dust upon
their heads.*

Here Joshua and the elders took responsibility after things
went wrong due to the greed of Achan, which caused the entire
nation of Israel to be defeated.

(46, 47) Joshua 8

8:10 *And Joshua rose up early in the morning and numbered the people and went up he and the **elders** of Israel, before the people against Ai.*

The elders and Joshua led the way into battle.

8:33 *And all Israel and their **elders** and officers and their judges stood on one side and on the other near the ark, before the priests the Levites, who bore the ark of the covenant of the LORD, the strangers, as well as the natural born among them, half of them over against Mount Gerizim and half of them over against Mount Ebal, as Moses, the slave of the LORD, had commanded before, that they should bless the people of Israel.*

Again it is very plain that the elders were an important part of the government of Israel.

(48) Joshua 9

9:11 *Therefore, our **elders** and all the inhabitants of our country spoke to us, saying, Take provision with you for the journey and go to meet them and say unto them, We are your slaves; therefore, now make ye a covenant with us.*

The elders of the Gibeonites were invoked as part of a major deception that hoodwinked the leadership of Israel.

(49) Joshua 20

20:4 *And he that flees unto one of these cities shall present himself at the entering of the gate of the city and shall declare his cause in the ears of the **elders** of that city; they shall receive him into the city among them and give him a place, that he may dwell among them.*

This is a reference to the responsibility of the elders in the cities of refuge.

(50) Joshua 23

23:2 *And Joshua called for all Israel and for their **elders** and for their princes and for their judges and for their officers and said unto them, I am old and stricken in age.*

Before he died, Joshua encouraged all the leaders of Israel, starting with the elders.

(51, 52) Joshua 24

24:1 *And Joshua gathered all the tribes of Israel to Shechem and called for the **elders** of Israel and for their princes and for their judges and for their officers, and they presented themselves before God.*

24:31 *And Israel served the LORD all the days of Joshua and all the days of the **elders** that outlived Joshua and who had known all the works of the LORD that he had done with Israel.*

The elders who received the Spirit with Moses in the wilderness and accompanied Joshua into the Promised Land were excellent elders. Many of the elders and people of the following generations, however, were deficient.

(53) Judges 2

2:7 *And the people had served the LORD all the days of Joshua and all the days of the **elders** that outlived Joshua who had seen all the great works of the LORD that he had done with Israel.*

These were elders who had learned to depend upon God. As men of faith, they had watched the unbelieving and disobedient generation die off in the wilderness, even while the mighty hand of God prepared the generation that would enter the Promised Land.

(54, 55) Judges 8

8:13 *And Gideon, the son of Joash, returned from the battle before the sun was up*

8:14 *and caught a young man of the men of Succoth and enquired of him; and he described unto him the principals of Succoth and the **elders** thereof, seventy-seven men.*

8:15 *And he came unto the men of Succoth and said, Behold Zebah and Zalmunna, with whom ye did upbraid me, saying, Are the hands of Zebah and Zalmunna now in thy hand, that we should give bread unto thy men that are weary?*

8:16 *And he took the **elders** of the city and thorns and briars of the wilderness, and with them he taught the men of Succoth.*

"Succoth" means "booths" or "tabernacles," and seventy-seven sounds like a goodly number, yet because of their terrible attitude, these elders were in need of some very sharp discipline at the hands of Gideon (who represents Jesus Christ in this example).

(56, 57, 58, 59, 60, 61) Judges 11

11:5 *And when the sons of Ammon made war against Israel, the **elders** of Gilead went to fetch Jephthah out of the land of Tob;*

11:6 *and they said unto Jephthah, Come, and thou*

shalt be our captain that we may fight with the sons of Ammon.

*11:7 And Jephthah said unto the **elders** of Gilead, Did not ye hate me and expel me out of my father's house? Why, therefore, are ye come unto me now when ye are in distress?*

*11:8 And the **elders** of Gilead said unto Jephthah, For this same reason we turn again to thee now that thou may go with us and fight against the sons of Ammon and be our head over all the inhabitants of Gilead.*

*11:9 Then Jephthah said unto the **elders** of Gilead, If ye bring me home again to fight against the sons of Ammon and the LORD delivers them before me, shall I be your head?*

*11:10 And the **elders** of Gilead said unto Jephthah, Let the LORD hear between us, if we do not comply with thy words.*

*11:11 Then Jephthah went with the **elders** of Gilead, and the people made him head and prince over them; and Jephthah spoke all his words before the LORD in Mizpeh.*

The elders of Gilead had the authority to choose Jephthah as the commander of their army and to offer him the leadership of their country if he won the war.

(62) Judges 21

21:14 And those of Benjamin had returned at that time; and they gave them as wives those whom they had saved alive of the women of Jabeshgilead, and even so they were not enough.

21:15 *And the people repented over Benjamin because the LORD had made a breach in the tribes of Israel.*

21:16 *Then the **elders** of the congregation said, What shall we do for wives for those that remain? For the female sex had been destroyed out of Benjamin.*

21:17 *And they said, Let the inheritance of Benjamin be saved that a tribe not be destroyed out of Israel.*

21:18 *However, we may not give them wives of our daughters, for the sons of Israel have sworn, saying, Cursed be he that gives a wife to anyone of Benjamin.*

21:19 *Then they said, Behold, there is a solemn feast of the LORD in Shiloh yearly in a place which is towards the Aquilon from Bethel and towards the rising of the sun from the highway that goes up from Bethel to Shechem and towards the Negev from Lebonah.*

21:20 *Therefore, they commanded the sons of Benjamin, saying, Go and lie in wait in the vineyards*

21:21 *and watch with care, and when you see the daughters of Shiloh come out to dance in dances, then come out of the vineyards, and each one of you shall rapture a wife of the daughters of Shiloh and go to the land of Benjamin.*

21:22 *And when their fathers or their brethren come unto us to complain, we will say unto them, Be merciful unto us for their sakes because in the war we did not take enough women for all of them; and you could not have given them to them, or ye should be guilty now.*

After war had destroyed the female sex from the tribe of Benjamin and the rest of Israel had sworn an oath to not give their daughters as wives to anyone from Benjamin's tribe, the elders of Israel intervened and came up with a solution to prevent the tribe from becoming extinct. Even so, note that the elders did not determine exactly whom any specific individual should marry.

(63, 64, 65, 66) Ruth 4

4:2 *Then he took ten men of the **elders** of the city and said, Sit down here. And they sat down.*

4:3 *And he said unto the redeemer, Naomi, that is come again out of the field of Moab, sold a parcel of land, which was our brother Elimelech's,*

4:4 *and I decided to cause thee to know this and tell thee to take it before the inhabitants and before the **elders** of my people. If thou wilt redeem it, redeem it, but if thou wilt not redeem it, then tell me that I may know, for there is no one to redeem it besides thee, and I after thee. And he said, I will redeem it.*

4:5 *Then Boaz replied, The day that thou dost receive the field of the hand of Naomi, thou must also receive Ruth, the Moabitess, the wife of the dead, to raise up the name of the dead upon his inheritance.*

4:6 *And the redeemer said, I cannot redeem it for myself lest I ruin my own inheritance; redeem thou; I cede my right to you, for I shall not be able to redeem it.*

4:7 *Now for a long time in Israel there had been this custom concerning redemption or contracts, that for the confirmation of all matters: one plucked off his shoe and gave it to his neighbour, and this was a testimony in Israel.*

4:8 *Therefore, the former owner of the right of redemption said unto Boaz, Buy it thyself. So he drew off his shoe.*

4:9 *And Boaz said unto the **elders** and unto all the people, Ye are witnesses this day that I have bought all that was Elimelech's and all that was Chilion's and Mahlon's, of the hand of Naomi.*

4:10 *Moreover, I also take Ruth, the Moabitess, the wife of Mahlon, as my wife, to raise up the name of the dead upon his inheritance that the name of the dead not be cut off from among his brethren and from the gate of his place. Ye shall be witnesses of this today.*

4:11 *And all the people that were in the gate and the **elders**, said, We are witnesses. The LORD make the woman that is come into thy house like Rachel and like Leah, who built the house of Israel; and be thou a man of valour in Ephratah, and be famous in Bethlehem.*

This is the story of Boaz, the kinsman redeemer (with many parallels to our redemption by Jesus Christ). The elders were very important witnesses of this event.

(67) 1 Samuel 4

4:3 *And when the people returned into the camp, the **elders** of Israel said, Why has the LORD smitten us today before the Philistines? Let us bring the ark of the covenant of the LORD out of Shiloh unto us that when it comes among us, it may save us out of the hand of our enemies.*

In the days of the corrupt priesthood of Eli and his sons, the elders made an extremely unwise choice that resulted in the ark of the covenant being captured by the Philistines.

(68) 1 Samuel 8

8:4 *Then all the **elders** of Israel gathered themselves together and came to Samuel in Ramah*

8:5 *and said unto him, Behold, thou art old, and thy sons do not walk in thy ways; therefore make us a king to judge us like all the Gentiles.*

8:6 *But the thing displeased Samuel when they said, Give us a king to judge us. And Samuel prayed unto the LORD.*

8:7 *And the LORD said unto Samuel, Hearken unto the voice of the people in all that they say unto thee, for they have not rejected thee, but they have rejected me that I should not reign over them.*

Here we have another very bad choice by the elders on behalf of the people, as they rejected God and wanted to have a king reign over them instead.

(69) 1 Samuel 11

11:3 *And the **elders** of Jabesh said unto him, Give us seven days' respite, that we may send messengers unto all the borders of Israel, and then, if there is no one to save us, we will come out to thee.*

Here the elders of Jabesh made a wise choice and gained enough time for help to be found.

(70) 1 Samuel 15

15:26 *And Samuel said unto Saul, I will not return with*

thee, for thou hast rejected the word of the LORD, and the LORD has rejected thee from being king over Israel.

15:27 And as Samuel turned about to go away, he laid hold upon the skirt of his mantle, and it rent.

15:28 And Samuel said unto him, The LORD has rent the kingdom of Israel from thee today and has given it to a neighbour of thine that is better than thou.

15:29 And also the Overcomer of Israel will not lie nor repent concerning this, for he is not a man, that he should repent.

*15:30 Then he said, I have sinned; yet honour me now, I pray thee, before the **elders** of my people and before Israel and turn again with me that I may worship the LORD thy God.*

15:31 So Samuel turned again after Saul, and Saul worshipped the LORD.

Saul seemed more interested in having the support of the elders than the support of the Lord.

(71) 1 Samuel 16

16:1 And the LORD said unto Samuel, How long wilt thou mourn for Saul, seeing I have rejected him from reigning over Israel? Fill thy horn with oil and go; I will send thee to Jesse of Bethlehem for I have provided me a king among his sons.

16:2 And Samuel said, How can I go? If Saul understands it, he will kill me. And the LORD said, Take a heifer with thee and say, I am come to sacrifice to the LORD.

16:3 *And call Jesse to the sacrifice, and I will show thee what thou shalt do, and thou shalt anoint unto me the one whom I name unto thee.*

16:4 *And Samuel did as the LORD said and came to Bethlehem. And the **elders** of the town trembled at his coming and said, Comest thou peaceably?*

Samuel was an old man with a staff, yet the elders of the town knew that God backed up every word that he spoke. These elders demonstrated a healthy respect for the word of the Lord.

(72) 1 Samuel 30

30:26 *And when David came to Ziklag, he sent of the spoil unto the **elders** of Judah, his friends, saying, Behold a blessing for you of the spoil of the enemies of the LORD.*

This helped to set the stage for the elders of Judah to invite David to be their king after the imminent death of King Saul.

(73) 2 Samuel 3

3:17 *And Abner had communication with the **elders** of Israel, saying, Ye sought for David in times past to be king over you;*

3:18 *now then do it, for the LORD has spoken of David, saying, By the hand of my slave David I will save my people Israel out of the hand of the Philistines and out of the hand of all their enemies.*

If David was to reign over all Israel, the elders had to invite him to be their king.

(74) 2 Samuel 5

5:3 *So all the **elders** of Israel came to the king in Hebron; and King David made a covenant with them in Hebron before the LORD; and they anointed David king over Israel.*

King David is an example of Jesus Christ. If Jesus is to reign uniformly over the entire people of God, all the "elders" should be in agreement and enter into a covenant with him.

(75) 2 Samuel 12

12:15 *And Nathan departed unto his house. And the LORD struck the child that Uriah's wife had given birth unto David, and it was very sick.*

12:16 *David, therefore, besought God for the child, and David fasted and went in and lay all night upon the earth.*

12:17 *And the **elders** of his house arose and went to him to raise him up from the earth, but he would not, neither did he eat bread with them.*

David knew that he was in deep trouble with the Lord and that there would be serious consequences as a result of his sin. Therefore he paid no attention to the elders, who attempted to comfort him.

(76, 77) 2 Samuel 17

17:1 *Moreover Ahithophel said unto Absalom, Let me now choose out twelve thousand men, and I will arise and pursue after David this night,*

17:2 *and I will come upon him while he is weary and weak-handed and will make him afraid, and all the people that are with him shall flee; and I will smite the king only.*

17:3 Thus will I turn all the people back unto thee, and when they have returned (for that man is whom thou dost seek), all the people shall be in peace.

*17:4 And this word seemed right in the eyes of Absalom and of all the **elders** of Israel.*

*17:15 Then Hushai said unto Zadok and to Abiathar, the priests, Thus and thus did Ahithophel counselled Absalom and the **elders** of Israel, and thus and thus have I counselled.*

Although the elders of Israel had made a covenant with David and anointed him king, they subsequently turned their backs on him and went along with the rebellion of Absalom. The Lord, however, overturned the brilliant counsel of Ahithophel by using David's friend Hushai.

(78) 2 Samuel 19

*19:11 And King David sent to Zadok and to Abiathar, the priests, saying, Speak unto the **elders** of Judah, saying, Why shall ye be the last to bring the king back to his house? Seeing that the word of all Israel has come to the king, to return him to his house.*

After the tragic death of Absalom, the elders of Judah were forced to do another about-face and receive David once again. They were reluctant, however, and David had to send Zadok and Abiathar, the priests, to reason with them.

(79, 80) 1 Kings 8

*8:1 Then Solomon assembled the **elders** of Israel and*

*all the heads of the tribes, the princes of the families
of the sons of Israel, unto King Solomon in Jerusalem
that they might bring up the ark of the covenant of the
LORD out of the city of David, which is Zion.*

8:2 *And all the men of Israel assembled themselves unto
King Solomon in the month Ethanim, which is the seventh month, on the solemn day.*

8:3 *And all the **elders** of Israel came, and the priests
took up the ark.*

The "solemn day" was likely Yom Kippur (the Day of Atonement or Day of Reconciliation), celebrated on the tenth day of the seventh month. All of the elders of Israel were present when the ark was introduced into its place in the Holy of Holies under the wings of the cherubim, the staves were drawn out, and the glory of God filled the temple so powerfully that the priests *could not stand to minister* (verse 11).

(81, 82) 1 Kings 20

20:5 *And the messengers came again and said, Thus
hath Benhadad said, Although I have sent unto thee,
saying, Thou shalt deliver me thy silver and thy gold
and thy wives and thy children,*

20:6 *yet I will send my slaves unto thee tomorrow
about this time, and they shall search thy house and the
houses of thy slaves; and it shall be that whatever is precious in thine eyes, they shall put it in their hand and
take it away.*

20:7 *Then the king of Israel called all the **elders** of the
land and said, Understand, I pray you, and see how
this man seeks only evil, for he sent unto me for my*

wives and for my children and for my silver and for my gold, and I denied him not.

*20:8 And all the **elders** and all the people said unto him, Hearken not unto him, nor consent.*

Although the king and the elders were willing to part with their wives and children and silver and gold in order to save their own lives, they weren't willing for their enemy to take their idols (which were more precious in their sight).

(83, 84) 1 Kings 21

*21:8 So she wrote letters in Ahab's name and sealed them with his seal and sent the letters unto the **elders** and to the nobles that were in his city dwelling with Naboth.*

21:9 And she wrote in the letters, saying, Proclaim a fast and set Naboth at the head of the people

21:10 and set two men, sons of Belial, before him, to bear witness against him, saying, Thou didst blaspheme God and the king. And then carry him out and stone him that he may die.

*21:11 And the men of his city, even the **elders** and the nobles who were the inhabitants in his city, did as Jezebel had sent unto them and as it was written in the letters which she had sent unto them.*

The elders and nobles went along with wicked Jezebel and participated in the death of an innocent man. This has happened with surprising frequency over the centuries, although in our modern times, the same effect is often achieved by merely destroying the reputation of anyone who gets in the way of the rich and powerful or confronts them with the truth.

(85, 86) 2 Kings 6

*6:32 And Elisha sat in his house, and the **elders** sat
with him; and the king sent a man unto him. But before
the messenger came to him, he said to the **elders**, See
ye how this son of a murderer has sent to take away my
head? Look, when the messenger comes, shut the door,
and hold him fast at the door; is not the sound of his
master's feet behind him?*

Elisha never ran from trouble. In this case, it appears that the
elders sided with Elisha instead of with the wicked king. The
city, however, was under siege, and the king's options were
limited, whereas the elders knew that Elisha had the power of
the Lord behind him.

(87, 88) 2 Kings 10

*10:1 And Ahab had seventy sons in Samaria. And Jehu
wrote letters and sent to Samaria unto the princes
of Jezreel, to the **elders**, and to those that brought up
Ahab's children, saying,*

*10:2 Now as soon as this letter comes to you, unto those
who have your master's sons and who have chariots
and horsemen and who have the arms and munitions
of the city,*

*10:3 see which is the best and most upright of your mas-
ter's sons and set him on his father's throne and fight for
your master's house.*

*10:4 But they were exceedingly afraid and said, Behold,
two kings could not stand before him; how then shall we
stand?*

10:5 And he that was over the house and he that was

*over the city, the **elders** also, and those who had brought*
up the children sent to Jehu, saying, We are thy slaves
and will do all that thou shalt bid us; we will not make
any king; thou shalt do that which is good in thy eyes.

These elders were willing to sacrifice wicked Ahab's seventy sons
(whom they had raised) if this would ensure their own safety.

(89) 2 Kings 19

19:2 And he sent Eliakim, who was over the household,
*and Shebna the scribe and the **elders** of the priests,*
covered with sackcloth, to Isaiah, the prophet, the son of
Amoz,

19:3 to say unto him, Thus hath Hezekiah said, This
day is a day of trouble and of rebuke and blasphemy,
for the sons are come to the place of breaking forth, and
she that gives birth has no strength.

There were elders of the people according to families, tribes, and
the nation of Israel. There were also elders of the priests, and
on this occasion they helped lead the people into repentance
under godly King Hezekiah.

(90) 2 Kings 23

23:1 And the king sent, and they gathered unto him all
*the **elders** of Judah and of Jerusalem.*

This is when King Josiah began his major reforms.

(91) 1 Chronicles 11

*11:3 Therefore, all the **elders** of Israel came to the king*
in Hebron, and David made a covenant with them in
Hebron before the LORD, and they anointed David

king over Israel, according to the word of the LORD by
the hand of Samuel.

Here is another witness to the covenant David made with all
the elders of Israel.

(92) 1 Chronicles 15

15:25 *So David and the **elders** of Israel and the captains*
over thousands went to bring up the ark of the covenant
of the LORD out of the house of Obededom with joy.

By bringing up the ark of the covenant, David demonstrated to
the elders and captains (and to all Israel) that he truly desired
God to reign and rule in Israel.

(93) 1 Chronicles 21

21:16 *And David lifted up his eyes and saw the angel*
of the LORD stand between the heaven and the earth,
having a drawn sword in his hand stretched out over
*Jerusalem. Then David and the **elders** of Israel, who*
were clothed in sackcloth, fell upon their faces.

The elders of Israel were an inseparable part of the government,
and thus they bore responsibility when things went wrong.

(94, 95) 2 Chronicles 5

5:2 *Then Solomon assembled the **elders** of Israel and all*
the heads of the tribes, the princes of the families of the
sons of Israel, unto Jerusalem, to bring up the ark of the
covenant of the LORD out of the city of David, which is
Zion.

5:3 *Therefore, all the men of Israel assembled them-*
selves unto the king in the solemnity which was in the
seventh month.

5:4 *And all the* **elders** *of Israel came, and the Levites took up the ark.*

It was very important for the elders of Israel to participate in bringing the ark of the covenant up to the temple and to witness the glory of God that filled the temple when the ark was positioned in its final resting place.

(96) 2 Chronicles 34

34:29 *Then the king sent and gathered together all the* **elders** *of Judah and Jerusalem.*

This is a second witness to the events immediately preceding the reforms of King Josiah.

(97, 98) Ezra 5

5:5 *For the eyes of their God were upon the* **elders** *of the Jews, and they could not cause them to cease until the matter came to Darius, and then they returned answer by letter concerning this matter.*

5:6 *The copy of the letter that Tatnai, captain of this side the river, and Shetharboznai, and his companions, the Apharsachites, which were on this side the river, sent unto Darius, the king:*

5:7 *they sent a letter unto him, in which was written thus; Unto Darius, the king, all peace.*

5:8 *Be it known unto the king that we went into the province of Judea, to the house of the great God, which is being built with stones of marble, and the timbers are laid in the walls, and this work is going fast and prospers in their hands.*

5:9 *Then we asked the* **elders** *and said unto them thus,*

Who commanded you to build this house and to found these walls?

The eyes of God were upon these elders of the Jews, and clearly it was he who commanded them to build his house and found the walls to his city.

(99, 100, 101) Ezra 6

*6:7 Leave the work of this house of God unto the captain of the Jews and to their **elders** that they may build this house of God in his place.*

*6:8 And by me is given the commandment regarding what ye shall do with the **elders** of these Jews, to build this house of God: that of the king's goods, of the tribute from the other side of the river, the expenses be given unto these men, that they not cease.*

*6:14 And the **elders** of the Jews built, and they prospered according to the prophecy of Haggai, the prophet, and Zechariah, the son of Iddo. They built and finished it, according to the commandment of the God of Israel and according to the commandment of Cyrus and of Darius and of Artaxerxes, king of Persia.*

6:15 And this house was finished on the third day of the month Adar, which was in the sixth year of the reign of Darius, the king.

God prospered the work of the remnant who returned from captivity, under the leadership of their captain and elders.

(102, 103) Ezra 10

10:7 And they made proclamation throughout Judah

and Jerusalem unto all the sons of the captivity, that they should gather themselves together unto Jerusalem

*10:8 and that whoever would not come within three days, according to the counsel of the princes and of the **elders**, all his substance should be forfeited and himself separated from the congregation of those that had been carried away.*

*10:14 Let our rulers of all the congregation now stand, and let all those who have taken strange women in our cities come at appointed times, and with them the **elders** of each city and the judges thereof, until the fierce wrath of our God for this matter is turned from us.*

The princes and elders took the lead in dealing with the "strange women" whose offspring didn't even speak the right language. Today there are many so-called sons of God who are seemingly married to congregations that can only be compared to strange women, where no one truly understands the universal language of the love of God. Now, even as then, a separation is called for, and the true princes and elders recognized by God must take a stand.

(104) Psalm 105

105:21 He made him lord of his house and ruler of all his substance:

*105:22 To bind his princes at his pleasure and teach his **elders** wisdom.*

This refers to Joseph in Egypt, when Pharaoh brought him out of prison to reign.

(105) Psalm 107

*107:32 Let them exalt him also in the congregation of the people and praise him in the assembly of the **elders**.*

There is *the congregation of the people* and also *the assembly of the elders.*

(106) Psalm 119

119:98 Thou through thy commandments hast made me wiser than mine enemies, for they are eternal unto me.

119:99 I have more understanding than all my teachers, for thy testimonies have been my meditation.

*119:100 I understand more than the **elders** because I keep thy precepts.*

This is messianic; it applies to Jesus Christ and also to those who are hid in him.

(107) Proverbs 31

*31:23 Her husband is known in the gates when he sits among the **elders** of the land.*

A normal place for the assembly of the elders was in the gates of the town or city.

(108) Isaiah 3

*3:14 The LORD will come with judgment against the **elders** of his people and against these his princes, for ye have eaten up the vineyard; the spoil of the poor is in your houses.*

3:15 What do you mean that ye beat my people to

pieces and grind the faces of the poor? saith the Lord GOD of the hosts.

When Jesus came, he didn't make positive reference to any of the Jewish elders. Within thirty-seven years after these elders condemned Jesus to death, the entire city of Jerusalem was laid waste, the temple was destroyed, and the rebellious Jews as well as their elders were dead. This was Jesus's first coming. What will happen at his second?

(109) Isaiah 37

37:1 And it came to pass when king Hezekiah heard it, that he rent his clothes and covered himself with sackcloth and went into the house of the LORD.

*37:2 And he sent Eliakim, who was over the household, and Shebna the scribe and the **elders** of the priests covered with sackcloth unto Isaiah the prophet the son of Amoz.*

This was a second witness to the national repentance under the reign of King Hezekiah, in which the elders of the priests were important leaders. Now we are in the priesthood of all believers, and the Holy Spirit is available to bring each and every Christian to maturity in Christ.

(110, 111) Jeremiah 19

*19:1 Thus hath the LORD said, Go and buy a potter's earthen bottle, and take of the **elders** of the people and of the **elders** of the priests;*

19:2 and go forth unto the valley of the son of Hinnom, which is by the entry by the east gate, and proclaim there the words that I shall tell thee.

*19:3 Therefore thou shalt say, Hear ye the word of the
LORD, O kings of Judah, and inhabitants of Jerusalem.
Thus saith the LORD of the hosts, God of Israel: Behold,
I bring evil upon this place, such that whoever hears of
it, his ears shall tingle.*

The elders of the people and the elders of the priests had the
responsibility to pass on this important prophetic message
to the people, but there is little evidence that they relayed the
alarm properly. Instead, many of them were part of the problem. It wasn't long before the city was destroyed, many of the
people were carried away captive to Babylon, and others fled
to Egypt and died there.

(112) Jeremiah 26

*26:16 Then the princes and all the people said unto the
priests and to the prophets: This man is not worthy to
die, for he has spoken to us in the name of the LORD
our God.*

*26:17 Then certain of the **elders** of the land rose up and
spoke to all the congregation of the people, saying,*

*26:18 Micah the Morasthite prophesied in the days of
Hezekiah king of Judah and spoke to all the people of
Judah, saying, Thus hath the LORD of the hosts said;
Zion shall be plowed like a field, and Jerusalem shall
become heaps, and the temple mount as the high places
of a forest.*

*26:19 Did Hezekiah king of Judah and all Judah put
him at all to death? Did he not fear the LORD and
besought the LORD, and the LORD himself repented of
the evil which he had pronounced against them? Shall
we commit such great evil against our souls?*

Here some of the elders helped to save the life of Jeremiah. However, the vast majority of the people and of the elders didn't take Jeremiah's prophetic warning to heart, and so in the end, they were killed, captured, or forced to flee to Egypt, where they died.

(113) Jeremiah 29

29:1 *Now these are the words of the letter that Jeremiah the prophet sent from Jerusalem unto the residue of the **elders** which were carried away captives, and to the priests and to the prophets and to all the people whom Nebuchadnezzar had carried away captive from Jerusalem to Babylon.*

Some of the elders and priests and even prophets were among those carried away captive from Jerusalem to Babylon. When Jeremiah wrote them a letter, I bet they paid attention! Jeremiah wrote that the Babylonian captivity would last for seventy years. Many kept that hope kindled in their hearts and in the hearts of their children and grandchildren until the time was fulfilled and a remnant was allowed to return and rebuild the walls of Jerusalem and the temple.

(114) Lamentations 1

1:19 *I called unto my lovers, but they have deceived me; my priests and my **elders** in the city perished seeking food to maintain their lives.*

Amos prophesied an end-time famine of hearing the words of the Lord (Amos 8:11-12). When this happens, many modern "elders" and "priests" will perish spiritually due to the lack of *food to maintain their lives.*

(115) Lamentations 2

*2:10 The **elders** of the daughter of Zion sat upon the ground and are silent: they have cast up dust upon their heads; they have girded themselves with sackcloth; the daughters of Jerusalem hung their heads down to the ground.*

Elders are mentioned five times in the short book of Lamentations. This is the second reference.

(116) Lamentations 4

*4:16 The anger of the LORD has separated them; he will never look upon them again. They did not respect the countenance of the priests, nor did they have compassion on the **elders**.*

The fact that someone was an elder or a priest didn't save them when judgment fell upon the wicked city of Jerusalem.

(117, 118) Lamentations 5

*5:12 Princes were hanged up by their hand; the countenance of the **elders** was not honoured.*

5:13 They took the young men to grind, and the children fell under the wood.

*5:14 The **elders** have ceased from the gate, the young men from their music.*

5:15 The joy of our heart is ceased; our dance is turned into mourning.

5:16 The crown is fallen from our head; woe now unto us, for we have sinned!

This happened to elders who didn't set a righteous example and who failed to lead the people of God into corporate repentance. Many groups today place an emphasis on the need for individual repentance, but they remain closed to the idea that they and their group may need to corporately repent of things that they have done and continue to do that are abominable before God. Some of this may have do with dogmas and traditions of "elders" that have become ingrained over time.

(119) Ezekiel 7

7:25 *A cutting off comes, and they shall seek peace, and there shall be none.*

7:26 *Destruction shall come upon destruction, and rumour shall be upon rumour; then they shall seek an answer from the prophet, but the law shall perish from the priest and counsel from the* **elders***.*

There will soon be another cutting off as we enter into what is known prophetically as the end-time day of the Lord.

(120, 121, 122) Ezekiel 8

8:1 *And it came to pass in the sixth year, in the sixth month, in the fifth day of the month, as I sat in my house, and the* **elders** *of Judah sat before me, that the hand of the Lord GOD fell there upon me.*

8:2 *And I saw, and behold a likeness as the appearance of fire; from the appearance of his loins downward was fire; and from his loins upward, as the appearance of brightness, as the colour of amber.*

8:3 *And that likeness put forth his hand and took me by the locks of my head; and the Spirit lifted me up between the heaven and the earth and brought me in the visions of God to Jerusalem, to the door of the inner gate that looks toward the north where the habitation of the image of jealousy was, which provokes to jealousy.*

8:4 And, behold, the glory of the God of Israel was there like the vision that I saw in the plain.

8:5 Then he said unto me, Son of man, lift up thine eyes now the way toward the north. So I lifted up my eyes the way toward the north, and behold northward at the gate of the altar this image of jealousy in the entry.

8:6 He said furthermore unto me, Son of man, seest thou what they do? even the great abominations that the house of Israel commits here to cause me to go far away from my sanctuary? but turn thee yet again, and thou shalt see greater abominations.

8:7 And he brought me to the entrance of the court, and when I looked, behold a hole in the wall.

8:8 Then said he unto me, Son of man, dig now in the wall; and when I had dug in the wall, behold a door.

8:9 And he said unto me, Go in and see the wicked abominations that they do here.

8:10 So I went in and saw; and behold every form of serpent and beasts; the abomination and all the idols of the house of Israel portrayed upon the wall round about.

8:11 And there stood before them seventy men of the elders of the house of Israel, and in the midst of them stood Jaazaniah the son of Shaphan, each man with his censer in his hand; and a thick cloud of incense went up.

*8:12 Then said he unto me, Son of man, hast thou seen what the **elders** of the house of Israel do in the dark, each man in the chambers of his imagery? for they say, The LORD does not see us; the LORD has forsaken the earth.*

God had Ezekiel publicly prophesy in the presence of the elders of Judah about the abominations that they were committing privately. Now they had seventy elders who not only didn't have the Spirit of God, but they had a spirit that produced abomination and every type of contamination, and they even had an image of jealousy that caused the true presence of God to leave their midst.

(123) Ezekiel 9

9:4 and the LORD said unto him, Go through the midst of the city, through the midst of Jerusalem and set a mark upon the foreheads of the men that sigh and that cry out because of all the abominations that are done in the midst of her.

9:5 And to the others he said in my hearing, Go after him through the city and smite; do not let your eye forgive, neither have mercy.

*9:6 Slay the old, the young men, and the virgins, the children and the women, but do not come near anyone upon whom is the mark; and ye must begin from my sanctuary. Then they began with the men, the **elders**, which were in front of the temple.*

When the judgment fell on apostate Jerusalem, it began with the elders. In our own time, something similar will happen soon regarding those who are apostate in Israel and the Church.

(124) Ezekiel 14

14:1 *Then certain of the **elders** of Israel came unto me and sat before me.*

14:2 *And the word of the LORD came unto me, saying,*

14:3 *Son of man, these men have caused their uncleanness to come up over their heart and have established the stumblingblock of their iniquity before their face: should I be enquired of at all by them?*

After a certain level of contamination, iniquity, and rebellion, God may decide to break off communication with certain elders.

(125, 126) Ezekiel 20

20:1 *And it came to pass in the seventh year, in the fifth month, the tenth day of the month, that certain of the **elders** of Israel came to enquire of the LORD and sat before me.*

20:2 *Then came the word of the LORD unto me, saying,*

20:3 *Son of man, speak unto the **elders** of Israel and say unto them, Thus hath the Lord GOD said: Are ye come to enquire of me? As I live, said the Lord GOD, I will not be enquired of by you.*

Here God doubled down on his decision to not be enquired of by contaminated elders who refused to repent.

(127) Ezekiel 27

27:9 *The **elders** of Gebal and the wise men thereof were in thee to repair thy breaches: all the galleys of the sea with their rowers were in thee to negotiate thy business dealings.*

This refers to Tyre, whose king is sometimes a symbol of the devil (Isaiah 23). The elders of Gebal (meaning "border" or "limits") and the wise men thereof were unable to "repair the breaches" with legalistic boundaries or limits. No amount of rules or submission to man will ever repair the breaches. The only way to solve the problem is by yielding to the internal presence of the Spirit of God (Romans 8).

(128) Joel 1

*1:14 Sanctify a fast, call a solemn assembly, gather the **elders** and all the inhabitants of the earth into the house of the LORD your God and cry unto the LORD.*

1:15 Alas for the day! for the day of the LORD is at hand, and it shall come as a destruction from the Almighty.

We are fast approaching the day when everything that can be shaken will be shaken.

(129) Joel 2

2:12 Therefore also now, saith the LORD, turn unto me with all your heart and with fasting and with weeping, and with mourning:

2:13 and rend your heart, and not your garments, and turn unto the LORD your God for he is gracious and compassionate, slow to anger and great in mercy, and he does repent of chastisement.

2:14 Who knows if he will return and repent and leave a blessing behind him even a present and a drink offering unto the LORD your God?

2:15 *Blow the shofar in Zion, sanctify a fast, call a solemn assembly:*

2:16 *gather the people, sanctify the meeting, assemble the **elders**, gather the children and those that suck the breasts; let the bridegroom go forth of his chamber and the bride out of her closet.*

2:17 *Let the priests, the ministers of the LORD, weep between the porch and the altar, and let them say, Forgive thy people, O LORD, and do not give thine heritage to reproach that the Gentiles should rule over her: why should they say among the peoples, Where is their God?*

2:18 *Then the LORD will be jealous for his earth and forgive his people.*

When a solemn assembly is called for, we are to gather the people, sanctify the meeting, assemble the elders, and then gather the children. It's obvious that the elders have a responsibility to keep the meeting clean and sanctified (set apart exclusively for the purposes of God). We can also see from this passage that the heart of God is to forgive and restore his people. It is essential, however, that he deal directly with each individual heart.

(130) Matthew 15

15:1 *Then certain scribes and Pharisees of Jerusalem came unto Jesus, saying,*

15:2 *Why do thy disciples transgress the tradition of the **elders**? For they do not wash their hands when they eat bread.*

15:3 *But he answered and said unto them, Why do*

ye also transgress the commandment of God by your tradition?

Why not accommodate the scribes and Pharisees in the interest of peace? Why not tell the disciples to wash their hands whenever there were any elders around? What could be wrong with washing hands before eating? Jesus knew, however, that this point was only the tip of the iceberg. Attempting to placate the elders would at best result in a false peace, for they would soon find other issues with which to quench the liberty of the Spirit and go against the will of God.

Therefore, Jesus did not accommodate *the tradition of the elders*. Instead, he turned their question back on them and accused them of transgressing the commandment of God by their tradition. This placed the ball back in their court in such a manner that the only way the elders could have made peace with Jesus would have been for them to have entered into corporate repentance and to have been willing to go back as far as necessary and undo tradition. Should we be surprised that they refused? This same type of situation has played out over and over throughout church history.

(131) Matthew 16

16:21 *From that time forth Jesus began to declare unto his disciples, how it was expedient for him to go unto Jerusalem and to suffer many things of the **elders** and the princes of the priests and of the scribes and to be killed and to be raised again the third day.*

The elders not only refused to corporately repent, but they also became Jesus's mortal enemies.

(132) Matthew 21

21:23 *And when he was come into the temple, the*

*princes of the priests and the **elders** of the people came
unto him as he was teaching and said, By what authority doest thou these things? and who gave thee this
authority?*

This is a direct confrontation between the human government
and authority of the priests and elders, and the God-given
authority of Jesus inside the temple that was supposed to be
the house of his Father.

(133, 134, 135, 136) Matthew 26

*26:3 Then the princes of the priests and the scribes and
the **elders** of the people assembled together in the palace
of the high priest, who was called Caiaphas,*

*26:4 and took counsel that they might take Jesus by
guile and kill him.*

*26:47 And while he yet spoke, behold, Judas, one of
the twelve, came, and with him a great multitude with
swords and staves, from the princes of the priests and
elders of the people.*

*26:57 And those that had laid hold on Jesus led him
away to Caiaphas the high priest, where the scribes and
the **elders** were assembled.*

*26:59 Now the princes of the priests and the **elders** and
all the council sought false witness against Jesus, to put
him to death;*

The princes of the priests and the scribes and the elders of
the people were hypocrites who wanted to condemn Jesus for
breaking the law, while at the same time they themselves had
absolutely no scruples.

(137, 138, 139, 140, 141) Matthew 27

27:1 *When the morning was come, all the princes of the priests and the **elders** of the people took counsel against Jesus to put him to death,*

27:2 *and when they had bound him, they led him away and delivered him to Pontius Pilate the governor.*

27:3 *Then Judas, who had betrayed him, when he saw that he was condemned, repented and returned the thirty pieces of silver to the princes of the priests and the **elders**,*

27:4 *saying, I have sinned in that I have betrayed the innocent blood. And they said, What is that to us? Thou shalt see to it.*

Even Judas learned a hard lesson about the hypocrisy of the priests and elders.

27:12 *And being accused by the princes of the priests and the **elders**, he [Jesus] answered nothing.*

Jesus chose not to defend himself, even against accusations that the priests and elders obviously knew to be false.

27:20 *But the princes of the priests and the **elders** persuaded the multitude that they should ask for Barabbas and destroy Jesus.*

The priests and elders persuaded the multitude to free a known murderer and destroy the innocent Jesus.

27:41 *Likewise also the princes of the priests mocking him [Jesus], with the scribes and **elders**, said,*

27:42 *He saved others; he cannot save himself. If he is the King of Israel, let him now come down from the cross, and we will believe him.*

It wasn't enough to present false witnesses and press false charges; they also mocked him. These types of people still do the same thing.

(142) Matthew 28

28:12 *And when they* [the chief priests] *were assembled with the **elders** and had taken counsel, they gave a large amount of money to the soldiers,*

28:13 *saying, Say ye, His disciples came by night and stole him away while we slept.*

Faced with undeniable evidence of Jesus's resurrection, instead of recognizing their own sin and rebellion, the chief priests and elders preferred to buy off the Roman soldiers. Doubling down on their hypocrisy, however, eventually caused the destruction of virtually everything they were so desperately trying to preserve.

(143, 144) Mark 7

7:1 *Then came together unto him the Pharisees and some of the scribes, who had come from Jerusalem,*

7:2 *who upon seeing some of his disciples eat bread with common, that is to say, with unwashed, hands, they condemned them.*

7:3 *For the Pharisees and all the Jews, unless they wash their hands often, eat not, holding the tradition of the **elders**.*

7:5 *Then the Pharisees and scribes asked him, Why do thy disciples not walk according to the tradition of the **elders** but eat bread with unwashed hands?*

7:6 *He answered and said unto them, Well has Esaias*

prophesied of you hypocrites, as it is written, This people honours me with their lips, but their heart is far from me.

7:7 Howbeit in vain do they honor me, teaching for doctrines the commandments of men.

This is a second witness of Jesus's confrontation with the Pharisees and some of the scribes regarding the tradition of the elders.

(145) Mark 8

*8:31 And he began to teach them that it was convenient that the Son of man must suffer many things and be rejected of the **elders** and of the princes of the priests and of the scribes, and be killed and after three days rise again.*

This is a second witness of the fact that the elders, princes of the priests, and scribes were Jesus's mortal enemies.

(146) Mark 11

*11:27 And they returned to Jerusalem, and as he was walking in the temple, the princes of the priests and the scribes and the **elders** came*

11:28 and said unto him, By what faculty doest thou these things? and who gave thee this faculty to do these things?

This is a second witness of the confrontation in the temple, pitting the authority and government of men against the authority and government of God.

(147, 148) Mark 14

14:43 And immediately, while he yet spoke, Judas came,

*who was one of the twelve, and with him a multitude
with swords and staves from the princes of the priests
and of the scribes and of the **elders**.*

This is a second witness of the betrayal of Jesus by Judas into
the hands of the corrupt priests, scribes, and elders.

*14:53 And they brought Jesus to the high priest, and
with him were assembled all the princes of the priests
and the **elders** and the scribes.*

(149) Mark 15

*15:1 And straightway in the morning the princes of the
priests having held a consultation with the **elders** and
with the scribes and with the whole council, took Jesus
away bound and delivered him to Pilate.*

This is a second witness of the crooked trial contrived by the
priests and elders and scribes.

(150) Luke 7

*7:2 And a certain centurion's slave, who was dear unto
him, was sick and ready to die.*

*7:3 And when he heard of Jesus, he sent unto him the
elders of the Jews, beseeching him that he would come
and free his slave.*

*7:4 And when they came to Jesus, they besought him
instantly, saying, That he is worthy that this should be
done for him,*

*7:5 for he loves our nation and he has built us a
synagogue.*

This is further evidence that some of the elders of the Jews, deep down inside, really knew who Jesus was.

(151) Luke 9

9:21 And he straitly charged them and commanded them not to tell anyone this,

*9:22 saying, The Son of man must suffer many things and be rejected of the **elders** and of the princes of the priests and scribes and be slain and be raised the third day.*

(152) Luke 20

*20:1 And it came to pass that on one of those days as he taught the people in the temple and preached the gospel, the princes of the priests and the scribes came upon him with the **elders***

20:2 and spoke unto him, saying, Tell us, by what authority does thou these things? or who is he that gave thee this authority?

These passages in Luke constitute a third witness against the elders and priests and scribes.

(153, 154) Luke 22

*22:52 Then Jesus said unto the princes of the priests and captains of the temple and the **elders**, who were come to him, Are ye come out as against a thief with swords and staves?*

*22:66 And as soon as it was day, the **elders** of the people and the princes of the priests and the scribes came together and led him into their council, saying,*

This completes the third witness against the elders of the people and the princes (elders) of the priests. According to Jewish law, every matter of life or death requires two or three witnesses. The elders and priests and scribes thought that they had condemned Jesus by their witness, but they were really condemning themselves.

(It's interesting to note that the gospel of John doesn't contain the word "elders.")

(155, 156, 157) Acts 4

4:5 *And it came to pass on the next day that their princes and **elders** and scribes*

4:6 *and Annas, the high priest, and Caiaphas and John and Alexander and as many as were of the kindred of the high priest were gathered together at Jerusalem.*

4:7 *And when they had set them in the midst, they asked, By what power or by what name have ye done this?*

4:8 *Then Peter, filled with the Holy Spirit, said unto them, Ye princes of the people and **elders** of Israel,*

4:9 *if we this day be examined of the good deed done to the impotent man, by what means he is made whole,*

4:10 *be it known unto you all and to all the people of Israel that in the name of Jesus Christ of Nazareth, whom ye crucified, whom God raised from the dead, even by him does this man stand here before you whole.*

4:23 *And being let go, they went to their own company and reported all that the princes of the priests and the **elders** had said unto them.*

Even after Jesus's death, resurrection, and ascension – even after the outpouring of the Holy Spirit upon the disciples on the day of Pentecost, with its mighty display of the power of God – the elders, scribes, and priests continued in their evil actions and their unbelief.

(158) Acts 5

5:21 *And when they heard that, they entered into the temple early in the morning and taught. In the meantime, the prince of the priests came, and those that were with him, and called the council together and all the* **elders** *of the sons of Israel, and sent to the prison to have them brought.*

All the elders of the sons of Israel included the seventy elders of the Sanhedrin who had condemned Jesus. Now they thought that they had the apostles securely locked up in prison, when in reality the angel of the Lord had let them out and they were standing in the temple, teaching. Scripture states that the real reason the elders locked up the apostles was jealousy (Acts 5:12-17).

(159) Acts 6

6:12 *And they stirred up the people and the* **elders** *and the scribes and came upon him* [Stephen] *and caught him and brought him to the council*

6:13 *and set up false witnesses, who said, This man does not cease to speak blasphemous words against this holy place and the law,*

6:14 *for we have heard him say that this Jesus of Nazareth shall destroy this place and shall change the traditions which Moses delivered us.*

The elders were behind Stephen's murder.

(160) Acts 11

11:29 *Then the disciples, each one according to what he had, determined to send relief unto the brethren who dwelt in Judea,*

11:30 *which they likewise did and sent it to the **elders** by the hands of Barnabas and Saul.*

This is the first mention of reliable elders in the New Testament,[145] and by this point an estimated eleven or twelve years, perhaps more, had gone by since the outpouring of the Holy Spirit on the day of Pentecost. Why were godly elders not mentioned sooner in the book of Acts? Maybe there weren't any! The Greek word for elders is *presbuteros,* meaning "older" or "mature." Perhaps it took this long for some of Jesus's followers to reach maturity in Christ and demonstrate mature fruit of the Holy Spirit. Many of the Jewish elders mentioned in Matthew, Mark, Luke, and the first chapters of Acts certainly demonstrated maturity in the fallen nature of Adam as they spread words of bitter poison like the seeds of tares at harvest time.

This Scripture also demonstrates that godly elders definitely have the authority to oversee financial matters related to the congregation or community that they represent.

(161) Acts 14

14:19 *And certain Jews from Antioch and Iconium came there, who persuaded the people, and, having stoned Paul, drew him out of the city, supposing he was dead.*

14:20 *But as the disciples stood round about him, he rose up and came into the city, and the next day he departed with Barnabas to Derbe.*

145 Joseph Benson, in his commentary of 1850, dates this verse at AD 44 and the outpouring of the Holy Spirit on the day of Pentecost at AD 33.

14:21 *And when they had preached the gospel to that city and had taught many, they returned again to Lystra and to Iconium and Antioch,*

14:22 *confirming the souls of the disciples and exhorting them to remain in the faith, and that we must through much tribulation enter into the kingdom of God.*

14:23 *And having ordained **elders** for them in every congregation and having prayed with fasting, they commended them to the Lord on whom they believed.*

Barnabas and Paul, as apostles of Jesus Christ, definitely had the authority to ordain or set in elders whom they selected. On this journey, Barnabas was clearly senior to Paul. They decided to ordain elders in every congregation (they may have ordained individuals who were more or less mature, having been formed in the Jewish synagogues, although many such elders would be prone to legalism). Later in his ministry, Paul appeared a bit more hesitant to do this early on in the formation of each congregation, preferring instead to wait until people came to maturity in Christ. Even after spending months or even a year or two in each place, after a prudent amount of time, he wrote to Timothy or Titus and requested that they set elders in place in each congregation. This fits with the situation described earlier regarding the congregation in Jerusalem, in which the first mention of elders comes eleven or twelve years after the outpouring of the Holy Spirit on the day of Pentecost.

(162, 163, 164, 165, 166) Acts 15

15:1 *Then certain men who came down from Judaea taught the brethren and said, Except ye be circumcised after the manner of Moses, ye cannot be saved.*

15:2 *When therefore Paul and Barnabas had no small*

*dissension and disputation with them, they determined
that Paul and Barnabas and certain other of them
should go up to Jerusalem unto the apostles and **elders**
about this question.*

15:3 *And they, being accompanied by some from the
congregation, passed through Phenice and Samaria,
declaring the conversion of the Gentiles, and they
caused great joy unto all the brethren.*

15:4 *And when they were come to Jerusalem, they were
received by the congregation and by the apostles and
elders, and they declared all the things that God had
done with them.*

15:5 *But there rose up certain of the sect of the
Pharisees who had believed, saying, That it was needful
to circumcise them and to command them to keep the
law of Moses.*

15:6 *And the apostles and **elders** came together to consider of this matter.*

15:7 *And when there had been much disputing, Peter
rose up and said unto them, Men and brethren, ye
know how that a good while ago God chose that the
Gentiles by my mouth should hear the word of the gospel and believe.*

15:8 *And God, who knows the hearts, bore them witness, giving them the Holy Spirit, even as he did unto
us,*

15:9 *and put no difference between us and them, purifying their hearts by faith.*

15:10 *Now therefore why tempt ye God, putting a yoke*

upon the neck of the disciples, which neither our fathers nor we were able to bear?

15:11 *For we believe that through the grace of the Lord Jesus Christ we shall be saved, even as they.*

15:12 *Then all the multitude kept silence and gave audience to Barnabas and Paul, declaring what great miracles and wonders God had wrought among the Gentiles by them.*

15:13 *And after they had become silent, James answered, saying, Men and brethren, hearken unto me:*

15:14 *Simeon has declared how God first visited the Gentiles, to take out of them a people for his name.*

15:15 *And to this agree the words of the prophets; as it is written,*

15:16 *After this I will return and will restore the tabernacle of David, which is fallen down; and I will repair its ruins, and I will set it up again,*

15:17 *that the men that are left might seek after the Lord, and all the Gentiles, upon whom my name is called, saith the Lord, who does all these things.*

15:18 *Known unto God are all his works from the beginning of the world.*

15:19 *Therefore my sentence is that those from among the Gentiles who are converted to God not be troubled,*

15:20 *but that we write unto them that they abstain from pollutions of idols and from fornication and from things strangled and from blood.*

15:21 *For Moses of old time has in every city those that preach him, being read in the synagogues every sabbath day.*

15:22 *Then it pleased the apostles and **elders**, with the whole congregation,*[146] *to send chosen men of their own company to Antioch with Paul and Barnabas; namely, Judas surnamed Barsabas and Silas, principal men among the brethren;*

15:23 *and they wrote letters by them after this manner: The apostles and **elders** and brethren send greeting unto the brethren who are of the Gentiles in Antioch and Syria and Cilicia;*

15:24 *forasmuch as we have heard that certain ones who went out from us have troubled you with words, subverting your souls, saying, Ye must be circumcised and keep the law, to whom we gave no such commandment,*

15:25 *it seemed good unto us, being assembled with one accord, to send chosen men unto you with our beloved Barnabas and Paul,*

15:26 *men that have hazarded their lives for the name of our Lord Jesus Christ.*

15:27 *We have sent therefore Judas and Silas, who shall also tell you the same things by mouth.*

15:28 *For it seemed good to the Holy Spirit and to us to lay upon you no greater burden than these necessary things:*

15:29 *that ye abstain from foods offered to idols and*

---

146 Greek *ekklesia* – called-out ones.

*from blood and from things strangled and from fornica-
tion; from which if ye keep yourselves, ye shall do well.
Fare ye well.*

This passage shows that first the apostles and then the elders
were responsible for leading the congregation and resolving,
according to the light and guidance of the Holy Spirit, any
spiritual or doctrinal problems that might come up.

(167) Acts 16

16:4 *And as they went through the cities, they asked
them to keep the decrees that had been determined by
the apostles and **elders** who were at Jerusalem.*

16:5 *And so the congregations were established in the
faith and increased in number daily.*

The decrees that had been determined by the apostles and elders
were essentially to place the Gentile believers at liberty to follow
the leading of the Holy Spirit in good conscience without being
under the burden of the law of Moses. Only four *necessary things*
were requested: *that ye abstain from foods offered to idols and
from blood and from things strangled and from fornication.*[147]

No obligatory religious rites or rituals were mentioned that
would require an intermediary clergy. No rules or regulations
were set forth in which the apostles or elders were to intervene
in or approve of personal decisions in the lives of individuals
or families regarding marriage, secular vocation, place of resi-
dence, etc. The people of the congregation were free to be led
of the Holy Spirit and to enjoy the glorious liberty of the sons
of God (Romans 8:21; Galatians 5:1; James 1:25, 2:12).

---

147 Essentially the rites and rituals of the entire book of Leviticus were fulfilled
and turned into reality by the one-time sacrifice of Jesus Christ. Now that we're
covered by the blood of Jesus Christ and led by the Holy Spirit, there are only
four things with which Gentile believers are asked to comply. This is nothing
short of amazing!

(168) Acts 20

20:16 For Paul had determined to sail by Ephesus, not to detain himself in Asia, for he hasted to keep the day of Pentecost, if it were possible for him, in Jerusalem.

*20:17 And from Miletus he sent to Ephesus and called the **elders** of the congregation.*

Paul called the elders, and they responded.

(169) Acts 21

21:17 And when we arrived at Jerusalem, the brethren received us gladly.

*21:18 And the day following, Paul went in with us to see James, and all the **elders** were gathered.*

21:19 And when he had saluted them, he declared particularly what things God had wrought among the Gentiles by his ministry.

21:20 And when they heard it, they glorified the Lord and said unto him, Thou seest, brother, how many thousands of Jews there are who have believed, and they are all zealous of the law.

Among the thousands of Jews who had believed, there were undoubtedly many elders who also continued to be *zealous of the law*. After consolidating the victory (largely brought about by the words of Peter and James) and after the general agreement among the apostles and elders not to submit the Gentile believers to the law of Moses, Paul didn't fight with the Jewish elders. Instead, he quietly accepted their suggestions, even though later this meekness almost resulted in his death (his life was saved when Roman soldiers snatched him from the furious Jews and cast him into a Roman prison). Within a few years, the temple was destroyed, and no one could offer blood sacrifices there under the law even if they wanted to. Since that time, no one has been able to rebuild the temple in Jerusalem, and it has been crystal clear that we are the temple and that God is the one who builds it out of living stones, without the help of human hands (Colossians 2:10-11; 1 Corinthians 3:16-17; 2 Corinthians 6:16-18).

(170) Acts 22

22:4 *And I persecuted this way unto the death, binding and delivering into prisons both men and women.*

22:5 *As also the prince of the priests bears me witness, and all the estate of the **elders**, from whom also I received letters unto the brethren, and went to Damascus to bring those who were bound there unto Jerusalem to be punished.*

When Paul (who had been Saul) persecuted the believers, he was given letters (or credentials) by all the elders of the Jewish establishment, as a governing body.

(171) Acts 23

23:14 *And they came to the princes of the priests and the **elders** and said, We have made a vow of anathema that we will eat nothing until we have slain Paul.*

The priests and elders, along with some activists, were involved in a plot to kill Paul.

(172) Acts 24

24:1 *And after five days Ananias, the prince of the priests, descended with the **elders** and with a certain* *orator named Tertullus, who informed the governor against Paul.*

The Jewish elders continued to plot against Paul.

(173) Acts 25

25:14 And when they had been there many days, Festus declared Paul's cause unto the king, saying, There is a certain man left in bonds by Felix,

*25:15 about whom, when I was at Jerusalem, the princes of the priests and the **elders** of the Jews informed me, desiring to have vengeance against him.*

Even though there was no valid legal case against Paul, the elders of the Jews wanted vengeance against him.

(174) 1 Timothy 4

*4:14 Neglect not the gift that is in thee, which is given unto thee to prophesy, through the laying on of the hands of the **elders**.*

It was known that the Holy Spirit could come upon a person by the laying on of hands by the apostles. This is the first indication in Scripture that a gift of the Holy Spirit (such as prophecy) could come by the laying on of the hands of the elders. It follows that apostles could also be elders (1 Peter 5:1; 2 John 1), although it's clear that not all elders are apostles. Another interesting thought is that when Jesus sent forth his twelve disciples as apostles, they were obviously not fully mature, and even Judas was among them (Luke 6:13-16). The signs of an apostle, however, were definitely upon these disciples (Mark 6:7-13).

(175) 1 Timothy 5

*5:17 Let the **elders** that govern well be counted worthy*

*of double honour, especially those who labour in the
word and doctrine.*

*5:18 For the scripture saith, Thou shalt not muzzle the
ox that treads out the grain. And, The labourer is worthy of his reward.*

*5:19 Against an elder do not receive an accusation,
unless there are two or three witnesses.*

Some commentators seem to think that the titles of elder, pastor,
and bishop are virtually the same and that these three words
are interchangeable. I am not of that opinion, although obviously there can be some overlap.[148] The meaning of the word
"pastor" is the same as the meaning of the word "shepherd."
An elder (someone who is mature in Christ) is not exactly the
same as a pastor (or shepherd), although it could be quite possible for someone to be both. David was a shepherd of sheep
well before he was mature, and today there could be many like
young David, who are definitely not elders but who yet have a
call from God to shepherd children or young people.

It's apparent in the above Scripture that some, but not all,
elders *labour in the word and doctrine.* Therefore, it follows
that not all elders are pastors and teachers. Some elders are
worthy of double honor and some aren't. (For example, in the
Old Testament, the eldest son received a double portion of the
inheritance.)

Elders can intervene in a given situation where, on the evidence of only one witness, something may have gone wrong.
For an accusation against an elder to be received, however,
there must be two or three witnesses. (Under the law of Moses,
all matters of life or death required two or three witnesses.)

---

148 The terminology of Scripture is precise, and when different words are used, there
is always a sound reason. This is why it's always good to track the use of key terminology through the Scriptures (as we are doing now with the word "elders").

(176) Titus 1

1:5 For this cause I left thee in Crete, that thou should correct that which is lacking and set in place **elders** *in every city, as I had commanded thee:*

1:6 He who is blameless, the husband of one wife, having faithful children who can not be accused of dissoluteness, nor insubordinate.

1:7 For the bishop[149] must be blameless, as a steward of God; not arrogant, not quick to anger, not given to wine, not hurtful, not greedy of dishonest gain,

1:8 but a lover of hospitality, a lover of good men, temperate, just, holy, gentle,

1:9 holding fast the doctrine according to the faithful word, that he may be able by sound doctrine both to exhort and to convince the gainsayers.

Paul confirms his verbal authorization to Titus to *correct that which is lacking and set in place elders in every city.* He also writes a wonderful description of an ideal elder. We must, however, keep in mind that the New Testament operates under grace and not law. Those who legalistically attempt to appoint elders by invoking the above passage of Scripture will fail miserably, because the application of the dead letter will kill. Peter, Paul, Timothy, and Titus were successful because they were led every

---

149 Greek *episkopos.* This word, translated "bishop," is used in only five NT Scriptures (in Acts 20:28-29, the bishop has the responsibility to feed and protect the congregation). Among early Christians, this was a person who was charged with exercising spiritual oversight, such as presiding at meetings, and who labored in word and doctrine (Philippians 1:1; 1 Timothy 3:2; Titus 1:7). Jesus is referred to as the Shepherd and Bishop of our souls (1 Peter 2:25). Most key NT Greek terminology has an OT trajectory in Hebrew that's very useful in defining its meaning in Scripture. If this is the case with *episkopos,* the prime candidates are *paqad* (Genesis 39:4-5; 2 Kings 12:11, 22:5, 9; 2 Chronicles 34:10, 12, 17) or *paqid* (2 Chronicles 31:13; Nehemiah 11:9, 14, 22; 12:42). They basically mean "to be an inspector" (i.e., an administrator).

step of the way by the Holy Spirit, and so were the elders whom they selected. Therefore, the grace of God was multiplied unto them (1 Peter 1:2; 2 Peter 1:2).

(177) Hebrews 11

11:1 *Faith, therefore, is the substance of things waited for, the evidence of things not seen.*

11:2 *For by it the **elders** obtained a good report.*

Elders who obtained a good report are listed as those who operated by faith, such as Abel, Enoch, Noah, Abraham, and Sara. The list also includes Isaac, Jacob, Joseph, Moses' parents, Moses, Rahab, Gedeon, Barak, Samson, Jephthae, David, Samuel, and the prophets. Note that there are three women on this list: Sara, Moses' mother, and Rahab (Hebrews 11:3-40).

(178) James 5

5:14 *Is any sick among you? let him call for the **elders** of the congregation; and let them pray for him, anointing him with oil in the name of the Lord;*

5:15 *and the prayer of faith shall cause the one who is sick to be saved, and the Lord shall raise him up; and if he has committed sins, he shall be forgiven them.*

When Jesus sent out the apostles, they anointed the sick with oil, and the sick recovered (Mark 6:13). Here James writes that the sick should call for the elders to pray for them and to anoint them with oil. It's very interesting to note that in the Gospels, Jesus himself never anointed anyone with oil. He simply put his hands on them or spoke the word and they were healed (even if they were far away).

(179, 180) 1 Peter 5

5:1 *The* **elders** *who are among you I exhort (I am also an elder with them and a witness of the afflictions of the Christ, and also a participant of the glory that shall be revealed).*

5:2 *Feed the flock of God which is among you, caring for her, not by force, but willingly; not for shameful lucre, but with willing desire;*

5:3 *and not as having lordship over the heritage of the Lord, but in such a manner as to be examples of the flock.*

5:4 *And when the great Prince of the pastors shall appear, ye shall receive the incorruptible crown of glory.*

5:5 *Likewise, young people, be subject to the* **elders** *in such a manner that you are all subject to one another. Be clothed with humility of will, for God resists the proud and gives grace to the humble.*

5:6 *Humble yourselves, therefore, under the mighty hand of God, that he may exalt you in due time,*

5:7 *casting all your cares upon him, for he cares for you.*

Peter exhorts the elders as a fellow elder. They are to lead by example and not by force, and to have no ambition of personal gain. The young people (or those who are immature in the Lord) are to be subject to the elders in such a manner that everyone is subject to one another. In other words, we are all to fellowship with one another in humility, with mutual respect and harmony, while recognizing and respecting those to whom God has delegated authority.

(181, 182) Revelation 4

*4:4 And round about the throne were twenty-four thrones, and upon the thrones I saw twenty-four **elders** sitting, clothed in white raiment; and they had on their heads crowns of gold.*

*4:10 the twenty-four **elders** fall down before him that is seated on the throne and worship him that lives for ever and ever and cast their crowns before the throne, saying,*

4:11 Thou art worthy, O Lord, to receive glory and honour and virtue; for thou hast created all things, and by thy will they have their being and were created.

White raiment is the righteousness of the saints (the righteousness of Christ if, by the Spirit, we are doing his will). Crowns of gold mean that those who wear these crowns reign and rule with Christ. They fall down before him and cast their crowns before the throne because they have no desire for personal gain and they recognize that they are an extension of his authority and government. Twenty-four is four times six, with four representing God's heavenly love that redeems by its very nature and six representing man and the animal realm of creation that will also be redeemed once the body of Christ comes to maturity (Romans 8:19-21). Even though it's easy for us to think of twenty-four literal elders (the twelve sons of Israel and the twelve apostles of Jesus), the number is symbolic of all those who have come to maturity in Christ and will reign and rule with him. Twenty-four is also twelve (representative of divine order) times two (symbolic of a corporate body).

(183, 184, 185, 186, 187) Revelation 5

*5:5 And one of the **elders** said unto me, Weep not:*

behold, the Lion of the tribe of Juda, the Root of David, who has overcome to open the book and to loose its seven seals.

5:6 *And I saw, and, behold, in the midst of the throne and of the four animals and in the midst of the* ***elders,*** *stood a Lamb as it had been slain, having seven horns and seven eyes, which are the seven Spirits of God sent forth into all the earth.*

5:7 *And he came and took the book out of the right hand of him that was seated upon the throne.*

5:8 *And when he had taken the book, the four animals and the twenty-four* **elders** *fell on their faces before the Lamb, each one of them having harps, and golden vials full of incense, which are the prayers of saints.*

5:9 *And they sang a new song, saying, Thou art worthy to take the book and to open its seals, for thou wast slain and hast redeemed us unto God by thy blood, out of every kindred and tongue and people and nation*

5:10 *and hast made us unto our God kings and priests, and we shall reign on the earth.*

5:11 *And I beheld, and I heard the voice of many angels round about the throne and of the animals and of the* **elders***; and the number of them was ten thousand times ten thousand, and thousands of thousands;*

5:12 *saying with a loud voice, Worthy is the Lamb that was slain to take power and riches and wisdom and strength and honour and glory and blessing.*

5:13 *And I heard every creature which is in heaven and upon the earth and under the earth and such as are upon the sea and all that are in it, saying, Blessing and honour and glory and power, be unto him that is seated upon the throne, and unto the Lamb for ever and ever.*

*5:14 And the four animals said, Amen. And the twenty-four **elders** fell on their faces and worshipped him that lives for ever and ever.*

Elders are prominent before the throne of God. If we take a careful look at verse 11, *And I beheld, and I heard the voice of many angels round about the throne and of the animals and of the **elders**; and the number of them was ten thousand times ten thousand, and thousands of thousands*, it seems to me that this could be referring to a very large number of elders. It's evident that God desires all of his people to come to maturity as elders so that they can reign and rule together with Christ.

(188, 189) Revelation 7

*7:11 And all the angels stood round about the throne and about the **elders** and the four animals; and they fell upon their faces before the throne and worshipped God,*

7:12 saying, Amen: The blessing and the glory and the wisdom and the thanksgiving and the honour and the power and the might, be unto our God for ever and ever. Amen.

*7:13 And one of the **elders** responded and asked me, Who are these who are arrayed in long white robes? and where did they come from?*

7:14 And I said unto him, lord, thou knowest. And he said to me, These are those who came out of great tribulation and have washed their long robes, and made them white in the blood of the Lamb.

7:15 *Therefore, they are before the throne of God and serve him day and night in his temple, and he that is seated on the throne shall dwell among them.*

7:16 *They shall hunger no more neither thirst anymore; neither shall the sun be thrust upon them nor any other heat.*

7:17 *For the Lamb which is in the midst of the throne shall govern them and shall lead them unto living fountains of waters, and God shall wipe away all tears from their eyes.*

This is another description of all the elders (the mature in Christ) who are before the throne of God.

(190) Revelation 11

11:15 *And the seventh angel sounded the trumpet, and there were great voices in the heaven, saying, The kingdoms of this world are reduced unto our Lord and to his Christ; and he shall reign for ever and ever.*

11:16 *And the twenty-four **elders**, who sat before God on their thrones, fell upon their faces and worshipped God,*

11:17 *saying, We give thee thanks, O Lord God Almighty, who art and wast, and art to come because thou hast taken to thee thy great power and hast reigned.*

The elders are able to fully appreciate the victory of the kingdom of God.

(191) Revelation 14

14:1 *And I saw and, behold, the Lamb stood upon*

Mount Sion and with him a hundred and forty-four thousand, having the name of his Father written in their foreheads.

14:2 And I heard a voice from heaven as the voice of many waters and as the voice of a great thunder; and I heard the voice of harpers harping with their harps;

*14:3 and they sang as it were a new song before the throne and before the four animals and the **elders**; and no one could learn that song but the hundred and forty-four thousand, who were redeemed from the earth.*

14:4 These are those who are not defiled with women, for they are virgins. These are those who follow the Lamb wherever he goes. These are redeemed from among men, being the firstfruits unto God and to the Lamb.

14:5 And in their mouth was found no guile, for they are without blemish before the throne of God.

Those who have the Father's name (nature) written in their foreheads have the mind of Christ. They are mature in Christ. They are not defiled with women. In this symbolic book (and elsewhere in Bible prophecy), women can represent groups or congregations. These elders have made no attempt to personally control the people of God. They used their ministry to help join people to Jesus Christ and not to themselves.

(192) Revelation 19

19:2 for true and righteous are his judgments; for he has judged the great whore, who corrupted the earth with her fornication, and has avenged the blood of his slaves at her hand.

*19:3 And again they said, Halelu-JAH. And her smoke
rose up for ever and ever.*

*19:4 And the twenty-four **elders** and the four animals
fell upon their faces and worshipped God that was
seated upon the throne, saying, Amen! Halelu-JAH!*

*19:5 And a voice came out of the throne, saying, Praise
our God, all ye his slaves and ye that fear him, both
small and great.*

*19:6 And I heard as it were the voice of a great com-
pany and as the voice of many waters and as the voice
of mighty thunderings, saying, Halelu-JAH; for the Lord
God almighty reigns.*

*19:7 Let us be glad and rejoice and give glory to him;
for the marriage of the Lamb is come, and his bride has
made herself ready.*

*19:8 And to her was granted that she should be arrayed
in fine linen, clean and bright: for the fine linen is the
righteousness of the saints.*

Those who have come to maturity in the corrupt life of fallen
Adam and have contaminated the earth with their fornication
and have killed (or have attempted to kill) those who belong to
God (as Cain did to his brother, Abel) will be judged, but those
who have come to maturity in Christ will participate in a great
celebration. It's no coincidence that the bride will be arrayed in
a manner similar to that of the elders described in Revelation
4:4, for only a righteous bride is fit for the Lamb of God.

Meet the Author

Russell Stendal, a former hostage of Colombian rebels, is a lifelong missionary to that same group in the jungles of Colombia. He is an influential friend to military and government leaders in Colombia, Cuba, Mexico, Venezuela, and the United States. Russell's ministry shares the gospel via twelve radio stations, hundreds of thousands of Bibles, books, and movies distributed through airplane parachute drops, and numerous speaking engagements for groups of leaders, prisoners, and individuals. Russell goes wherever the Lord leads, whether it's to speak with a president or to go deep into the jungle to help an individual in trouble. He has witnessed thousands commit their lives to Christ.

Connect with the Author

Website: www.cpcsociety.ca

Newsletter Signup: www.anekopress.com/stendal-newsletter

Russell and his coworkers have built dozens of radio stations in Latin America that concentrate a clear message on remote and dangerous areas where persecution of Christians is rampant. More than 120,000 Galcom solar-powered radios have been deployed to those being discipled. Most of the programming is in Spanish, but they also transmit in almost a dozen native languages where a great move of God is presently taking place. Russell  preaches through the Bible, a chapter or so per message. More than 1,000 messages have been recorded and aired repeatedly. The chapters of this book are samples of these messages preached on the radio in the Colombian war zone about ten years ago. The key website is www.fuerzadepaz. com. Pray for Russell and his team as they expand Spanish-language radio coverage into places like Cuba, Venezuela, Mexico, and Central America.

Internet radio station on the air with worldwide coverage: For Spanish, go to www.fuerzadepaz.com (or download the free Fuerza de Paz App from the iTunes store). Or, the Jubilee Radio in English has a free App on iTunes (or you may go to www.cpcsociety.ca). This station is for people who speak English as a second language or those who desire to better their English, as well as for English speaking people everywhere. There are many in Africa, Asia, the Middle East, and Latin America that are drawn to this station. Two short wave stations continue international broadcasts from Colombia: Radio Alcaraván on 5910 khz. and La Voz de Tu Conciencia on 6010 khz., both on the 49 meter band.

Connect with Russell's Ministry

Website

www.cpcsociety.ca

Receive newsletter updates

http://goo.gl/amBsCD

Buy books

http://amzn.to/1nPLcNL

Other Similiar Titles

By Russell M. Stendal

Elijah & Elisha

While the kings served the gods of this world, Elijah and Elisha did not. They were dedicated only to the Word of the Lord, and if the Lord didn't speak directly to them, they didn't move at all. And when they did move, it was with the authority of the Lord, resulting in dramatic calling down of fire from heaven, a three-year drought, people raised from the dead, and many other miraculous events. But did Elijah and Elisha take any glory? No, Elijah didn't even accept Naaman's token of appreciate – so completely was he relying only on the Lord's provision.

The lives of Elijah and Elisha, as well as the corrupt lives of the kings, serve as important lessons for us today. In addition, there are many prophecies in 1 and 2 Kings that are now being fulfilled. Your own life will be changed forever if you apply even one truth that the Lord reveals to you in this book.

Available where books and eBooks are sold.

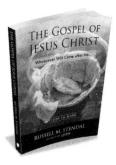

The Gospel of Jesus Christ

The gospel of Mark speaks of the Son of God who will soon return and manifest an incorruptible kingdom that differs greatly from the kingdoms of men. When Jesus said that his kingdom is not of this world, some were very disillusioned. They did not understand that Jesus came to announce a very different kingdom, which he started by planting an incorruptible word (for he is the living Word of God). Over the long history of the church, many have made and are still making tragic mistakes as they attempt to take over the corrupt kingdoms of this world in the name of God.

Jesus was ordained by God and approved by God. He had no human credentials, no certificates from Herod or the Sanhedrin or the high priest, and he gave no written diplomas to his apostles. At the Last Supper, Jesus said, *Verily, verily, I say unto you, He that receives whomsoever I send receives me, and he that receives me receives him that sent me* (John 13:20).

Available where books and eBooks are sold.

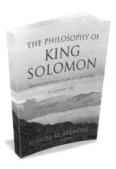

The Philosophy of King Solomon

What if we have it wrong? What if happiness is not found in having a better paying job, a wife and three children, knowing the right people, or even going to church?

What is the secret of successful living? After getting more gold, wives, fine houses, and wisdom than any other man on earth, King Solomon discovered the secret. The Book of Ecclesiastes is not as much a book of lament for himself as it is a message for the people, for us. King Solomon wants to leave us with his final conclusions after having attained all. Let him show you how to store up treasures in heaven, treasures that surpass even that of him who gathered all things under the sun.

The Philosophy of King Solomon explores Solomon's wisdom, the folly of man's ways, and the still-unfolding prophecy found in the rich book of Ecclesiastes.

Available where books and eBooks are sold.